You, Yourself & Source

Our Energiez
Your Power
Your Purpose

Cathy Copperthwaite

You, Yourself & Source

Cathy Copperthwaite

Copyright 2025

ISBN: 979-8-9890008-1-4

Series

√* **Me, Myself & Us**
   Our Energiez, Your Power

√* **You, Yourself & Source**
Our Energiez, Your Power, Your Purpose

* **Me, Source & You**
Play Shoppe Journey & Journal
Our Energiez, Your Power,
   Learn how to Play the Roles for Your' Reality

* **You, Me & Us   Relationships**
Your Energiez, Our Power, Your Lovez

* **Save Space for Source**
My Journey Our Energiez, Our Power

What is Inside of You?
What is Your Table of Contents

Chapter 1	You, Yourself & Source	11
Chapter 2	We Organics Are Very Similar	19
Chapter 3	Communication with Source	29
Chapter 4	Your Heart	40
Chapter 5	Our Senses	51
Chapter 6	Action & Reaction	54
Chapter 7	It is Always Done Your Way	64

It is Always about You

Chapter 8	Contrasts	72
Chapter 9	Big Impacts or Traumas	79
Chapter 10	Love Your Addictions	89
Chapter 11	Careers & Chapters	99
Chapter 12	Overwhelmed or Stagnate	111
Chapter 13	Judgements & Comparisons	117
Chapter 14	No One Loves Me	128

I don't Love My-Self

Chapter 15	Your Fears	135
Chapter 16	A Victim	152
Chapter 17	The Past	162
Chapter 18	Ego, Your Protection	177

& Perspective

Chapter 19	Live in the Now for Your Future	189
Chapter 20	Release & Refill Again	199
Chapter 21	Patience	209
Chapter 22	Our Imaginations	215
Chapter 23	Who are You Today?	224
Chapter 24	The Highest Alignment	243

Choosing You

Chapter 25	Relationships	257
Chapter 26	Parent'ing & Kid'ing	277
Chapter 27	Your Desires	289
Chapter 28	Manifesting	305
Chapter 29	Our Happiness Scale	327
Chapter 30	Changing the Situations	341

Using Your Power

Chapter 31	Good Vibes &	354

The Best Company

Chapter 32	Create Something New	362

Writing Your Own Book

Chapter 33	Meditation, Y'allz Time	376
Chapter 34	Grounding or Earthing	393
Chapter 35	Eat Healthy & Move	405
Chapter 36	Intention & Freedom	425
Chapter 37	Practice & Play	443

Your Negativity Detox

Hello, Thank You for joining Me again for My second book in the series, **'Our Energiez Your Power'.** This Journey is all about You and the things We could go through in Our lives, and how to make them 'better for You'. These ideas and facts are already working for so many people, it's not just Me, and I'm not here to talk anybody into anything because eventually You will find out on Your Own. *'It is better to love and have fun now, today while You are living on Mother Father Earth, then to wait until..'.*

Each individual's timeline is their Own to change. We all have that power. We just kind of forgot about it, in a gradual way, over many, many, many thousands and thousands of years and through multiple generations. But it's okay, because We're starting right now. You just have to release what You got caught up in while living Your life that does not serve You anymore. Those timelines and the expectations of society, the presumption of using the protocols of medicine, and the programming from the memories of what has happened with You, Your family, and of past generations. Your Source is here to help You every single time. There is always an answer to be found when the question is asked at the right time.

Your life starts with a dream; and Everyone has unlimited potential.

If You are having fun in Your life and trying to find the positives, Your life is going to flow, and when You get to those little hurdles, You can easily step over and accomplish them. You will easily accept things that are happening around You, because of You, and then You can change it to the way that You want it to be. Your ancestors are all here with You saying, *'Oh yea, We are glad You finally got it. Let's play'.*

Really, the only way to get out of any situation is to know Yourself 1st. Trust that Best Friend in *You, Yourself & Source.* You will know that, *'how You feel'* will always give You the right answer. *Please read the chapters in order the 1st time, and then You can go back and practice and play as many times as You wish.* By the end of this book, You are going to be floating on air, grinning from ear to ear, walking down the hallway and giggling to Yourself, playing with Your new Best Friend and talking about Yourself with the highest respect and love. Only the positives from all aspects of Your life so You can flourish knowing where You came from, how You are living right now, and where Your potential is in the future. You have to love life, so that life loves You back even more. Accept and allow life to dazzle Your Source's favorite person, **YOU!**

There is a Vitality or life's force, an Energy, a quickening which is translated through You into action, & because there is only One of You in all time, this expression is Unique. If You block it, it will never exist through any other medium & it will be lost, & then the world will never know it or You.

Martha Graham

Chapter 1

You, Yourself & Source

Hello and welcome to *You, Yourself & Source, 'Our Energiez, Your Power, Your Purpose'.* Hopefully, You've read *Me, Myself & Us,* which kind of got You started in a new relationship with Your Source, Your BFE. I heard the word *'Source'* and I loved it, so that is what I speak of now, because to Me it encompasses Every One's Creator. Our Source is always living in the highest frequencies only. Your Source always puts in a good word for You, 100% of the time. Talk about friends in high places! Source loves positivity, loves fun and they know the Laws of the Universe. They gave Us Our lives and somewhere to live it, with nutrition from Mother Father Earth. Most of Us received all of Our senses and Our organ systems work without Our assistance. If You want to know more about what Your Source does for You and how 'They' live, please read Chapter 3 in *Me, Myself & Us.*

In this 2nd book, We're going to be talking about You, which is the most important Physical Person and the most important Energy in this Universe, period! You are unique, You are special, one of a kind and I know You've heard that many, many times and it is so true. You are made of two parts, physical and energy, and Your mind is in there somewhere. If I say 'You', I mean You and Your Best Friend. If I say 'We', I mean Us and Our Best Friends. Energy is Your Source, Your Inner Child, Your bigger part and We are all connected to every Organic on this Earth, to all of Your Ancestors, Angels, Guides, the Universe and to Mother Father Earth. *Everything that is Organic in this Universe is attached to Your Soul or to Your Energy already.* It is **You, Yourself & Source** first and *then* every aspect of the world that You live in. It is always *Me, Myself & Us* and then My son. It is *Me, Myself & Us* and *then* My family, friends and the world. It's *Me, Myself & Us* first and then working with My physical body and remember, Your physical body is already and always helping You, because every single cell that You have, every single microbiome that You are made of (Remember the ratio of microbiomes to cells is a 10:1 ratio), is already attached to Your Spirit, to Your Source, to Our Creator, to Our Energy. Our Mind and Our body link Us to Source, to Our Soul, Our Subconscious, or to Our Energy. Your 2nd Best Friend should be Your physical body.

The physical aspects are what You and I need to take care of consciously, by learning and adapting to what is happening in Our lives and by practicing '***Preprevention***'.

And if You don't have a religious preference, You can still have a relationship with Your Best Friend. Yes there is something else, there is another part of You. You are mostly Energy and *then* Your body. The nonphysical portion of You and Me that is attached to Source, that Energy part, is so powerful, calm, knowing and at peace, because there are no worries, doubts, resistance or uncertainty flowing. Imagine just one day like that with Your Source, easy, unlimited and fun. Visualize all good things happening to You, one after another, changing Your life to a more positive one. Your existence is going to change with so much benefit for You, and for everybody else around You. Now, imagine a week, a month….. Oh MY! Be eager for more.

Your Source is like Your driver, Your Spiritual chauffeur who is also Your Best Friend, ready to take You any place that You want to go. All You have to do is pick somewhere that's going to make You feel good. You have to pick some place without any regret, guilt or how's attached. You have to pick each path,

each segment without any feelings of scarcity or fear. *'Well, if I do that, then I can't do this; if I spend that money, then I have to go back and save'.* You have to head towards an area where You are not going to criticize, complain, judge or cut others down with Your negative emotions. You can assess the situation yes, but if You find Yourself doing anything like those above, You know that You are not in the higher frequencies where Your BFE is. If You live that way, the things that You ask for are going to sit at that red light for a little bit of time before You get them. Your BFE wants You to head in whichever direction that You need to go happily along with them: North, South, East, West or a mixture, it doesn't matter. Imagine all the pathways that You are going to be able to choose and use. You can do it very quickly, very quantumly or You can be slowed down at every stop light, stop sign, yields, warnings, traffic jams or speed humps. If You travel with Your Source, Your BFE, You're not going to need to go through a lot of congestion, You will be right there.
😍 Remember Your driver is going to know all of the shortcuts and the best pitstops along the way. Tell Your chauffeur where You want to go every single day and in the meantime say, '*Thank You and ask Yourself*

often, 'are We having a good time today? Have We laughed a lot already?' Your chauffeur is here and Your team is waiting for You. You might be the boss, but Your Higher Source is here helping You along the way and giving You the desires and gifts You ask for. We have Lots of love *if We* let it in. All of Our Wealth, which covers health, prosperity, safety and the desires and wishes We have individually, can be Ours if We believe in Us. It must start with You. If You live this way, Your life is going to be funner, it's going to be simpler, and it's going to flow in the perfect way for You to have joy and to have everything that You want every single day, every single time.

The older You are, the more set in Your ways that You follow. A lot of people have been suppressed for many, many years and for many generations, and if You are not happy in every aspect of Your life, the further away You are from that larger part of You. Consciously or subconsciously, it doesn't matter. Some people are afraid to let it be and allow their control and power to be fully supported 100%. There are only great things that can come from being with Your Source as a Best Friend.

When You don't need anyone, who do You wish to hang out with?

Imagine the emotions that You will have learning about Your ultimate power with Your Source. A knowing that You will be able to get out of any situation or any segment that comes up for You in Your environment. Yes, that power. Think of the desires in this life that You want and then include all the feelings and emotions that You would have if they came true. If You had all the money that You ever needed, never to worry about that again, oh My goodness, the Freedom! What if You had the healthiest body, Strength, Flexibility and Freeedooom! Imagine the emotions of having a blissful relationship with anybody in this world, especially with Your special person. Fun, Freedom and Ecstasy! Just imagine those feelings, wouldn't they all be wonderful? Think about this though, money can only help with certain things, well, a lot of things actually. Having a healthy body can get You to the next minute and having a really great relationship with people can only get You so far. The only thing that can honestly and continuously keep You going and get You to the top of the Happiness scale is Your relationship with *You, Yourself & Source.*

This connection will surprise You; it will delight You and it will make You so excited for more fun and games with Your new BFE. Don't You want to have a good time, all the time, giggling and laughing with everything going Your way? Once You get to playing, You're not going to ever, ever, want to go back to Your old thought patterns and life.

The Laws of the Universe are part of Your life. When You know how to *'play the games, as I call it'*, when You know how to have fun with Your Source, it will All work out in a better, easier way for You. Find Yourself 1st and be loving, gentle and kind to You. Love on all Your parts, the physical, mental and Spiritual. You have to live Your life for Your purpose and not living for the physical things that You want. Every Organic's purpose in life is the same, which is to find *Joy, Happiness, Peace and Love for Yourself, for all the Organics, and also to find Your way back to Source in the end.* In every segment and with every second, You always have that choice to live the way that You feel great about. Everybody is an innocent at each moment in their life, even if it is the same scenarios. If You don't know what to expect, that is even better, 'Yaeee, the unknown'. Have that Self-assurance that it is going to be ok and that everything is always going to work out because of You and Your Source. Once You get that down, it will be so much easier to spread Joy and Love around the whole wide world. Yes, You do affect everything that's around You and You Can affect the whole world too. :) *You, Yourself & Source, Our Energiez, Your' Power.*

To Me, Energy sounds so **Powerful**. My Source, My Energy is vast and fills the Universe and so does Yours. That's why You need to save at least 15 minutes A-day, just a little quiet time to be part of Your Source consciously, and the rest of the day You want to play and be with them with no resistance. Let Your Source do the driving, let Your Source do the talking as You move towards Your wonderful, blissful, joyful, happy, abundant, an anything You want to happen kind of life. Let Your Source do the things that need to be done and You just have to follow and play along with the Laws of the Universe. Laws that You can't do anything about except to frolic along and see how Your life changes. Trust and have more fun daily while 'They' take care of every human and every Organic on this Mother Father Earth.

I am going to motivate You to just let some things go and to let better be allowed in Your life. You have a new Best Friend, Your Energy, Your Source, so act like a Best Friend would. Now, since You've met Your new BFE, don't You want to talk to Them all the time?

100% of You are going to get this. The Ones who Play the most are going to have the Greatest Fun along the way........

Love,. Learn &
 Take Control &
  Yes, We Are......

Chapter 2

We Organics Are Very Similar

Yes, Yes, We are all unique individuals in Our own little ways, but We are also very alike in many ways too. Here are some thoughts I have gathered together that show Our similarities.

*We are the same, as in the fact that We are all *humans living on this Earth*. We refer to Us as human and We call Ourselves, 'I' and 'Me'. There are such varying degrees between individuals because of what? *'Our physical aspects and conscious minds'.*

*Every human body, animal, insect or plant has a *Soul* that came with it. Our Soul or Spirit is directly linked to and a part of Source. That Pure Positive Energy is Our Source, Our BFE and Our Source lives through Us while We are here on this Earth.

*We All have the same *Best Friend Energy* and their names are what We choose them to be in accordance of how We grew up. We All have the emotions and the ability to communicate with Our Source, Our BFE through Our *intuitions.* Intuitions are Our link to Our Higher Divinity and it is given to

Us freely before birth and it stays with Us throughout Our lives.

*We are all the same, deep down under and spiritually. It is already proven by science that We are made ultimately of Energy. Yes, We are made of *Pure Positive Energiez* and We are related to everything that is Organic on this Earth, and that includes Mother Father Earth, the atmosphere and the Universe too. Organic means to be alive. So now think about everything else that is alive on this Earth, the non-humans. Our diverse vegetation without minds to think negative thoughts, communicate, have emotions, take care of each other and of Us also. Imagine all those other Organics on the Earth too, the animals and insects. Their Pure Positive Energies are supporting You too, All for You, at any time. Such beautiful Energies all around each other contributing Love and support. Imagine if Your communities were like that, where Everybody lives their true purpose in life, just the way that it is supposed to be and will be.

derOur purpose in life is the same for Every One. There are individual desires and contributions for Us to share with the World, yes, but Our main purpose is to live with Joy, Fun, Happiness, Peace, Love and to find Our way back to Source. Whether it is spiritual or physical, Your Purpose is having a really, really, great time with Your Best Friend Energy.

*We are All *inventors*. We are All geniuses and bad asses to the core! Oh yes, absolutely We are. We all have and use Our imaginations, and because of those ideas You become a creator. This is what We came on this Earth to do*, 'to co-create with Source a life that We would love to live, all the while making the World a better place'.* We imagine things every single day that nobody else has thought of before and because You thought of it, it will be here for infinity, for Our thoughts are never lost.

*Another similarity is that *You are number One* and You are the creator of Your own reality according to the Law of Attraction. Reality is the physical world in relationship to Our minds. You have thoughts that You believe, that You can change at any time to make anything You want happen. Your Source is helping You feel the love and giving You clear solutions to every question that You have. We/You got this. You are #1 alongside Your #1, Who is with You always, Your BFE, Your One and only Source.

*We are similar in *Our thoughts* of the things that We *desire* here on Earth. There are usually between 4-8 aspects of what everybody wants in this life, the common denominators. Everybody wants to have a *safe* place to live and *nutritious food and drink* to be as *healthy* as We can. Most people want enough *money* to live and enjoy life. Most people want to *laugh and be happy* most of the time. People also want to *love what they do for work or career*, and everyone wishes for a *supporting family, or community, or someone special to share their lives with.*

Our fears in life are also comparable and there are many definitions of fear. No one wants to suffer, nobody wants to be sad, angry or to be afraid. If You have a fear or worry just think, *'is there any evidence to back up this thought process or is it just something that I brought up and are thinking about? What if it isn't even Your business and You're making it Your own, adding in stress. Is My fear something that I can't do anything about anyway?.* I wrote a whole chapter on fear, Chapter 15 to help You out.

*Another comparison to note is We All have the capability and the right to *release* anything from Our lives, Our Minds and Our bodies. Even a women's monthly menstrual cycle or hot flashes are a cleanse of pent-up energies and of materials and toxins that are no longer needed in the body. Your body does that for You, are You trying to stop them? You have to release what no longer makes You feel Your best every day and open up for more positivity in Your life, and Your BFE is right here to assist and make it so. There are so many ways of how to do this. To help, You can lay down or walk on Mother Father Earth. This is Grounding and it is freely given to All Organics to use. Chapter 34. Other ways to dissolve unhappiness are to dance, laugh, scream, cry out loud, take a nap, read, meditate, listen to music, etc., and also there are special people who are trained, that can help You to release and clean up Your stored Energies.

*Another kinship is Our *innocence*. In every segment of Your day, in every single part of Your life, You are an *innocent*. You are in fact an innocent with a Powerful Loving Best Friend included. Our naïve Inner Child has all the wisdom of the Universe because of the relationships and links to Our Energiez. Being an innocent means You are able to make a different choice with each segment if You want to, and You can change and evolve into something brand new and possibly opposite of the way that You have lived until now. Listen to Your Inner Youth. Compared to an adult mind, Your Inner Child will not overcomplicate things, which means You don't think or talk about the parts of life that You can't do anything about. Which also means that You have no judgements about other people and their ideas. If You ask a child a question that You also ask an adult, children are going to have more answers for You and they will not decrease the potential positive outcome with the 'what ifs' that could happen. Even if You think some of the answers are 'way out there', I bet if You really thought about it, they are kind of hitting the point in a different way. Remember, that children already know the Secret and Our purpose of Happiness and Love until society kicks in at about 2 or 3 years old. All the 'stuff' that You learn from Your parents and grandparents from generations past, and of course from Your friends and teachers. The programming actually starts adding up when kids are in elementary and middle school. I believe what really matters is what You do at home in their haven, in Your shared paradise. Kids just want to be positively acknowledged and to have fun, (just like adults do). So don't disregard Your Inner Child, or hide it, or keep it suppressed. Start every segment and any questions that You have with Your innocence first and then see the great results that will occur.

*What about the other Organics? Even the animals and insects treat Us the same. That wasp or ant will sting You and the tick or the mosquito will bite You, but they don't say, *'oh My goodness, a girl, Caucasian with brown hair and blue eyes, kind of small, talks a lot; I wonder if she will suffice?'* No, they're like, *'Oh yes, warm blood and food'.* What about an animal that could eat You because they are hungry or they need to feed their children? They're not saying, *'look at the color of that skin, what is their religion?, I wonder where they live?, look at that bad attitude or that sweet, loving person. Ha, absolutely not'.* They just want their next meal. Animals or insects, I believe do not second guess their intuition or power.

What about the foliage and fungi? They feel Us and say, *'hey let's trade, You give Me love and I will give You something beautiful to look at, smell and touch. We will also give You shade. You give Me Your air and We will give You Our air, and Our air is going to have a whole bunch of nutrients in it. We will also provide nourishment to help You live a happy, healthy life'.*

And Mother Father Earth, a huge energy We are connected to, loves ALL OF US. Mother Father Earth and Source co-create the things that are beautiful, strong and magnificent or tiny and powerful that help Us live. Just think of All that You know that comes from Mother Father Earth: every insect, every animal, every plant, every mountain, every stream, every body of water, every body of land, the minerals, the vitamins, the nutrients, Our bodies, Our microbiomes, Our cells etc. This is a great deal to Me. The only thing that separates Us, is Us. All the Organics in the world treat Us the same, as a powerful Energy Source living on this planet with Them. They see Our divinity, just as Our Source does.

*And My final light of thought is that We are all similar in the reality that We are all *different*. Thank Goodness for Our diversities, similarities and the common denominators. Our similarities physically, deep down under and spiritually are real and Our abilities to connect with other people and Organics is amazing. Even when We don't speak the same language, there is also a kinship to be found. Think of All the

Beautiful People, Organics and Souls out there in the World waiting to connect with You somehow, either face to face or with Our Energiez. To Me it is so exciting to think of everything We can learn and All the fun that We can have together as a Whole, positive, loving Universe. We can accomplish the same outcomes and resemble how we do it with others, but there is NO ONE in the whole world that can achieve it with the uniqueness or with the exact individuality/duality (with Source), the way that YOU CAN, ever. These are Your gifts to the World, Your Dharma. You can change the Universe, All with Your '*Happiness & Joy*'. So much fun and it so awesome that it works that way.

You see Yourself as many..

Isn't that enough to Love Yourself more, so You can Love other people more; or isn't that enough to Love other people more, so You can fall deeper in Love with You?

Chapter 3
Communication with Source
Your Intuition

We all have some degree of knowing how to communicate with Our Source. If You use praying, asking, meditating, singing, dancing or a praise to Them from You, how do 'They' respond back to You? Your *intuition* is the message from Your Source or the Universe to You. Those little bits of information here and there prompting You to ask Yourself, *'is this good for Me or not?'* Your intuition will never lie to You. Intuition is like the trailer to Your movie, book or documentary. How Your life will be is dependent on how *You use* those ideas and which way *You choose* to go. Things in Your life are going to happen whether You are in a higher frequency or not, but it's funner if You're up there in the positive emotions most of the time when You see a sign, or hear a certain sound, or smell or taste or touch a message. (When I say, 'higher frequency' I just mean living with positive, happy emotions). Everybody and anybody can use their intuition and energy to receive messages, You just need to open up Your mind to realizing it. How many times have You looked at Your pet and they look back at You and they're actually telling You that they have to go out, or that they are hungry, or that they want to cuddle? They're not talking to You by meowing or barking or squeaking or squawking, they are using intuition. A beautiful Spirit that trusts You and loves You is communicating to Your Spirit, from their Spirit with their intuition.

An instinct and a reflex are from Your mind, but first it is a spark from the Spiritual part of You. An instinct is Your intuition. Instinct could be for survival or for nurturing and it is usually associated with wildlife. With animals, they don't usually second guess their decisions, only humans think about and argue with themselves about a hunch. Yes, You know Your mind, or You think You do. Haha!

Intuition is actually Your Soul's guidance, and for You to understand it, it has to be in a language between Your mind, Your Spirit and Source. Intuition always happens for You, because of You, so make it what You want. Do You remember how You and Your Best Friend when You were younger, had Your Own little special language? We made up Our Own words and signals and sounds. Well, Intuition is the secret language between You and Your Source. You have to speak to Your Best Friend Energy in Y'allz Own language, and You will know those words and those little signs that are shared because Your signs are going to be Your Own. Intuition is a feeling, a picture, a color, a sound, a thought in the back of Your mind that can come from Your senses. They can be pretty, they can be bold, they can be funny. They can be anything that You think of. For Me, I always say, '*make it funny and beautiful and make Me laugh and smile. I love to see hearts and smiley faces, vibrant colors and repeating numbers. While sometimes they let me know with one or two words.*' When Your BFE is talking to You, discover the way You feel or what You sense and then learn what They mean for You to do.

Your communication to Source is through Your thoughts, words, emotions and actions. To add to Your point or to Your wish and make it more potent, accompany them with Your emotions. Emotions are what Your Source will pick up on easier, because emotions with words are much more powerful than words are alone. Emotions are very powerful by themselves too. When Your emotions are at high, Your thought processes are out of here. Have You ever been so angry or Happy that You just couldn't think straight and then You said or did something not like You?

Some people just live with their thoughts and they don't use their emotions very much. Hiding Your emotions, these boundaries that You put up keeps Your true identity from people, that wonderful truth about You and it also unintentionally buries it from Source. When You hold back Your emotions, You are blocking Yourself off from Source. If You are hiding behind Your walls to protect Yourself or if You are waiting at that red stop light, You are in a self-imposed prison. Your true emotions, the ones You really want to let out, eventually You will and it will be a big blow up or Your physical body will reap the pent-up energy in a negative way.

Using Your Intuition is being on the feminine side or letting Source do most of the work. You can talk to the Universe about the desires that You want. You can have questions answered about what's going on in Your life right now, and You can also say, *'Thank You for being around Me always'*. Use Your special connection to get clarity not confusion, which is what You're probably going to get from another person. And I'm not talking about life-or-death situations or

Your health, heck yes at those times You need to talk to Your doctor about something that could be wrong with Your physical body. Yes, Your physical body is healing itself, but please get help when You need to. You also have intuition between Your mind and Your physical body. That awareness of Your body. You need to know that language of Your physical body and listen to it notify You. If it tells You that You don't like that, with many different ways, then listen! All the parts of You communicate all the time through Your *Interstitial Matrix.* Even when You're not thinking about it, Your cells and Your microbiome co-create with Source for a healthy space for them to live in. They're making sure that You are balanced. They're making sure that You know when You're hungry. They're making sure that Your immune systems are working and that Your elimination systems and circulatory systems are flowing smoothly. If You really want to be healthy, then use Your Spiritual side to assist with Your body.

If You are anxious, doubtful or worried all of a sudden or maybe even scared. If You start feeling unsecure and keep thinking about 'it' in a harmful, challenging kind of way; that is Your intuition speaking to You. An example of an intuition, '*You just had this kind of feeling, that little nudge of something that feels off inside of You. You couldn't put Your finger on it and because You consciously couldn't address it and decide what was bothering You right then and there, You brushed it aside'.* Then it became a memory that You realized later on. *'Yep, I knew, I felt something off. I should have done that, or I should not have done that'.* Your better judgment and the bigger part of You would have ended it, but that's okay. I'm not saying feel guilty about any of Your decisions from the past, even from an hour ago, You can't. Why waste Your beautiful mind on those negative emotions that You can't change. Start right now and do it differently this time.

Also know this, Your Source, Your Spirit, Your Subconscious does not want You to be dependent on Them. They do not want You to have a codependency to anything. Although You do co-create with Your Source all the time, Your higher, powerful Source really wants *You to be You* on the inside and on the outside. If You trust Your intuition You are going to have less fear and doubt, and You will know the right answers to any questions that You have along the way. You have that power within Yourself and they want You to know that You are their BFEF.

If You have a little feeling that You are supposed to do something for Yourself or for the World, that is Your intuition. A feeling that You have, to push forward, figure it out and also have fun along the way. This is why You smile when You talk about it. This is why You glow and get little butterflies and get excited when You think about it. Listen to Your intuition, it is Your Source, it is the Universe saying, *'absolutely, let's do this'.* You don't have to search for Your path or Your individual purpose when You are Your true self, it will be easy to face the right way on Your journey. Using Your intuition and doing what You love, Your pathway is going to show up right before *You*.

For Your protection and a positive perception, when You're meeting new people let the bigger part of You kick in, Your intuition. That first impression from You is a judgment or critique. We are not supposed to judge people any way, it is not Your place at all. You can assess them absolutely. *Thank You Nurse Blake for saying We assess. I am a nurse and We Assess. I love it!* In Your initial opinion, remember that You actually have *no* truth about them yet, except for the way they look, smell and speak. If people want to fit in or hang with the crowd, they will change some of their behaviors to adapt, so You have to get to know the person or not, and that's Your choice. What I believe is, *'Who gives a c*** about 1ˢᵗ or 2nd impressions',* it takes time to get to know someone. First, second, third and fourth... Those times can also add up to years before the revelation. I know It takes Me several meetings just to remember their names. I only know for sure that they are important for My journey and I am important for theirs. Most people that I meet now, because I've changed My attitude and I try to find the positive in everything, are going to be in a higher happy state too. I know that there will be the others and I will be able to tell with My assessment. Maybe they are ready to learn something from Me or vice versa, they are definitely on My path for a reason. I wonder what will their first impression be about Me?

With meditation when Your mind is quiet and Your communication is none, all of a sudden a conversation between You and Your Source, between You and Your Spirit is opened up in a whole brand-new way. It makes You feel good for the rest of the day and You become closer to Your BFE. You deserve all of this positivity for You. Anything with Source is easy-peasy, fast and flowing. It is exciting, fun, expansive and unknown and You should hardly wait for more. What are we gonna do now, and now, and now? They make it so simple because there are only 2 answers to every question or dilemma or hurdle that We have. *Do I feel good about it? Yes, let's do it then. And then there is the other side of it, nope, I don't feel good about it so I am not going to do it.* This answer does not necessarily mean forever 'no', it could just mean to take it at a slower pace and don't answer or take action right now. Remember, logic might not always be right. We have 3 brains: Our heart, Our gut and the thinking one, Our conscious mind. The most important one to use at the beginning of any segment is Your Spiritual brain, or the Heart and Gut combined, Our emotional side, the feminine side, Your intuition. Which one comes first in a situation? Could it be measured in nano seconds or less? That gut wrenching knot in Your Solar Plexus or that Loving feeling in Your heart. Is it separate or is it simultaneous?

Source, Mother Father Earth and everything that is Organic already speak to each other. Every plant, animal, infant and Our bodies talk to Source every single day. Our minds are the ones that botch it up. It's Your mind that needs to learn this new language and absorb it. I believe that with Your Source, it should be one of Your first and it should be one of Your last conversations to have about a segment You are going through. Actually, it should be continuous, if You allow. If You really listen to Your intuition, to Your Source, You can have information on every single thing that anybody could possibly think about and a knowledge of Self. It is right here. If You involve Source and Your intuition in everything You do, Your life will be flowing smoothly right into the next situation. Commit to finding the perfect lingo between Yourself and Your BFE. Learn, practice and play with Your languages and Everybody speaks at least 2 languages, Your primary language and then Your language with Your Spirit, which is Your intuition. I always thought I could only speak one language and a bunch of man-made bad words, Pleases and Thank Yous, hellos and goodbyes from other languages. But no, I know 2 full languages and then come to think about it, I know baby talk too, because You can kind of tell the differences in cries. And oh yea, I know the language of Mother Father Earth and the animals and plants too. Oh, My goodness, I am a genius! Your intention now should be to learn Your intuition or Your secret code with Your Best Friend. Use Your Spiritual side and let Your intuition work with

Your Source to employ Your Spirit. Use that Power in anything that You do, first. You want to build up Your confidence between You and You and intensify Your Spirit. Amplify Your strength and then with the Law of Attraction more of that positive knowledge is just going to come to You, it has to, it is a law! So, to break free of Your easy to open cage or to step out from behind Your wall, You have to stop the protocol, the training that You've been in little bit by little bit, layer by layer and then that aspect of Your life will change. Keep Your confidence just between **You, Yourself & Source** in the beginning. You must see and feel Your Own Divinity first and then You can play more in the world. So yes, You can read Your intuition, anybody can and it's Your choice to be able to discern which way is the right way that would make You feel better. You don't need to follow the steps of Your ancestors at all anymore if it doesn't make You feel good. Your best life could start as soon as today. Speak Your Own language and open up Your world... The only way to learn anything is how? Just to *Practice and Play!*

'Intuition is the Whisper of the Soul '

Jiddu Krishnamurti

Chapter 4

Your Heart

Your heart brain works from and knows emotions better and Your heart energy connects You with the Universe. Think about You and Your Source with a difference in emotions or having a different perspective, because that's what You will feel 1st. *A notice of something not right or missing.* Your Source does not feel bad or negative, ever and what that basically means is, Your guiding system, Your Source is right there with You saying, '*yeah We don't like that and We are not going there with You. That's why You feel that discord, anxiety or that separation'.* If it's something that's good or better than satisfaction or anything that's positive at all, Your Source is saying, '*Yes, We are here, let's go'!* Be glad that They are here with You trying to help You see it in a more positive light.

One important fact is that God, Your Source made You out of Love, made all humans and Organics with so much love. Our Source made the Earth out of Love and made this wonderful Universe out of Love from Their Heart to Yours. When You feel the love and accept the love from the Universe, it is going to change Your mind forever. Go to service every day spiritually, only between You and Your Source. Go to A&A every day with You and Your Source, Yes, Ask and Allow. My friend Carlton and I were laughing and talking on the phone one night when she said, *'ask & allow' and I was like, 'well I go to My A&A meetings every single day'.* Yep, Ask & allow and I use that while sending so much Love, Respect and Happiness to everyone who goes to AA meetings for their health.

There are many things from everyday life that You have to make better for Your Heart strings. You have to heal Your heart about what is said on the news. You have to heal Your heart about the negative things that people talk about. You have to heal Your heart from the criticism and judgment from others. We all have to heal Our hearts at times from a loss of something or someone. Sometimes You have to heal Your heart about Yourself, while in other segments You have to heal Your heart from not accepting its Best Friend. Your Source feels what Your emotions are every segment of the way and They know You want a change. They know that You don't want to be in the lower emotions because it does not feel good. Your body tells You when it doesn't feel good and Your Spirit lets You know when it doesn't feel good too. Your mind knows these emotions also and can pick up on this communication, and it is in the mind where You need to make the choice of staying in Your frustration longer or just adding a little bit of fun into Your day. Your big ole heart is very powerful for You to use at any time that You wish, and the way to go is always in a path that makes **You** *feel good.*

If You lose a person or a pet, You go through many emotions depending on the circumstances. You feel bad, sad, sick to Your stomach and sometimes angry, blaming or not believing. It is a sequence and cycle that We all go through. We don't want to feel bad; We want to be that happy, joyful self that We were, but…. IT broke Your heart. Yes of course, We must absolutely go through Our grieving times, and it is definitely an individual's experience, but there's no reason to feel bad, if possible, for significant amounts of time. A cycle does mean that there is an end. The other Soul is where they are supposed to be. They are happy and They want You to be happy also. They want You to know that they are safe and still with You. A Pure Positive Energy. It just takes a second to Feel that love around You and that will enlighten Your whole body with them.

I believe in MY heart, even if someone chooses to end their life, it is not a negative occurrence for them, even if they were in a 'bad place' according to society or Us. They finally have peace and calm in their existence. Just know that everyone has the sovereign choice when to leave, it is not up to others. That choice to have, is so powerful, liberating and wonderful for each of Us.

What if You lose Your job or didn't get the one You have been trying for? Your loss means something better is happening on the side lines, a better career and Your Source knows it. Open up Your intuition and find it.

If You're unhappy about where You are right now or it's the same thing every day. '*Oh, My goodness. I feel so bored, something needs to change*'. All that is, is Your Soul, Your Energy telling You '*it doesn't like where it is either*'. That's why You have these feelings. Don't feel bad if You feel less than satisfied or have negative thoughts, or if You feel bad about not being happy where You are and You want more, those thoughts are here for a purpose, Your purpose.

What about relationships? Say You break up with somebody. Don't You hear just every flippin song about heartbreak and loss? Are Your emotions of loss bringing those in? It is Your choice to listen to the song or not to. After any sadness You have to heal Your heart, but is it healing from that person or that situation that is not there anymore? It takes less than a second to change Your feelings and to notice something beautiful around You, something positive. Find a happy song and happier emotions will follow.

You can heal a lot from any situation and it is easier in the beginning just to forgive the situation, not the individual. Eventually You might want to forgive them, or not, but just remember, the more You hate, the more hate is gonna come back to You in Your environment. See their divinity the way Jesus or Your Source would do. If You see their divinity, even if it is just a smidge and love them no matter what, and that doesn't mean like them or the event, the power that You are going to have, that abundance of love that's gonna come back to You from the Universe, Oh My goodness! And because You're being awesome and loving and living Your purpose of happiness and joy, You will bring that to the whole world too.

There are 2 sides to every person and which one is dominant is the one We will see, hear and acknowledge. Every Organic has a physical side and a Spiritual one. When You diminish Your Spirit, WELL.. You will lose Yourself. When people get in a way where We would say, '*Oh My gosh, what did they do*'? If somebody does things that are that negative or out of control, it's because they are working on their survival, their very essence, their individuality, so that they feel worthy and they just don't know how to go about doing it. There are many aspects that change a person's behavior. Sometimes it is because of drugs, their nutrition status or overwhelming stresses. You cannot blame, criticize, or judge others because You don't *live them 100% of the time, even if You live with them.* From the past something happened to them and You can't say how it affected them in their mind or in their Spirit. You don't know who they have become on the inside or why they do what they do. No matter what it is, they were hopefully once in their life a happy, loving person, even if it was just for a little while. Think about that and love that part of them that still exists somewhere.

There are so many easy ways to lift Your Spirit and heal Your heart and You could feel a positive difference by tomorrow, some people feel different within an hour. The more You communicate with Your Best Friend, the faster You'll be moving forward. And the fastest way to find Yourself and the fastest way to happiness, is to have fun and be grateful for whatever You can think of at the moment. Being open minded and seeing things from all 4 sides, Your side, Their side, The truths and what everyone else is talking about. Be Happy from the inside out first, not outside in and not because a condition or person made it better.

One of the things to do in order to get rid of something hurtful in Your past is to change the way that You think about it and that will change the issue that happened in the past. You can also write down the things that bother You, but not about the people themselves, because You are not condemning people, You are just not agreeing with the actions. '*I am releasing it, never to come back again, it is no longer for My benefit. I am grateful for the thoughts and the growth that I've had from it, but no more.'* As You are releasing these things, make sure You take some deep cleansing breaths and bring that nutrition into Your body. Bring all the good Energy in and help fuel Your fire to move forward in the most loving, warm, positive and beneficial ways.

Another way is to work with Your mind occasionally and remember to let Your Universe do what it needs to do for You too. Take Your breaks several times a day to calm everything around You. Let the things that You want to happen, the way that they are supposed to happen, not necessarily the way that You planned them. The Universe will make it better for You. They'll make it more extravagant, more abundant and more fun every time, if You just let it. Listen to Your Heart, Your Source is with Your heart. Your Source knows those special emotions, that's what they read from You. They say to, *'follow Your heart' to the things that You want, that You love and that would make Your life more fulfilling'*. Your heart, Your emotions will never let You down. If You live through Your heart, Your emotions or Your gut feelings, You are working directly with Your God, Your Source or with Your Energy, and that is so much more powerful than Your mind. It will always take You to the right place.

One of My goals in life is to please others. I love to make people happy. I love to make people smile or grin or chuckle or shake their head and say, *'What did she just say'? It makes them stop and think, and yeah, they are gonna smile.* That's My job and I love doing it, and I love seeing the happy expressions on people's faces. It is all worthwhile. So, Me pleasing people and wanting to make people happy is different than a lot of people in their lives trying to please others. It could be Your boss, Your mother, Your dad, Your spouse, or Your children. If You do not feel-good trying to please others or making them happy, for whatever reason, it's probably because You're possibly not really making them happy anyway. You are following a routine that is semi comfortable and You are letting Yourself be controlled. There are many things that You can do to avoid those situations and to decrease those negative emotions on Your heart and it's all out of Love. It has nothing to do with anybody else, so don't let them make it that way and don't give anyone Your Power. Don't let them take it personally either, You're looking out for You, which is what they should be doing also and they probably are. Who are You letting be Your adviser? Who are You letting control You? You need to look out for You to get started and then You'll do it all the time, naturally. You are the one who has to achieve the balance, You're the one with the choices for You. You just need to switch it out a little bit and put Yourself first. If You work on Yourself first, with the help of Your BFE, Your children will look up to You and see Your happiness and joy and they'll want to be just like You. Doesn't that make You feel good when Your kids say, *'Mommy, I wanna be just like You, or Daddy, I wanna be just like You?'* Doesn't that make You feel warm and snuggly and tender inside? Play with Your Source and work on Yourself and then guess what, Your children will see Your divinity, the true YOU.

So yeah, please do follow Your heart. Do the things that You love, and in every single one of those aspects, open up Your heart. Live on that scale that is above satisfaction and have fun. *'This is what I want, it is going to be awesome, let's live right now and be Happy'*. You know when Your heart is happy everything around You is just wonderful, so do things for Your heart. *Be selfishly selfish*. Heal Yourself, but not the exact 'who, what, or when', work on the whole of You. Start grand, start big, why start small? The steps You are trying to heal from are in the past, it is done. Change those emotions about You, change those emotions about Your environment and see how fast the Law of

Attraction is going to bring You the good stuff. Know that You can change if You want to, at Your pace, anyone can. Then You just practice and play, practice and play, practice and play, and because You're in a happy manner, a happy place thinking about what You want next, You can skip along and have fun getting to know Yourself and Your Energiez on the way to Your future.

The more You accept Yourself as You are, and the more You love Yourself as You are, the more that You are and that You want to be, is

Chapter 5

Our Senses

Our 5 senses help Us to interpret the world and We understand it differently because We are different people. A white cat cannot be a black cat ever, unless We translate it differently from the situation that We are in. Most would say that in the dark, that cat through Our eyes is going to be black. Then Our imaginations and emotions make it that way and it becomes true to Us for that moment. Then, when You see the cat in the light the story changes, interpreted differently because of the environment. Both sides are true at those times. For Me it is never just black or white either, there are way too many colors of both black and white, each on their way to the other, with so much diversity and with so many choices in between. Isn't that wonderful to know? Everyone has picks of whatever they wish to choose, including the colors for their shadow sides.

Use Your 5 senses in a positive manner and that will help You every single day. Sense the beauty in everything and use All of Your senses to enhance Your life. Play with Your capabilities and be excited for the next segment, just like Your Source is. Your ears can boost the sounds of things, especially those tones that make You feel good to listen to. If it doesn't make You smile, then turn it off or sing Your Own song or make Your Own music. Your senses of smell and sight and taste and touch can be amplified if You choose and practice. The sky can be a beautiful color blue with wispy white clouds, or it can be freaking gorgeous with many colors. Add in the smells of the wind and greenery or flowers, and maybe even the smell and feel of the rain that comes with the clouds. Your senses are free and readily available for You to use as You wish, and if some aren't functioning or flowing, the other faculties can be strengthened for Your benefit.

Use Your senses while allowing others to use theirs, We all deserve that. You also should practice turning off Your senses or focusing on something else when it is not Your business. It is their life, only help when You really need to. We are all correct in Our Own way and everyone is always doing the best that they can. They have their Source just like You do, and if they are ready, they will see and know their Own light.

If We break Us down to the nitty gritty, We are 100% energy and We are all connected through Our senses. Your 5 senses that are already connected to Your Source. The only part of You that really needs to 'sense the difference' is Your mind, and Your mind is such a small but important percentage of who You are totally. Your mind and Your body only mean something to You while You are here on this Earth, which means both are controlled and changed by the things that happen for You and around You in Your environment. Use *All* of Your senses and don't limit or be confined Your life by only using five of them. Acknowledge and accept Your BFE in the morning and throughout the day. **Save Space for Source** and this will give You the 6th, 7th, 8th and beyond senses, which is far more powerful for You and anybody. It will never hurt You or overwhelm You to expand what Your mind can do for You. Add in Your Higher Consciousness to Your physical senses, it is Your choice. Believe in Yourself and in Your 6th sense and beyond.

'Belief creates the actual fact.'
William James

Chapter 6
Action & Reaction

Action and reaction are ways that We communicate with each other to let someone know just how You feel or how You can handle a situation. Different situations call for different reactions, and altered states of mind give different actions or reactions. *Action means: action or no action*. Action also means just to look around Your environment and observe, which is still an action. When You do respond, are You going to respond from a calmer Source sort of way, or are You going to stay forward and take a more action-oriented reaction or a speaking reaction to the circumstance? Ask Yourself if You are taking action, 'where is it coming from'? Fear and ego, or is it coming from Your heart and above, with peace and calm knowing that it is going to be okay? Your action or Your reaction to what's coming towards You decides which way You are going to go and how much fun You are going to have along the way.

People say and do things to get a reaction out of You and that could just be by simply asking You a question. There are several things that You can do or say to that person to make it all good for You no matter the circumstance. For some of Your actions and reactions, just think about it first, *'does it, the situation or the person need or deserve a response? Is the answer about Me or someone else? Is it going to benefit Me now to respond?*

When We react, Our egos are involved most of the time. Your ego is trying to protect You even if You don't really need to be saved. What have You been programmed to do? What cycles or habits remind You to do or not to do? The more contrasts that You've been through in Your life, the more that You're going to be in that reactive mode, that ego mode for Your survival. The bottom line to people's conscious thoughts and actions are from their programs and routines learned from what Our brain has picked up from society and from whomever You were with growing up, Your parents, grandparents, Your teachers or from the circumstances in Your environments. The reactions that You live every single day, are based on experiences real to You or not.

There are four actions or reactions that I counted as important to Me. First is quickly, as in fight or flight, a drastic action to save a life. The second is reacting fast without really thinking it through, though no threat is nearby. Third is not knowing what to do and slowly choosing wisely, and last is just plain taking Your time and letting things unfold as they will and then responding as it progresses forward.

First of all, most things do not need to be done right now. There might be some benefits of doing some things right now, but then to think about later on, 'how are You going to feel'? In most scenarios You can take Your time and gather Your thoughts, and You have to gather Your thoughts from all of Your brains and the most important ones are what? Yes, Your heart and Your gut. Only then do You use Your thinking brain. Don't just use Your conscious, practical mind, it will limit You so much. If You are stressed out, You are only working with Your conscious mind. If You just take a little bit more time, You learn more and You take less risks. Remember, stress is only working in Your mind. If You can calm Your mind just for a little bit every day, that is when You can become whole and all the perfect answers for each moment can be revealed within seconds if You are already balanced before You even step into a situation.

The first action and reaction happens only a few times in Our lives, hopefully. This is where We have to move quickly. A 'save Your life right now kind of segment or fight or flight'.

The second reaction that You can have, is one that You just can't control and then it is done. It can be positive or negative. It's not even a second before You're there in that emotion and You fly off the handle. Do You yell, pace, laugh, storm out or reach for something to help You? When You get to that point, I think it's harder to control because You have passed a certain level. Please ask the right person for help if it happens frequently or if You or a loved one becomes afraid.

The third reaction I have had many times, which is My answer of 'maybe, or I don't know, or I am not sure yet'. This just means that when You are ready to say Yes (if You do), it's going to be something that You really want to say Yes to. Have a little patience, it is not forever, it is just a smidge of time. Imagine if You just jumped right in and started a momentum not exactly where You wanted that segment to start. The Laws of Attraction and Momentum are going to start right when You decide. If You have that clarity, self-assuredness and remember that You are backed up 100% of the time, You don't need to quickly react most of the time. Again, most things don't need to be rushed. You can wait, contemplate and then the best will happen for You.

The fourth reaction or action, I believe is the best one and I have to practice and play this frequently. After the stimulation and acknowledgement, be the observer of the question and let the situation pan out on its Own. You will know when and what to do and a lot of the time it'll work itself out. Yes, sit back, observe it and don't do anything, don't react but assess. You really do have that easier choice to step back and possibly realize that, *'hey, this is not really My business'. I know that it is My family or My friends and I love them very much, but this is an opportunity for Me to back off so they can get their own clarity as I send them love, support and respect*. It doesn't matter if it's Your boss in Your workplace, it's not going to do any good unless You know how to respond. Because using conscious consideration and waiting to answer, even if it's just for a few seconds, You'll know just what to say or do. Let the response be on Your time when You can. If You need a moment and You ask for it and it's not given, then they probably don't have very much respect for You. Yes, they might have to get the job done, but You don't have to play that game in some situations. You don't need to respond promptly unless it is when there is a deadline at work, use Your discretion. To Me, the best way to be successful quickly is to let everything fall into place. Start Spiritually first with You in charge and be on that feminine side which gives You a chance to reflect. Use Your Source and trust Your Spirit with You standing back and observing it from an outside position with Your Source saying, '*yeah, oh My goodness, this could be a little different and better for Me'.* Stepping back for a moment, to Me, increases Your honor, Your integrity, Your humbleness and Your power. It increases all of the positivity about You. Look for signs and feel Your intuition from Your Source. Intuition works fast, but don't feel rushed about anything or from any person at all, and usually if somebody is telling You something that needs to be done right now, hurry up or else, that is a red flag to slow down. Nothing needs to be discussed about how You're acting towards the situation and You do not need to explain Yourself or try to prove what You're doing. Most of the time patience is the key, and patience is an answer about taking action or not.

And it is definitely okay to say, 'No', I mean 'no thank You'. When You say no because it makes You feel better at that moment, go with it. Saying 'no' to things gives You potential and an opportunity for something even greater to come in.

Sometimes You do have to take action because if You don't, Your physical body will make You. If You feel tired, sleep; if You just don't want to eat and it is 'that time', don't, drink some water; if You want to walk outside, nature is calling You; if You just don't feel like going out, don't then, go home; if You don't want to talk, then it is not the right time to speak. Sit quietly with Your BFE. All Your choice, but listen to Your body.

As You move through Your life, of course You know that everything changes. It doesn't mean that a similar scenario from the past should be treated in the same way now. There are many ways to handle situations. I came up with four and the common denominator is **You**. You can change Your love and You can change what brings You joy. You can change Your programming and You can change controlling factors. You can change cycles in Your life and You can change Your routines. You can update Your faith, belief and Your trust and then Your action and reactions, depending on what is going on in Your environment right now, could be similar or something totally opposite. For You to start this journey and to find Your true self. You might get to the lowest of lows just for You to go in the opposite way and be where You are meant to live. Do not be misled, trust what You are being shown and don't question Your intuition if all of a sudden it would make You happy to do it another way this time instead. Nothing is ever really over; it is always just a recycle of something that You can make a little bit different or a lot different. The choice is up to You on which way to move forward and act.

Situations that made You flip out, that made You worry, that kept You from sleeping or made You bite Your nails or eat all that s*** quickly, or made You reach for a numbness alternative, or made You lash out to somebody else, be mean or even snippy with Your loved ones, if You respond after You've calmed down, took a deep breath and grounded Yourself, when You do speak or act, this is what Your Source would do. Those actions will always move YOU forward, maybe not with the person, but with Your higher Source. There is always a nicer way to speak the truth or handle a situation. Stay true to Yourself, don't lie and don't roll Your eyes if You can help it. When You lie to somebody, it's just showing that You're afraid to be Yourself, that You have a hesitancy to stand up for Yourself and to show up with Your full potential. A lie is a lie and it's only going to make You have a worse time throughout Your segments, and whoever You lied to, it does affect them too, more than You know. You can acknowledge it and smile on the inside, but don't say anything. Sometimes an action or reaction will not help to change a thing. The more You play this reaction game, the calmer You're going to be and if You can calm down, then You can take the right action at the right time.

Using and playing within the Laws of the Universe can help everybody win by helping You pick Your right kind of action, and please know that there is absolutely nothing in this world that You cannot handle with Your BFE by Your side. The Universe brings You towards the things that You want in life, You just have to be able to pick out which way to go and which action to take, and it's easy because They show You exactly which way to do it. And when You do respond, make sure

You do it with peace, happiness and joy in Your heart. Make sure You do with unconditional love for them and Yourself. Make sure You appreciate the situation and ease into freedom flowing in that direction. You just have to play the game, open up Your intuition, listen to that communication and answer Your question, *'Do I like it or not? Does it make Me feel good or doesn't it?* When You start to take action, be excited, like when You can't write fast enough for it to happen. Everything with ease and grace and flow and fun and oh My goodness's... the whole time. That is the way that You want to feel before You start doing any kind of action. And because You worked on the Spiritual side of You first, that action becomes exponential. Your Spiritual side always has to be 1st, which means You need to talk to You, Yourself & Source at the very beginning of a segment and ask Yourself, *'What do You think, does this make ME feel good? No, well maybe not then, I'm not going to make that decision right now. Or ok, that makes Me feel good, so heck yea, oh My gosh, let's do it then, absolutely!'*

It is not what You say & it is not the life that You choose. It is actually the actions & reactions in life that You live, which shows You Your life and reveals who You are.

Chapter 7

It is Always Done Your Way
It is Always about You

You create a lot more than You think, yep, You manifest all the time. When You are co creating You are trying new things and working on Your desires and goals of something that You would Love to bring into this world. Source and The Laws of the Universe help to bridge whatever You want into a reality and then You can keep moving forward towards what You want and where You want to be. According to Your Universe and Source, it is always about You and it is always done Your way.

You create Your own reality even if You have to follow the guidelines of where You work, family guidelines, the governments rules, societies and Our friend's thoughts, and the expectations of Your religion. *You have to be at work at a certain time, but You choose the path that You want to be on to get there. You can set up Your work space, for the most part, exactly the way You see fit. Family, friends and society, those 'ways' can be changed in Your favor. The government, well poo, they are doing the best they can, and as for Your religion, that is totally up to YOU.* Even when We have to follow the policies and regulations, We still always do things Our way.

There are a lot of people out there who don't believe that they are in control, and some people who know that they have control but don't want to take that chance and admit it. You always do it Your way even if You don't believe that You have that power. Power! Just the sight and thought of that word causes fear in people because they are reliving or associating 'power' with control, pain, negativity, conditioning, coercion, manipulation, fear, the unknown, etc..

So, think about the people that would have physical control over You. Are they bigger and stronger, or higher up the ladder, or are You just afraid of them for some reason? Some people act really big and strong and they look really big and strong, but they're not that way in many aspects at all. There are 2 sides to their story and one of them We don't know. If You are in a situation with physical control over You, Your family or Your possessions, please find someone to help. *There are angels all over the place.*

Think of someone that You believe controls You mentally with the things that they say to You or the things they say about You to other people. Eventually over time You will think and believe that You don't have that ultimate power because they could change Your mind about Yourself. They can't harm Your mind if You don't let them program You. You can stop their words, which is all they are, by humming and thinking quietly to Yourself and Source, Your Best Friend Energy about how great that You are. You know there are 2 sides to their story too and what they say is really what they actually think about themselves. To Me, they just don't see *You* and they are definitely afraid to see how powerful You actually are. And, no one can ever command Your Spiritual mind except for You, that is between You and Your Source, no matter who tells You differently.

If it is an environment that You don't appreciate anymore, like work or community, there are methods to help You cope until a change can occur. One way to do it, is to find amusement and fun in it. Another way is to find the positives, because You can always find the positives, and if You do that, pretty soon You'll see the positives that You didn't notice before. Another way is to be grateful of what You do have and there is plenty to choose from if You look around. One of the easiest paths to environmental happiness is to mind Your Own business about situations around You. Most scenes have nothing to do with You anyway and don't let people around You try to involve You either. It is Your choice to say, 'no thanx'. During these segments in Your life, try to focus on You and Your BFE changing things around for the better of You. This is when You practice smiling. This is when You play Your games quietly with *You, Yourself & Your Source* and be in Your Own little world.

We all go through dark or shadow segments also. We learn from both the light and the shadow sides. Our shadow side nurtures Us unconsciously and helps Us cope with the environments We are in. If You unconsciously or consciously stay in the shadows, in those lower habits or routines, then You can consciously move on up by never giving up on You, Your' integrity, Your honor, Your True Self and Your Oneness with Your' BFE. It is still in Your control to change. In those trying or uncomfortable times in Our lives, We need balance to be able to step out into Our light again, the balance being between You and Your Source.

We don't live the same lives, but We all go through the same rotations when something happens. Some people don't move forward, they don't step out of the cycle when they can. Sadness, guilt, anger, fear, the why's, feeling alone, trying to see what You missed and repeat. Those emotions are on the lower part of the Happiness Scale. Being in a lower vibration is NOT a bad thing; We need those feelings to know We want change. If You stay however in the lower emotions or less than satisfied on the Happiness scale, eventually it will affect Your mind and then Your physical body in a not so positive way. Don't wait until it reaches Your physical body and something happens like a disease or an illness. Our cycles moving in and out *do not need to be revisited* to show You which way You could go. We are all innocents at any deciding moment. Repeating painful or fearful cycles are not necessarily negative, if they are a slight move up in some way, because repeated cycles or routines are never done in exactly the same way, ever. It is a smidge different at some aspect. Each time You go through cycles, new energies always come in, so use that with Your power for right now or forever if You wish. Our Energy is Your Energy.

You can change anything about right here and the way that Your future is going to be 100% of the time. If You've imagined something, then You will succeed. Don't sit there stagnant, blaming, or worried that somebody else's going to do it before You, what a waste of time. What a waste of play time. Any adversities that were thrown at You, don't curse 'em and give away any more of Your power, use it to Your advantage. *Play time, relaxation time and fun time to the end.* You have to trust in the fact that You will accomplish it, so don't use the excuse that You are not in control. The life that You are living right now, You have to accept, You have to be positive about it and be having fun with everything else along Your path, and then You will find everything that You are asking for. Whatever You've ask for has already happened. It's not Your job to worry about the who, what, when, where, or how, it is just not. Be in the feminine mode, You've asked for it, and 'They' (Your Source, the masculine) has it now and They're trying to get it to You in the best, funniest, most positive ways. Do not worry about what other people think. There's a time in a place for other people's input. Most of the time it should be between You and Your Source. 90% of the time it should be between You and Your Source and 10% of time, You are sharing Your ideas with the resources provided to You by 'Yours Truly', Your BFE.

No matter what anybody tells You, You're always going to do what You want to do, but is it, *'You for You' or is it 'You for someone else or even everybody else'?* For some of You, and *I Love You So Much* and I know it's not what You want to hear right now, but Your Source knows what You need and sometimes the Universe has to make it so uncomfortable, that You actually must leave. A power that You might have given away for a smidge of time, and it doesn't matter what the time frame was, You can have back, right here and now, and at any time. It Is Your Power. You can always say that You do not create Your reality and if something is happening in Your life that You do not like, that You won't change for whatever reason and it is staying the same, You have made Your decision for that segment. If You are still there, then You are most definitely participating with Your thoughts or Your continued actions or non-actions. Again, please, if You or Your family are not in a safe place, please seek help and protection, grab Your necessities and go. We have the resources, Speak up. Your sanctuary is here somewhere around You and possibly not where You would think of finding it. In the meantime, be as close as You possibly can to Your Source and become Your Best Friend. Let Them be a part of You and Your life, because They already are that bigger part of You. There are so many avenues to get things done and it might not be the route that You would have taken to change Your life, but You do have the power to change Your mind and to do it Your way. So, who do You think is the biggest controller now?

You are Your <u>Bestest Self</u> right here & now in Your reality or in Your imagination, because You can't live in the past & You can't live in the future either.

Chapter 8

Contrasts

With every segment there is wanted and unwanted, negatives and positives. This is just how the Universe plays. Even if it's something that is so positive to You, there's always going to be an opposite aspect, a 180˚ twist, a contrast. All the contrasts that come around in Your life are just challenges to help You grow, not to make You fall down, not to make You be stagnant and not to make You get a disease or an illness. It is just a segment that You are supposed to go through and adapt to or not. Do not feel bad because You have contrasts, We need those to live. This is the way how We know what We want and what We don't want.

Ask Yourself how You would want Your environment to be from the contrasts that show up and then just ask and allow. You can break up Your world into all of the aspects that You live in or of all those roles that You play in Your life and say something like, '*From the contrast available to Me now, I want to have more fun and I want to find the positives. I want to work around great people. I want to be able to create and do positive things for the world and co create great segments for Myself. I know I can choose great nutritious foods for My body and I want to notice that it is a beautiful day every day. I do have the confidence knowing that I can make My life any way that I wish.'*

Your life is led by Your emotional *flavors*. Even when You are receiving something not quite right, it is still somehow for Your benefit. I always teach people that they can consciously find the positives in any situation, but You can also unconsciously find the negatives in any situation too. I heard someone say, 'it is easier to find the negatives. 'No, it is Not'! Once You play and practice, positives come to mind first, second and third. Now the question is, 'Which one You are going to focus on'? It is all up to only You on how You relate to and go forward in Your segments. It is Your choice.

Isn't it true the things that You consider 'negative or bad' that happened and You reacted to, the more negative things that keep coming in? These are the Laws of the Universe at Your service. Imagine if You could not react as easily and be a little bit calmer before You do or say something that is negative. What if You could just sit back and let it be or giggle at the situation and let it pan out for the benefit of You? The Law of Attraction will also bring that to You, because when things are working out, they are going to keep on working out. You have to find the positivity in every situation especially if it really, really, bothers You, and if that is a true statement, then it also means *it* is that important to You.

The contrast within Our minds, Our inner narrative will cut Us down faster than anything in the whole wide world. *'What You think about Yourself, what You say about Yourself, the way You feel about Yourself or what You say about You to others, if it's negative, those contrasts are going to stick with You instead of You growing while being the True You. What You say about Yourself, is what other people are going to say about You too, or that is what You're going to think they are saying. Do You judge or criticize Yourself? Well then, those are the people You are going to draw in. Thank You Source for not bending the Laws of the Universe... Yep, those kinds of friends that are going to judge You and others. They will know the way society sees it, or that the way that they did it is the best alternative.* Those unfavorable thoughts can keep You from Yourself, if You choose. To help You move forward, and I know it sounds weird, but You can't be negative about the things that You think are negative about You. You can't say damaging things about the parts of You that You don't appreciate or of the circumstances within Your life. You are adding contrasts in where they do not need to be. It just can't work that way if You want to move forward to where You actually want to be. And if You let things affect You in a harmful way for too long, especially if it is negative, it will be harder to retrain Your ego into believing what Your Source knows about You, that *You are the best just the way You are.*

If You actually believe that there are many things that are that bad in the world and that We are not going to be taken care of, then don't You want to have a Best Friend that You can always depend on no matter what? The Ones who are already with You all the time, the Ones that made You, the Ones that have been here before the beginning all of time. Don't You want to change Your relationship with Your Source and have more love and back up 24/7 to help You maneuver the contrasts that pop up? Well Yes You would, I can answer that for You. Now would be a great time to change Your alliance with Your Best Friend, and this Best Friend is so much more for You than a human Best Friend. And I'm not saying anything negative at all, because I have lots of friends that I call family, absolutely. I have a lot of Soulmates too. Everybody that You meet that has an impact on Your life is a Soulmate, even if it's just for a minute. Isn't that awesome? Soulmates can bring contrasts in or the opposite and their Energy is going to be with You until You decide otherwise. So don't make Yourself separate from Your Source, Your team or from You, because remember, You guys are of the same Energy and already connected since the beginning of Your time.

With a lot of things, if You leave it alone and don't give it any of Your power, eventually it will fade away and there are many situations that You can actually leave alone. If You leave it be and continue with the positive parts of Your life, eventually it is going to dissolve away. Just like the fog fades away, just like the street lights fade when the sun comes to shine, or when the clouds fade and move through cycles with all sorts of different weather as the outcome. **Nothing lasts forever the same** even though it has been a very long time for some things, for some of You. Nothing lasts forever exactly the same, it is constantly changing and You can alter any part of it, anytime, expecting better to come.

There are many ways to decrease the impacts of contrasts in Your life. Have positive emotions, find the good things in Your surroundings, be grateful for where You are, don't make anything a problem. Another way to change things around is You have to let go of the dilemma just for a little bit, let it go to the wayside. Go do something You love to do, meditate or take a nap. You have asked for the changes You want, so let it go for a minute and let the answer come to You. An 80/20 rule I read: If You try to fulfill Your life by just doing things and taking action (80%), it is going to take longer and You are not going to have as much fun on the way. If You turned it around and let Source do most of the action part, so now You are taking intuitive, inspired action only 20% of the time, You are going to start feeling better sooner and having more fun. Source will show You how to do things and where to go to get whatever You need. The *best* way to decrease negative thoughts or emotions from the contrasts in Your mind I think, is to spend some time with Yourself and Your Source. A short space of time where You can set Your mind and Our Spirit back to One. Yes, calm Your mind and pick a time to be by Yourself and step away. You are here on Earth with Your Source, Your Energy to create the life that You want for You and Your family and sometimes it's because of the contrasts that occur. It is not a problem to solve, but questions to answer through Your hunches. It is so much better using Your communication with Source. Accept the contrasts as they come and not before, because conflicts will keep on coming and going, so don't fret about the future's ups and downs that You can't do anything about right now anyway. If You wish, You can learn, adapt and expand with a positive momentum, moving on to the next set of contrasts and lessons. Be excited and strive for the next little hurdle, hiccup or question to be answered between You and Your Source. It could be fun, if You let it.

Have the conviction that You are going to Live the Life that You want to live from this moment forward.....
♡♡♡

Chapter 9
Big Impacts or Traumas

There are so many different thoughts associated with words like, 'huge, big or large'. (and no, We are not going there) When I worked in Emergency Medicine it was, 'multiple' diagnoses or a 'massive' MI or stroke. With using words like 'b*ig*, *massive,* having '*large* amounts', or even 'older', makes it 'something' that seems a little more difficult to let go of. These moments are going to stay in Your mind for a longer time, because what happened was labeled as *big*.

What about words like 'major trauma' or 'ancestral trauma'? Trauma can also be a continuous cycle that stays within Your here and now, for months or years later. There are so many things that are traumas to people too, fracturing Your first bone, failing a test, being abused in some way, losing a job, breaking Your tooth off, hearing, smelling, seeing or feeling something negative, even the little disappointments to some people could be a traumatic event if they keep happening over and over. Some even think that their life's negativities are from their ancestor's mess ups or their past life screw ups. No, no, no, that is so not true.

If things aren't working in Your favor, a lot of people put the blame on others, on situations or even their Source. *'I can't believe that My God or My Source would let that happen to Me'.* It doesn't work that way; Source has nothing to do with any kind of negative. If You are blaming someone or a situation for what is going on with You right now, You are also waiting for 'them or it' to fix it. Don't use too much of Your precious time talking about who to blame, what You don't want to happen or what has happened that You don't appreciate. Release all of the betrayals from Your life, everything and anything negative that any one has ever done to You, because right now it is All about You feeling better, not about them at all. Cut the cords, dissolve them. Take Yourself away from Your Ego and Your blaming pride.

With a lot of people, the pain, suffering, grief or the disappointments are all in their minds now. A memory that is being replayed or reexperienced over and over again. The way You feel and talk about Yourself and Your life is a truth, it is Your reality. The more You talk about that 'big' thing, the longer those feelings last and the more exponential it becomes. If You hear it enough or if You think it enough You will feel it, and then it's going to be true to this day and it will be in Your reality now. Also, with those thoughts being relived over and over again, You could have that feeling in Your mind that it could happen again. Well yea, You are focusing on it, it could.

All occurrences in Your life impact Your 'whole being', Our Mind, Body and Spirit, and Your hurt and betrayal definitely will make You a believer. The longer You stay in situations or think about circumstances that don't make You happy, whether it is real now or in Your memory, the more wounds that You are going to have Physically, Mentally and Spiritually. Sometimes for the benefit of Your life and happiness, You need to adjust the people around You. If You can't find mutual respect on a path, then You should go Your separate ways and it doesn't matter *who* it is. Do not endure unhappiness, suffering, or uneasiness. Please do not stay, it will make You physically ill. It is bad enough to have somebody actually change Your mental health, but if it gets too far, then Your physical health can take a turn for the worse. There are other people on this Mother Father Earth that are better for You.

Time doesn't always heal all wounds because You are always going to remember some part of it. Time does help You however to see it from Your other perspective, the one with Source, and then You can change the storyline or not talk about it anymore. You must know this true fact, that there is a 180° version, another part of You and a complete opposite or a variance of those emotions and actions You were having and could still be having, happening at the same time. Humans can train their minds to believe another aspect, which is still true. Anyone can rewrite those words and emotions if You don't feel good about a subject. You just need to switch up Your thoughts and replace what else You remember with something positive. For some of You still, You might never really heal all of it, which is ok, because You can always move on and be the True You with an alternative, positive recollection.

Some people say, '*the things that happened in the past made You stronger.*' That is true, You hopefully learned and grew, but You know what else I heard somebody say, '*that it doesn't make You stronger, because You were already as strong as You are ever going to be right then, You just gave **some** of Your power away*'. Now, You just have to believe that Your power is back, all that strength and courage that We all have inside of Us. Everybody has this power, yet some people don't believe that they have it. If You don't realize and accept that You have this Love and power with Your Source, then Your reality could be that of despair, depression or powerlessness, those lower or lowest of the frequencies or emotions. Nothing is too big for You to overcome. You can do it because You are right here and now with a HUGE POWER behind You that NO ONE can change or take away. If You believe that, Your healing can happen really quickly. You are already as strong as You can be right now and You can always practice and make it greater.

A lot of people if You ask them, not the ones that You hear on the news, but most people when You ask them if they have found something positive from a traumatic or negative event in their life, they have found something wonderful and positive and now they've moved on. There is lot more of that positivity growth than We are led to know.

Slow healing from anything most of the time is because the people around You or society kind of make You go the long way. I have listened to people say, and I've heard this multiple times, *'I've been in therapy for many years for... the same thing.'* What You are actually doing is not moving away from that trauma, that big thing, You are just relocating it forward to today with every re-thought. You could be finished with it, except You're bringing it back up in the now part of Your life, back into Your heart and in between the love You could feel from Your Source. You know deep down inside that it happened or is happening and that You really need to move on and heal, but... You can go to as many sessions as You need and please do. If You need to, also take Your medicine to help You calm down a little bit, or to be more focused or whatever Your medicine does for You, but also ask Yourself, *'what else am I doing for My mind, for My body and My Spirit?'* Hopefully, You are keeping Your physical body healthy, because that helps to balance Your mind, absolutely. But more importantly for the bigger part of You, I hope that You are taking the time for Your BFE and You and talking to Yourself and to Your Source in a good way. You don't need to bring up that past and try to find out what happened. Your mindset back then was correct and Your mindset right now is correct and also has evolved because You've lived and learned for those past days, weeks, months, or years. Every time You go through an episode in Your life now or from the past, You find something new, something different that You didn't see before. When something comes up that reminds You of 'it', start to think about it differently. Reminders are going to happen and if You could just narrow it down to, *'oh s***, yeah, that happened'. Laugh about it if You can and be blah.* Imagine what Your Conscious Mind, Your Spiritual mind and Medicine can do together for Your healing and health. Your body has already been working on it. You can change anything if it doesn't make You feel good anymore. You do have that power somewhere inside You and You have the choice to live Your reality or to live Your truth. They could be the same or they could be different scenarios. Which one will You choose?

Don't make the things that You think are big and holy s*** that important unless You make them positive, then things will change around for You. Try to revamp those major icky things, those holy crap thoughts to something less powerful within You, within Your conscious mind, Your 3rd brain, Your ego. If You make them no big deal or decrease their importance because You are here now not back in the day, it will make them not as impactful as they once were. You just have to change Your mind about things. The more positive and more fun You have now, the faster they'll change around with You.

Anything that happens in Your life is because of You. It is because of Your doubt, it is because of Your confidence, it is because of Your strength, it is because of Your weakness, it is because of Your understanding and clarity and it is because of Your choices a minute ago, a day ago, or even years ago. Now You know that You might not be able to heal every part of Your past traumas, but You can move forward in Your reality without them. You don't have to deal with past traumas if You are done with it. Today is a different day, so start Your day differently. Don't ever forget that You have Your Source here with You all the time, 24-7/365 days a year. Even if You do not believe this, they are still here with You and for You. You know, every time You get Goosebumps does that actually mean that You are cold, or is it Your Pure Positive Energy saying, *'Heyya, We are letting You know that We are here'.* Your Spirit or Your BFE wants You to think and live Joyous, Happy, Positive thoughts about the present and the positive things that *did* happen in the past. It is perfectly ok, honest and expected for You to live Your Purpose of Joy, Happiness, Love and Fun every day. Speak differently about the things that are bothering You in Your life, and also heal as much as You can from the crap that happens in Your life daily. Don't let it build up, or if You don't let it bother You then You won't have to heal, start before it even happens. You, Your Source and Your Team have this. Let Your intuition from Your BFE lead You the right way to Your better life. Imagine Your Team all around You and feel that soothing Energy. Don't try to do it all Yourself. It is a 50/50 chance if You do it Yourself. If You let Your Best Friend lead You on the right path, it will be 100% success. Be excited about what You do want and the right people will find You and help You move forward with the life of where You want to be. Just let Yourself be guided away by Your Source to a new, happy true reality for You. If You keep practicing and playing all those 'negative' **big** things, become smaller. Open up Your heart and love Yourself even more now. Introduce Yourself to the true clarity that the outcome is always going to be okay if You let it, and eventually, even if You don't.

A cycle does mean that there is an end.

If there's something that You really do not like or even hate, put Yourself in that position just for a minute, You won't hate anymore.

Chapter 10
Love Your Addictions

Love, love all of Your addictions, the ones that are harmful to You, those that add to Your self-limiting beliefs and especially the ones that lift You up. An addiction can be good for You or they can be bad for You. It can be unhealthy for Your physical body, Your mind and Your Spirit. Now with that first sentence some of You are going to say 'what?'. I want to get away from those unsafe cravings that put Me high on that Happiness Scale for specific amount of time. I wish to stop those short bursts of satisfactions with the highs and then lows that are harming Me. *'Why should I love them, are You crazy Cathy'?* Well Yes I am the good kind of crazy, but for You to succeed You must accept and love them first and then You can move forward with or without them.

A lot of the time Our dependencies start in Our lives unconsciously and then stay with Us and eventually become a habit. Even things that are bad for Your mind and body and that hurt You, You can still unintentionally make those a habit. A habit is an impression on the brain that has been reinforced by repetition, and if it also makes You feel good, well then….. All of Your addictions have to do with *'how You feel about Yourself'*, but they mask what We are truly feeling, cover up what We would normally do and they disguise who We really are. Your addictions begin by helping You to be somebody else, because for some reason You think that You aren't, that You can't, or You won't. They quickly intoxicate You with a potential relationship or a feeling from an opportunity, to where You don't really consider the outcome. You go right in to do it without really thinking so You can feel that instant gratification or that immediate bliss that sometimes puts smile on Your face or that gives You the 'what a relief' kind of feeling. You just think of that pleasure, satisfaction or release no matter the consequences or how long it's going to last. If something starts to trigger You or happens that is not above satisfaction, it is consciously and physically up to You to do 'it' again or not, but with the cravings those considerations don't get to that thinking brain or to Your heart and gut brains easily. It is like a reflex, quick and done. Addictions help You to get lost, so You are able to run away from You, Your reality and unfortunately and incidentally away from Your power and Your Source.

Addictions can be to *material things, food, people, or emotions* just to name a few. Addictions can be *thoughts* that You have constantly just to feel that satisfaction for the moment.

You can be addicted to having *negativity in Your segments* too. You think these thoughts immediately before giving Yourself a chance. They come so quickly without You really considering them and then the outcomes are what happens to You all the time. *'See, I told Ya and I didn't even do anything, this always happens to Me, it is ……. fault.'* Addictive thoughts, quick and protective from Your one and only ego, because if You don't succeed, You have already predicted it and it seems to make You feel better.

What if someone has *You addicted to them* because of what they can provide for You? You must be with them to use their provisions for You to live and then all of a sudden You are dependent on them for some reason or another. That is an addiction with a huge fear added in of possibly being out there alone in the world if they weren't around. Have You or someone else convinced You that there is no way You can change it?

Do You believe that it's going to be too hard and that You can't do it? Also having pent-up resentment towards Yourself for letting it get this far or for You allowing this kind of activity in Your life could be Your addiction. With certain people, it is often multiplied because You also have to take care of and raise Your children. Believe in Yourself and Your Source will show You the way out.

If You are the one holding prisoners for whatever reason, You are also masking and detaining Yourself many times over. Ask Yourself what You are obsessed with or afraid of, what are You addicted to?

Excuses can also become an addiction. *'It's ok, I am comfortable enough, I'm fine, it has always been this way, there is nothing I or anyone can do, they don't really mean it, they are going through a lot, ...'* Coming up with reasons 'why' quickly can hold You back. If this continues because it makes You feel better, You will miss out on wonderful things that could be in Your life.

Being ill can also be an addiction to some people, and yes, You can make Yourself sick. You're feeling Your body and it is telling You that it's not happy, so You talk about it and try to get love and attention from people. You could be addicted to the attention that

You get when You are saying that You are feeling poorly, because most people want to help comfort You. You can also talk about others discomforts or problems for that immediate satisfaction of concern from others. For some reason You don't see the love, compassion, or Your importance that You already have from friends, family and the medical community.

You can be unconsciously be addicted to *stresses* too. The daily ones that bother Us just a little bit at a time and the bigger ones that come occasionally. Remember, constant non-released stress is the number *One toxic silent killer..*

You can also be addicted to *'Diamond Art'*, right Helen, Mary and Gail? I love You guys so much!!!

You can be addicted to *adrenaline or to danger* too, because it gives You that 'high, euphoric, accomplished' emotion.

The circumstances in Your mind from Your realities are the ones that make You crave those feelings, and a lot of it has to do with what You eat. You ingest foods with so many additives and crap inside that Your body cannot digest it correctly and then all of Your elimination systems get sticky and bound up and You store it. Eventually it becomes a toxin and inflammation starts in and continues throughout the whole body, and that in turn causes Your diseases and illnesses. It also messes with Your resistant thought processes. Since Your brains can not think appropriately, eventually You don't even try to think about it or reason with Yourself on how 'bad' it is for You. If You don't get rid of that crap then Your body will tell You initially with digestive and skin problems. Some ignore them and some take medicines here and there to relieve the side effects. If it is really hurting Your physical body, You have to think about 'it' first to stop it, because it has become a part of You.

What if You are craving certain foods and drinks? These addictions from the side effects of Your *food* are not necessarily Your fault. Sometimes it is Your body systems telling You that it needs certain nutrients and other times it is because Your microbiome are not balanced. After a little while of junk or processed foods, Your microbiome, the controlling bacteria in Your gut/brain connection, will be addicted and tell You what You should eat or drink next and when to do it. Please l*earn about 'The Stickiness in Your 7 Circulatory Systems' on My You Tube channel,*

Preprevention & AlignAge. Just type in My name and all My videos should be there. Thank You very much and don't forget to Love, Like, Subscribe and Share so We can help more people stop their food and drink addictions.

Along that journey of You cutting down what You are doing or quitting all together, You might need to step back from the community that You hang out with now and that could include Your family and best friends. You do not have to explain Yourself at this time or ever. So be careful and make sure that You have positive, happy, caring people around You. It is so much better to hang out with likeminded friends or to talk to somebody else who's been through it and is doing really well. You will also realize that Your new Best Friend, Your Source has always been there and is so awesome and supportive. They know the things that You guys can accomplish together!

To help Yourself out and away from these situations, it matters that You start with the love for You and only You, Yourself & Source first. It's easy to switch and get that lovin feeling back, that inspiration that comes from everything in Your being that loves. Then You need to acknowledge all Your addictions and cravings and accept them. Yep, they are here and You can change them easily. Welcome the past dependencies that bother You with some Appreciation and Love. Embrace those addictions with gratitude for the lessons, and by embracing it I mean not to complain or think negative thoughts, especially those 'what if's'. Accept and allow the contrasts in Your life and be questionable at times, because the answers are always there or right around the corner. Find positives in the contrasts, and pretty much every single time, You can always find a positive for You to be better. Maybe not right at that specific time or in that specific reality, but sooner or later, You can. Then replace 'it' with some positive things into Your daily or Your weekly situations. Whatever makes You Happy for right now is leading You on the path to Your individual purpose and away from certain habits. The longer and longer that You are away from addictions to certain substances, situations or a person, the more and more You are going to see things in a different way. Those contrasts that started all this in the first place will not matter anymore and it can relate in a positive, funny, or in an amusing way if You choose. They defined You back then, but it does not need to identify You right now. You can change what You say about it and not even speak of what the dilemma really was. It will always be a continuation onto something else better, if You let it. When You accept it and You say, 'bye, bye' and You beat Your addiction whatever it is, and yes You can without a doubt, especially if You use the Laws of the Universe to help You, because They give You an extra little boost, *oh the places You can go.* You do have so much support, energy and power from Your BFE behind You, in front of You and on all sides. They know that 100% of the time You can switch anything around to receive more and more of everything that You want, all because You've changed Your attitude and thoughts. With each dilemma We grow, We expand hopefully in a positive way and We transform. That transformation in any segment of Your life, will be a revelation to something happier, to something delightful and joyous just for You. Once that mask is removed, the real wonderful You is going to emerge and Your true feelings are going to come out for the whole world to see and love more.

Any emotions You put out there will be felt by the Universe. So, what about those good addictions that make others around You also feel that way? I am not going to mention any negative ones, because again for Me today, it

is too wonderful of a day to consciously think negative and mess it up. So, the heart stuff for Me is, lots of smiling, kindness, gratitude, assisting, complimenting, loving, positivity or even acknowledging all the greatness in Your environments and spreading that Joy.
Become addicted to more Happiness, more Fun, more Bliss and to the anticipation of more exciting days with great things that are going to come next. Be addicted to that kind of adrenaline and life instead. Believe in Yourself, We do and then You will have continuous sunshine, even on cloudy, uncertain days.

Becoming aware is to become conscious of Your choices every day. Be strong and happy about Your intentions..

Chapter 11
Careers & Chapters

We all have the same purpose in life of living with Joy, Happiness and Love, but what could We do individually on Earth to have fun, pay the bills, love on Mother Father Earth and live the life that We desire? Right off the bat with anything in life especially a career, whether it's Your first, second, third or fourth chapter it doesn't matter, the main thing is... *You have to make sure You are doing something that You LOVE to do. A task that You want to do every day that You would not associate with the word 'job'. Something that excites You enough to want to share it with the world and make it even better. This is My Darma to the Universe.* What You put out there in the world is what You bring back to You, and those people putting that inspiration out there, are worth millions. The emotions that come with believing in how much You are worth and that what You are doing that will benefit You and the world, are way up there on the Happiness Scale. Imagine waking up with that flutter of anticipation every morning for the next step of expansion and learning more about it so it will grow. You are going to expand and grow anyway, right, so which way are You going to do it? Reluctantly, trying to make Your millions or to keep that title, or with enthusiasm, happiness, fun and having the clarity knowing You are doing great along Your journey and it is all going to work out in Your favor? Playing with the Laws of the Universe, Your joy in Your careers and jobs will bring more success back to You.

There are entrepreneurs out there that have started their Own industry from scratch and they became successful with their Own definition of success. It could have been from their hobbies or their ideas, weird or not, but it was usually from something that they loved to do, that they are inspired by and are passionate about. They also believed in themselves and their purpose, no matter what others said. If You were to ask them, *'How hard do You work? Were You worried about saving for when You retire and for when You take Your vacations? Did You think You were going to fail?'* They would say something like, *'Yeah, I worked My butt off. I had ups and downs and what some would consider failures, but they weren't. I knew somehow that I could do it. I learned a lot of things and look at Me now. I don't consider it a job and it was definitely not as 'hard' as doing something that I don't really like to do to make money. I do this that I love with more smiles on My face and it just seems effortless in My flow of ideas coming in.'*

So, You young'uns, if You don't know what You want to do in life, that gives You more time to work on Yourself and become a Best Friend with Your Source. If You just don't know what You want to do next, then start with the little stuff that You do like to do, that You would look forward to doing every day even as a side hustle and go from there. There is an infinite number of things that people can think of to do, so there has to be at least three or four topics that You could like to do. In finding Yourself, Your journey will evolve in front of You in the best ways possible. It is easy with Your BFE to adapt to Your new life as it moves along. Go with it, You know what I'm saying?

If You chose a job because of the money that could be made, You have kind of already made it harder for You. You will have more hurdles to jump over and You will have to work harder, taking the longer route to Your fulfillment, unless You fall in love with it. I've heard a lot of people say, '*Oh, You need to get a job that makes the most money or You need to go to school to do this because You can make a lot of money'. Yes, there is a lot of responsibility involved. Yes, there's a lot of schooling that goes with it, but if You want to be successful and make the 'good money', these are the things that You need to sacrifice and do.'* Again, choosing a job because of the money involved, especially if You are not interested in that profession, You've already put a little shadow over the way that You could easily be making money and possibly hidden something that You could be doing as a career that would make You burst at the seams with excitement every single day. If You did get a job because You saw the numbers, You are very special to be able to eventually learn to love what You're doing and stick with it. If You do Your job to make money just because You love to make money then that is Your reality. Go with it and good job!

If You must stay in the job that You are in now waiting for Your dream job to come to You, You must at least like where You are right now. To make it easier on You and so You get the employment that is best for You, You have to leave this current job in a good place in Your heart and mind. Find the positives in what You have right now and the positives will always show themselves to You but, *You have to be ready to see them*. Also to move on from one job to the next in the best possible way, You could switch some segments to make it funnier or more amusing doing the activities that must be done. Make Your responsibilities and the things that You have to do every day, something that You want to do. Look to those positives and then the things that are bummers, won't affect You negatively as much anymore. Also, don't go looking too hard for that new career or job, let it come to You. Don't think about the who, when, what, where or how, just think about the way that You want to feel when You are working that perfect job. If You're not sure what You want to do, that's fine, just know for sure how You want to feel. I say, '*I want to feel safe. I want freedom. I want to do the things that I want to do to help Myself and the world in My career. I want to feel love and have the best friends and cocreators and for the money to be overflowing*'.

If somebody says to You, who is Your superior or someone who is mentoring or teaching You something, '*You got a lot of stuff to learn*'. Most people would say to themselves, '*this is gonna take forever it is going to be so hard*'. Maybe change it to, in Your Own mind, '*Oh My goodness this journey is gonna be so fun. I'm going to have such a great time learning'.* Make it positive, make it fun and be grateful. That should be Your attitude. When somebody says, '*You got a long way to go', say to Yourself, 'oh, thank goodness and You know what, I can learn and accomplish it faster than what You believe of Me'.* It'll work out every single time if You play that way. Celebrate everything that You possibly can in Your chapters of work, including other people's wins. Congratulate them with sincerity, love and joy. Celebrate with them and celebrations will come to You also.

If You are a controller and You feel like You need to manage things so that You believe they will work out better, the Universe is gonna bring You more people to control, more subjects to teach and employees who won't really have initiative. If You work by Yourself and if You try to control every little aspect, especially future ones that *potentially* could happen, there are going to be more aspects for You to control and figure out. You know, those things that You would have to work hard on or force Yourself to do. Do what You need to do for the *right here and now* to accomplish Your goals for the day, and let Your Best Friend Energy figure out the other parts. Do the things that You need to do now and love it. Be positive about what You want to happen and the Universe will do the rest. Say, *'this is the end goal, this is what I want it to look like and feel like, this is what I want others to get out of it', and the Universe will bring You the right people, resources and ideas.* If You plan Your day with Source, it will not have to be controlled, it will be working together and cocreating. Even if You are the boss, You could still have that kind of atmosphere within Your workplace. We can all love and learn from each other. With Your passionate career or anything in life, You have to deal with Yourself first and then the others *might* follow. By doing something that You love, You will be meeting the people that *will* inspire You to be You and all of Your endeavors will be a success, right on to the next segment and celebratory party.

With the chapters and cycles within Our lifetimes and with every time that You do something, it should become easier and easier, right? If it doesn't, then ask Yourself why. Do You keep saying that it is hard? Are You making it harder than it actually is? If You really believe 'that' about anything You are working on, then ask Yourself if You really want to keep up the action of what You are doing right now. Try something new, don't always do the same things as Your life evolves. Another 80/20 rule, 80% of the time try new things and 20% the time, do the things You need to do. If the first thing You think of when I mention that 80/20 rule is, *'no way and then You think maybe',* then change that thought process and expand Your horizons. Instead of saying, *'no or maybe',* just talk to Your BFE and think of how great it could be and how much fun Y'all could have and then go from there.

Start by writing down those passions that You have. Note the happy things that You're actually doing now and how much time You spend on it in a week. Think about what You would really love to do and possibly make an income from. Source is ready have some fun with You, their Best Friend human (BFH), so what can We do, living on this planet to make it enjoyable for Us and for Them? Are those interests called hobbies or recreations? Those vocations that You relish doing by Yourself or the activities You enjoy with Your family and friends? When You are trying to answer those questions ask Yourself, *'does it feel good to Me or not'?* Don't worry about the bills being paid with Your new career for right now, or Your spouse being happy, or what Your friends or coworkers would say. This is about You, so add in the diversity of

Your choices to Your list. Think of a passion that You have, because if You *love* to do it, it means '*You are probably already successful at it*'.

To begin anything, You should talk to people doing something similar to what You are doing, which is usually not Your family or the friends at this job. Join those new communities, meet different people and learn from them. Learn something new every day from Your Source, because they are the ones who actually bring all that information in anyway, and if You think about it, You have all the Energies of everybody who is alive now and anyone who has ever been alive. For Me it is all those geniuses, all those kind, generous, rich, wonderful people. All the inventors, healers and all of those comedians. This is just Me talking, because like My friends and family know, I love to make people laugh, I am a comedian. So yes, new information from everybody, even the ones You have just met. This activity should be a constant throughout Your life; You learn something new or several new things every single day that keep You moving forward, and it will make You more excited to check that out and maybe try this or even that. Talk to Your Source and feel what a great day it is and the path will show up right in front of You on what You could be doing today. Start part time if You want, working with You and Your BFE and then expand. Work on it with You and Your Source and You are going to be building that bond, that trust between You and Your Energies and it's going to be the best thing for You.

Everybody lives these realities, and either You work and play with it and have a great time, or You don't. If You care enough to freaking love it and have a good time being YOU, You're going to be easily successful doing anything in Your life, whether it's in a career, family or hobbies, it doesn't matter. Doing what You love will increase Your power and the happiness everywhere in Your life, and it will also open doors to more opportunities that You haven't even thought of yet! I think these thoughts, *'What would bring Us joy to do today? Yes, I have My chores and work. Yes, I have things to do, but what will bring Me joy today? Besides meditating and saying hello to Mother Father Earth throughout the day, My little pauses, and Yes talking to Me, Myself and Us makes Me happy too.* **It makes Me happy & it makes Them happy too! :)** They, Our Source, Our Universe loves to be here and acknowledged. *'Yep, I am here. I am God, I am Your Source and We are here for You.*

Thank You for saying 'Hello' and yes, what another wonderful day it is.' Do something that You already love or like to do and then the Universe takes over and makes it even funner for You. Think about Your future using the 'emotional parts of You' having great times and playing the games of life. The Universe is jamming out in Your favor 100% of the time. You have a greater chance of having a better outcome if You let them do most of the effort. Don't go crazy searching for that perfect job or paradise or home to live in, let it find You. Feel all the happy emotions and imagine being in that segment. Don't go and look for that perfect relationship, let them come to You, let Your Source help You cross paths. *It is just magical if You can see it.* In the meantime, work on loving Yourself first. If You try to do all the work that You previously did when You found this job, relationship or home, it might not work out as well and You will be in the same situations. Be flexible when it comes to the plan and dream and live the outcome now. Do the things You love and complete it with Source, then You will find Your niche. You will break the cycle and You will be happy in every single part of Your life. So yep, You do really, really, need to work on Yourself 1st and I'm not talking about being selfish, at least not too much... When I'm talking about thinking about Yourself 1st, You can also say, '*Me too!*'. Just a few minutes for Yourself, every single day. I'm telling You to make Your life easier, work on Yourself 1st and surrender to success in every aspect of Your world, because isn't that what everybody wants, '*the easy life*'?

Congratulations on Your new, fun successful life, even if You are staying where You are. I celebrate **You** with so much Love, Respect and Appreciation and I can't wait for what You can teach Me.

Selfishly focused, selfishly in Love with Yourself & Source. That is using 'selfishly' with a better definition.

Self-Love Always

Chapter 12

Overwhelmed or Stagnate

What about being or feeling stagnant? Is every year kind of unchanged? Do You have consistent squabbles with Your person, or is it similar amounts of money going into and out of the bank account and saving as much as You can? Are the same thoughts running through Your mind daily? Is Your life one big routine? Are You bored and feel like there could be more out there for You? If You're not growing within Your life, then You are stagnant and You will feel like something is wrong or missing.

Do You procrastinate or become stagnant, saying *'I'll do it this week, or in a month or a year?' Procrastination* is a form of fear and it adds stress into Your life, and stress does what?...........

Using the Laws of the Universe is natural and it starts unconsciously. We are all supposed to go on the path of least resistance, and that doesn't mean being lazy either. There is no Law of least resistance, but it is a natural thing for Us to do, trying to do little for a lot. In Our society sometimes it is shunned, '*oh*

You took the easy way out'. Well, that is actually the correct road to take, it is the way We should be moving. The path of least resistance should be fun and it should be simple and pleasurable. Our Spirit takes the straightforward route because there are only 2 answers, do I feel good about this question or direction or not? Our body takes the path that is the easiest with healing and digesting and eliminating. Our mind loves the same routines and habits, because it is easier to accomplish the same things We have to do every day in Our lives in the same way. Isn't that being stagnant? To Me it is definitely boring, so switch a few things up and excite Your mind and body again.

If You feel overwhelmed, agitated, or if You feel all over the place and You just can't get started on something. If You feel uncentered or unbalanced or if You think You're moving too slow, these could mean that You are *impatient*. It could also indicate that You are trying to control everything or take action too soon. You have to let the feminine side kick in most of the time. *Yes, there are all these things that You have to do to get it started, and then this will come up, and then You have to do that and then this…* There is such a huge list. Break it down to the little things that You can do right now, not in an hour, not tomorrow, just get started with little increments. Write a list, an outline, or rough draft first. Then it's, *'I can do this within 30 minutes and I can do this in an hour'.* If the time is not exactly right, don't get frustrated, You are supposed to have those extra moments. Be happy about it and move forward and then with the Law of Attraction and the Law of Momentum, those Laws of the Universe that We live by daily, consciously or unconsciously, all of a sudden those little hour things are all done and You have something that You desired completed. If You've cocreated with Your Source, You also met the best people and found the perfect answers at the exact time that You were supposed to. Now You have lifelong friends or Soulmates that will grow with You in Your business and life.

Do You feel *overwhelmed by somebody else's presence,* by their Energy? Then that's Your body's way of saying, 'this is not a good person for You, Your energy is higher than that. Sometimes You need to change Your environment and the people in it. You are not alone, You always have *Me, Myself, and Us or You, Yourself & Source* to help You play along the way. Isn't that a great feeling to have and to know is possible? Do what matters most to You every day and then You will see that the world does revolve around You.

If You feel overwhelmed about something that You want to do, something that You desire, something wonderful that Your senses picked up on or something that You just received, especially if it's 'big', You know sometimes You cry. What that could mean is You just don't believe that You deserve it. I cry easily with happy things or sad things. *'Overwhelmingly Happy'* I call it, and I know that it is also Not A Bad Thing at all. Now with all the great things occurring in My life, I just have to believe that I deserve it and I let the tears flow. It does not last for very long before I am laughing and playing around again.

If You start feeling overwhelmed, break it down, start general, start smaller and enjoy that journey :) And don't fret, if You don't think that You understand how, You will and You already do. You were born with this knowledge; You just have to let it in and learn again. *One way that I did it was to listen, pretty much every day for a year, something new from Abraham Hicks with any questions I could think of. A new tidbit daily to change My attitude and My thought processes to something more positive, and to keep Me from feeling stagnant and overwhelmed with My life. I realized eventually that I had to make Me #1. Since then, 2022, so many great things have happened to Me, so many wonderful things that some would say miracles. Nah! Not miracles to Me, I like the word Magical better, yes.* You just have to step on a new pathway, still headed in the same direction that You want to go, just a little bit higher up on the Emotional Happy scale. If the world or Your environments get a little bit too much, play around Your home in Your paradise and spend more time with You & Your Source.

Be Happily Overwhelmed with all the Love that You are receiving, all those resources, all that kindness and all of the intuitions and ideas that are coming in that keep You from becoming bored and stagnant! Even if You believe that You are stuck, You could still be in balance. Have fun doing what You need to do to move along in Your endeavors, with You being a priority and then all of a sudden. *'Oh hey, would You look at that, I finished it and all My questions were answered'. :)*

Even if it is the same mundane things over & over again where Your Creations are concerned, in all that time You are Mastering something....
...... & if You are doing something You Love, You are Practicing Your Destiny.

Chapter 13
Judgements & Comparisons

We split up Our environments into what We need to do, where it happens, and to who will be involved. The opinions of others from the conversations that We have, also help You to know what You want or what You do not want. It can be a contrast or You can concur. We find similarities by comparing it or them to Us and to Our lives so that We can decide the right path to go on at that time. If You live mostly by judging others, add in all the Laws of the Universe and either Your life can go really well or it can go really sour and continue on a cycle in that form.

You know *some people* seem to get everything that they want and You compare Yourself to them because You want to be happy and have all that You desire too, just like You *think* they do. You would love to live the life that they live or to have Your physical body healthy like theirs, but do You know exactly what that person's life is like and how their journey was 100% of the time? If You did know, it might not be the path that You would choose. Please remember, it is not every part of You that

You want different, because most areas are good or even great. It is just certain aspects that You feel bad about because somebody or society told You that You shouldn't be that way. Comparing Your life to someone else's that You would like to live, is unconsciously putting You in a closed space. If there are some things that You like about them, then You can be similar, but still be Yourself. The only thing that You can be the same with, because You are part of 'it', is Your Inner Being, Your Soul, Your Source. This comparison is the truth, because We are all One Energy, all related. You can be anyone You wish to be, so concentrate on that smiling, happy personality within You and be proud to let it come out.

There is also the other half. You know, those people that just can't get anything they want and their life keeps bringing in more negativities. Are they focusing on all the bad, unfavorable aspects, expecting better? What You focus on happens, and judging or comparing with a poor emotion in You will keep bringing that to You and Your life, never to the other person.

When judging or criticizing something that You believe needs to be fixed, You concentrate on that and all the bad parts about it. You talk with others and then everybody focuses on it, and all that power makes Your thoughts a bit more chaotic, it brings forth that negativity more and it separates You from Your Source at an even greater distance.... Please and Please.. Don't ever judge or compare Yourself to the extent of despair or of anything that would make You believe that You are not good enough or not worth it. Again, any kind of negative judgements of You or anyone else will close You off more and more, and it will keep You spiraling down into Your little shell or into Your deepest darkest shadow areas, all because You want a part of or all of Your life different. Just know that Your shadow side is there to teach You and it is a form of ego and protection.

And if it is You or Your friends judging or criticizing others in a mean way, then *'Who the …. are YOU to do that?'* You are not with the person in the spotlight 100% of the time. They might have certain tendencies that You don't appreciate or that You do, but come on, no tags on people or situations. *If You are criticizing, You believe what is happening will affect You. If You underestimate a person, You also underestimate Yourself. Remember, You see people as You Are.* If You Yourself are judging, having anger towards others or ridiculing people or their actions, these are thoughts that would put a barrier into the good things in Your life. Those feelings will make Your energiez lower. Be quiet, be like Jesus and love. Look at, focus on and appreciate their innocence and their divinity when determining responses to situations. No harmful judgements, only assessments with Love, while finding and complementing their positive attributes, or ….. just mind Your Own business.

Don't let people who do not know You label You, which means anybody and everyone, because nobody knows You 100% the time. If people label You, sometimes it can be hateful, unkind or teasing, and it could be because deep down they are trying to understand You from their point of view. They will never admit that though, neither to You, to their friends or to themselves. If somebody says something about You that You don't appreciate, don't accept it and even better, don't acknowledge it with them. The characterization is only bad, no matter what was said or shown, if You let it be. Never let anyone try tell You who You are especially if You know it is not true. They do not know You, only You and Your' BFE do. You are perfect where You are right now and yes, if You want some aspect different, then things can change with the help from Your BFEs. When You finally realize this, You can let things and people go with confidence and love for Yourself and for them. The people that You believe hate You, are the people that want what You have the most. Don't worry about their dilemmas. It is their life to figure out. You are an individual not to be measured up to anyone. Haven't You heard that somewhere before? It starts at home with, *'Your brother or sister does it this way. Or in school when We are ranked against another for so many different reasons. Status, grades, skin color, heights, weights, hairstyles, friends, Your parent's incomes, having the 'newest things', etc. The list can go on and on and it does move forward into Our adult lives, because Your kids get that mean, judging, bullying criticism from You. Yes, they bring Your attitudes into their spaces'.* In sports and in competitions should be the only times We are compared and they should be fun for all involved, both the winners and the losers. To Me, *everyone is a winner in some way.*

If You do not want criticism about something that You really believe in that You are doing, then don't tell people and You won't get Your feelings hurt. Do You really want people to know Your business anyway? People aren't going to have anything to run their mouths about unless You bring it up in the first place, because rumors start from there. Yes, there are some out and out lies, but Your true friends will know the difference; they know the truth and can pick out the fiction. They love You and will have an intelligent conversation with You if needed. If You do get ridiculed, it'll teach You not to talk about it right now. Most of the time it is because they just don't understand, they want attention or secretly, they don't want You to leave them behind. There are 4 sides to every story, Your side, their side, the truth (which would be on both sides), and what people are talking about. Don't speak until You can confidently show the world Your successful ideas and You can shut off other's views. The right people You need to talk to will come to You and Your Source will make sure that happens.

Learn how to make constructive criticism a positive. I try to find a positive when I am criticized or judged now and I always can, but in My past I didn't really know how to change it. Usually, I would take it as being cut down, because of their words or of their tone. I would have tears in My eyes, hold them back and go cry afterwards sometimes. Yes I learned, but what a way to go, Ya know? Then I became stronger because I found My Source and My power to take 'it' as a good thing for Me. It doesn't matter the way that person portrayed it or stated it either. Yes, I saw their facial expressions; yes, I saw their body posture; yes, I heard others laughing; yes, I heard and felt the words they said and emotions attached, but it is up to Me to make it beneficial to *Moi*. You should care less how they intended it when they told You if they were malicious. Make it constructive and productive, even if it wasn't designed that way. You can take it 'Your Way' and make a criticism, favorable always!

If You want attention from certain people then work on Yourself and they will wonder what You are doing. Self-awareness first with love and then You'll be higher up in Your frequency. Maybe then they just won't be as important in Your life as You thought they once were. You should be the most important One, this is what Your Source knows. *'You are the most important One to Them'*.

When You come in contact with people to help, what You do is try to put Yourself in their place, to make it be about You with a comparison or possibly a judgement. Most people do it this way. Me first, put into their situation. When You are trying to assist to better a solution, sometimes You can improve it according to what has happened to You. If You have not been in that situation or if You really do not know best, then have the honor and integrity to speak up and say so. Don't go on what You have heard from someone else, because You never know where they got it from. I just say, *'I have not been there so I am not the person to ask, but maybe so and so could.'* It doesn't mean ever to talk about their business with others either, unless it is a life-or-death situation. Remember to Always send them towards Source, so they can meet their Best Friend for Life that comes with 100% support included, 100% of the time.

I heard that every saint has a past and every sinner has a future. I thought that was so awesome. And the 'sins' were labelled by man telling us what they are and what is 'bad' and how to deal with the person. Anybody can change for the better and most people do try, so Mind Your Own Biz. One main reason to mind Your Own business and not judge or criticize is because Your body and mind do not know the difference. Your body, mind and Your Spirit are all about You. If the emotions that You are feeling, or the actions and thoughts are from judging, criticizing or blaming, Your body and mind do not know the difference if You are talking about You being that way or somebody else. Even if You are saying someone else's name and speaking it aloud about them, Your body and mind relate that to You and only You. Only Your Spirit, Your Source know the truth. So that's one reason they say, 'when people are mean, they are also mean to themselves, consciously or unconsciously; when people hate, they also hate a part of them; when they criticize, they are criticizing themselves and they are living the life that they are talking about'. Maybe the people that they are around do this to them. Anyone can change, be who they want to be, no matter what happened in the past or what other people think about it.

If You can't imitate him,

don't copy him.

Yogi Berra

To have the life that You want is a reality that You can train Yourself into. That *power* is in everyone and then Your Source and the Laws of the Universe are going to keep that momentum going. Decrease judgements within Your life and just concentrate on You, because if You judge, the question always comes back to You, *'who am I'?* You will question who You are. Please, no comparisons that could push You too far. Don't give a crap what You think people believe about You and concentrate on what Your Source feels and knows about You. Fixate on that truth and then You could strut right on out and have no problem at all with any circumstances that happen within Your day. While You are in that mode of joy and happiness for Yourself and for the environment around You, the more positivity will come to You. You know the way that You're supposed to feel, so love and appreciate Yourself and be grateful for Your uniqueness. *'I love this.. about Me. I am so confident that I really am that special, and I'm so glad that My Source loves everything about Me too'.* When You compare Your life and wish Yours was 'that way', guess what? What! Because that thought is there, *You can!* If You are actually going to look at someone and compare Yourself and say, *'that's the way I want to live'*, it is telling You right up front that You can do it. Also, Your Spirit is saying, *'yeah, We could do that, it will be fun'.* See how long You can stay

Happy during the day without judgments or criticisms of others and just working on You. With practice that time frame will get longer and longer. Play the games with **You, Yourself & Source** and see Your results of the life that You wish for. You got this!

We are All One Energy. You are a part of everything that is Organic on this Earth. We are related both <u>Physically & Spiritually</u>.

Have Unconditional Love for Everyone, especially for You!

....♡ ♡ ♡ ♡

Chapter 14

No One Loves Me

I don't Love My-Self

Are You feeling lack of Love in Your heart from You, from Your Source or from other people? Were You so bombarded by all the less than satisfied thoughts in Your head from You and other people, that You just locked it up inside Your ego and haven't let out yet? You might be mad at someone or Yourself and it is holding You down, but Your Source never lessens Their love for You and ever dislikes how You are living or surviving. First of all, *Please don't say that 'nobody Loves You or that You are alone',* because You know deep down in Your heart that it is *'Not True'. You are only thinking of certain people and it might be blocking love to You from the ones who would be a sweet friend.* No matter what You think or believe, You have never, ever been alone. Your Source, Your Spirit was and always is with You. Even in Your deepest darkest hour or hours Your light was still there, it is always there, just dimmed down a little bit. Your glow or Your pilot light never goes out and it flies freely into Pure Positive Energy at the end of Your time on Earth.

We All have a shadow side. You are a shadow version of Yourself when You are in those lower frequencies and You believe 'it' to be true. Your shadow side is that darker part of You, the negative side, the anything less than satisfied side on the *Happiness Scale,* Chapter 29. It is that little vulnerable part, that special part of You that You hide or that You are trying to suppress from society for whatever reason. While You are in Your insecure place, Your light, Your divinity is hidden even from Yourself. You have to know in that state, You are hiding from Your true self, the real You. Your shadow side is dominant when You have cut out Your Source, and You can be in Your shadow side where You are with Your Source. This is the only time You can pick the color of Your shadow. I will repeat this many times, Your Source, Your Soul, Your Subconscious, Your Inner Child, that bigger PART OF YOU, They Love You a lot and they can easily Love the *hell* out of You so You are free and clear of any negative energies, thoughts or beliefs.

Do You punish Yourself saying that You can't do or have this… until You do this…? *Maybe after I complete this, then I can enjoy the thing that I want right now.* **Who says You can't do it right now or simultaneously? If there is time, then fit Yourself in. If it is something that You would love and it is going to make You feel good, then absolutely go for it and make Yourself smile. The task You were trying to accomplish will work out even better in the long run.**

If You believe You are unworthy to other people, to Your Source, or even to Yourself, it's going to make it harder for You to live the life that You want to live. If something happened, You are already forgiven by Source. Hopefully what You did to have those emotions now of regret, sorrow, guilt, anger or even resentment for Yourself or somebody else has dissipated, and what You are doing presently is different. The past has passed and it has to be fine, because You can't change it anyway. The only thing that You could be doing to keep it here, and the only thing that matters is that You are still saying them or living in those terms now. The whole battle is in Your mind and it will make it more difficult for You to believe in Your Own core values and for You to find those clear solutions to Your little hurdles. You need to forgive Yourself and live differently from now on. Let go of the Self-made labels, no matter *where* they came from.

Every plant, insect and animal already know that they are worthy. It is only humans who change Our minds about it, because We are told who We are, so We listen, We compare Ourselves, We feel it, We think about it and then We believe. You do not have to prove Yourself to anyone at all unless You are applying for a job. You don't even have to prove Your worth to Source, to Your God no matter who tells You otherwise. There is no proof or sacrifice that They require, because Your Spirit looks at You with divinity, Love and adoration only. They know that You are worthy, just like every Organic on this Earth and in the Universe is.

You don't need to carry anybody else's burdens at all either, and that includes anyone who did something to You. That is their burden. Yes it affected You, but it can only mess with You negatively for as long as You let it. If You go back into the negative feelings, it's because You are separated from Your Source. To begin and continue this journey, You need to have Self-Love and Self-Appreciation and then pretty soon You'll get to a great point in Your life, and You are going to love it when You do and when You say, '*yes, I'm glad I am where I am, and I'm glad for all the challenges, hurdles, for the contrasts and the questions that I needed to, that We needed to figure out along the way. I am grateful for My shadow side, because it shows all of the different colors of My personality. Thank goodness I can make it any color that I want and that I can jump out of it easily with the support from My Source'.*

Humans know that they are smart and We are, but We are not the smartest of the Organics on Earth. We are maybe the most capable of adaptation, but not necessarily the smartest about doing what We are supposed to be doing, like living the way We should be living in 'Our purpose'. Animals are existing the way they are meant to and they are actually living at higher frequencies than humans are, with no 'shadow side'. Then You have to think about nature, Our foliage. We have plants who are actually the smartest I think, of all the Organics. They are one of the highest frequencies on this Earth because they are 'One' with the Earth's body. They wait for their light, nutrition and water to come to them. They are Yin, which is on the feminine side. You have so much support around waiting to help You accomplish anything. By letting the Universe work for You is being Your True Self, an Attractor. If You live this way, You are moving closer and closer to an alignment with Your Source and with Your individual purpose.

Actually, You have a lot of votes on Your side already and there is a lot of Love pouring in. We have the same Energiez that flow towards You and Me, so feel that Love and make sure to Love it back. Every single thing that is alive or Organic, Loves You. They have their Souls also; every single animal loves You. Every single insect loves You, think about that. If the animals or insects hurt You, they're just doing what they're supposed to do, it's nothing personal, they still Love You. The Earth loves You with all of the plants and that is huge powerful Energy at Your side All of the Time. If You feel lost, always work with Your BFE and if You think that it's worse than that, then please get some help. Talk to somebody who knows what they are talking about, not just somebody who will listen.

Working with Your BFE means to do Your meditations every day and light a candle to release anything You need to. Let the light calm the air and the energy around You. Add in Your 'little pauses' throughout the day to talk to Your Best Friend, Your BFE and to thank Mother Father Earth for the happiness that surrounds You. You are going to feel so good practicing this every single day that You're going to want to do it more often. If You can't believe in Love for Yourself yet, then step aside and observe 'You' from Your other vantage point, where Your Source is. Be like Your BFE, Who Adores YOU SO MUCH! It Must Begin and Continue with You loving You first, second, third …. ~

Live life, trust in Your Source & Light it be.

Chapter 15

Your Fears

Either You are happy or You are sad, what really is there in between? Well, there is *FEAR*..

The feelings of fear come from Your consciousness or basically Your mind, and Your ego is what sees fear as real. Fear is a person made word and a person made emotion and is usually not a fact. Most fears are from the 'what ifs and the unknowns' that *could* potentially happen along the way. They say that over 90% of what We worry about never happens, but it still affects Our day to day lives. Fear as a title, has many definitions, emotions, subtitles and appendages, and the list of 'fear identities' is endless. All fears have a unique name attached to make them *special.* If You are intimidated by something then You are consciously thinking those thoughts and yes, they can overflow into the unconscious mind and then yes, You can dream about them too. Fear is different for everybody, and it includes Our individual reactions and actions due to that concern. Fear is one of the things that is so diverse that it should be worked on individually, but then again if You think about it, once You start talking with the positive community around You, You'll realize that You are not the only person who feels 'this way' and together, yet still by Yourself, You can kind of clump those #*:@! into a few headings and it will be easier to decrease most of those dilemmas in Your mind and from Your life.

Fear has to do with a relationship to something. Whether it's a connection to Organic things like family, friends, acquaintances or Mother Father Earth, or to the attachments to monetary and material aspects, or to the relationships with Your safety and security. Being confused about anything is a type of fear. Anger is a type of fear, it is a defense mechanism starting in the lower, lower, frequencies. The sources of fear and addictions, (material things, food, people, emotions) are kind of similar don't You think? Fear is a huge burden to put on to anybody or to hold on to Yourself. With Your interconnection to Source, Your God or Whomever You look up to, a fear of not being able to relate, of being left behind, or the feelings of unworthiness creep in, especially if Your life is not how You wish it to be or someone says it to You. This negative aspect can be marked off right now, because those fears are an untruth for anybody, every time.

Both introverts and extroverts can internalize their fears, their doubts, their worries and keep that fire burning up inside them. Both of these types of people can also outwardly let others know how they feel, by the way that they act or from the things that they say or don't say. Even if You think that You are an extrovert, You still might internalize those things that bother You.

So, who or what are You afraid of? God, Ghosts, control, insects, the dark, the light, certain people or emotions? If You are afraid of ghosts, is it because a ghost basically is from the past? Was it an action? Was it a person? Was it just from a thought, or from watching all those scary movies, or from what people have said and experienced with ghosts? What about the fear of change? What do You think about the world possibly ending? Are You afraid of an unhealthy body, or of suffering, or dying? Do You have a fear because *it* happened to somebody else? What are the things that You say to Yourself that add in fear because of what You have lived and learned from Your environments? All those factors in Your mind from You, Your family, Your teachers, Your friends, movies, the people around You or society as a whole, which one is the scariest? Which one do You believe is controlling Your ego, Your actions, or Your thought processes now?

How about the top 2 identities to be afraid of that control people in every country: religion and government. Are You more afraid of the government or of Your God? The government, and I am talking about where I live, along with the media scare people with all sorts of things that are happening in the world, or within this country, with our finances, with the lands, how things could be, or to be weary of this person or those people, of new diseases, or what happens to *some* if You don't follow the rules. They show Us the *'scarcity factor'* of fear. If You put that element in, it will knock Your ego down several notches and panic could ensue. The thoughts of scarcity come in from many influential factors, and the wave starts only from Us humans trying to manage Our lives in the same fashion thinking that there won't be enough. Holding on to that 'potential lack of' mindset, will continuously keep You dominated.

And what does religion scare You with? The fear of being judged by Your God or to suffer under his wrath. What has Your religion taught You? As for any religions in the world, and I am not being negative about any person's preference, these are My beliefs. *You do You, as long as no others are disgraced, harmed or judged because of their ideas or by the way they live, especially if they are peaceful.* You don't have to like them, but You should love everyone without prejudice, verdicts or gossiping about their special programs and beliefs. We all can learn from each other's loves. I believe in God; My Source and We love everyone, and I hope You are happy with Your special community too. Just remember though, religion just like government, is also a business trying to keep You there by any means available. You can always be with and talk to Your Source, Your Maker, Your other half any time You wish, with no person in between.

If it came right down to it, I think that most people would be more afraid of God compared to the fear of the government. If Your Source showed up in front of You and said, *'What the heck are You doing?'* What would You do or say? You cannot lie because they already know it all, just like the government likes You to believe that they do too. Fear plays a huge role in control. So, who are You afraid of the most, Your governing body who wants to be in power over You and of Your life or Your governing Spirit who is the Power?

The fear of *abandonment*, of being left alone to do everything on Your Own, that is going to psych You up to want to hold on to things or to tolerate things that nobody should put up with for a second. If You believe that there is no way You can make it on Your Own with all of the responsibilities that You have, You climb up and down on Your emotional scale, and then staying in the lower frequencies You give Your power away to situations or to people. You do the best that You can to make sure that everything is just the way that it is supposed to be so everyone has a good life and You put Yourself in the background. There are only specific things that You are really responsible for: You, Your children, Our elders and Your pets. The others in Your life are adults and they can make their own choices of feeling good or not, and they also decide on their own fears.

What about the fear of *change* that holds a lot of people back? If You are struggling with anything or if You are constantly unhappy, it could mean that You are being resistant to change. In any situations, You not knowing what is going to come next can become a little fearful, and that unknown aspect, that vagueness can make any situation bigger than what it actually is. We tend to over analyze when change is trying to happen because We are not sure about what to do, or what could happen, or if We aren't certain that the answer is the truth. The common denominator to know how to transform easily in pretty much in any situation, is having clarity in knowing that it will all be ok for You no matter what. Know that things need to change to keep up with the adaptation of Mother Father Earth and the Universe, and they are going to keep on expanding whether You do or not. You also need to modify certain aspects just a little bit at a time, because growth is a necessity for You to live the life You want. You have to revamp along with Your evolution, or You will only be living a boring, constant satisfaction with no excitement or freedom in Your life.

What about the fear of *an issue to be confronted*? First of all, try not to think of the things that You're going through in any aspect of Your life as a challenge. Think of them as 'questions to be answered and pathways to continue to follow or not'. I don't like the word problem anymore; I use the phrase, *Ask a question about what to do about this or that, not 'solve a problem'.* You have to change the pathway sometimes and if You think it's a challenge, it is gonna be a challenge. Don't think that it is hard, because then it *is* going to be harder. '*Well, I work really hard for My life'.* If You are working hard, Your life is probably not as happy as it could be. You might be accomplishing things, but You're going to have a lot more hurdles to jump over. The phrase, 'if only....' adds in stress and pressure to Your life too. You are attaching an undo worry to Your story and it is suppressing You from moving forward. Cocreate with Your BFE and don't think it's difficult. If You think it is a struggle, You are the only one who can change Your attitude about it. You will always get through it; the struggle You have made is not going to last. It will get to the end and hopefully You will have made the journey a little bit better than what it could have been, all because You just released Your fearful concerns about it and trusted in Your Source and Yourself. When You know that You are going to find the right solutions, because You will, Your path is going to flow with ease, fun, excitement and with new opportunities that You didn't even think about, showing up.

What about the fear of *not being able to do something that You have already started* because You believe that You cannot finish? That is a fear of *uncertainty*, those '*what ifs'* pertaining to the future. It is *You* that is the dilemma because You are afraid that You won't find the solution or get the help You need. If there is something that You want to do and it is going to make You happy, You will find the resources in time, *if You don't have that little doubt.* That smidge of disbelief is a huge set back because it's messing with Your imagination and You know what?, it is messing with Your future too.

Some people have a *fear of the past, some of right here and now, and some people are afraid of the future*. Any of these can put a halt on You moving forward. Those conscious fears of whatever You're worried about could stem from the right now reality or from past situations. Imagine if You have that fear of the past because You keep bringing it back to now? Fear could also be carried forward on how things were from Our ancestors and then it is brought forth into the next and the next... generations. If You try to live adding all those in, Your now, past and future, basically You are not living at all, You are just being. Putting all three of those together puts a tremendous burden on You and it will hold You back from so many things in the here and now. One thing You can cut off really quickly is Your fear of the time ahead, because You can only live right now and You can only make something happen right here and now to make Your future. Forget about most of the past happenings too, because Your heart and Your Source can only live here right now with You. So, ask for what You want for the future, then dream and be happy about the way that it could be. Why not just get it over with once and for all and always start Your reference point from right here and now, knowing that You are safe, secure and loved.

What about *phobias*? Phobias are stronger than fear itself. In similar situations, other people around You do not react the same way about it because they know it cannot hurt them or it is not as terrible as it seems right now. For both of You at that time, it is the truth. Everybody gets startled and afraid at times, and it is the way You handle it that will help You move forward or become powerless to the feeling.

At times with things that You are afraid of, You can also have a *panic attack* and panic attacks can spiral to where You are out of control. One single thought can escalate and affect the whole body, and then the Law of Attraction and the Law of Momentum make it more. It is not always because You are afraid, some of the time it is because You are mentally and or physically exhausted.

With the presence of fear in Your mind it is a sure sign that You are trusting in Your Own strength. You know Your power is here for You to use, You just need to ask God or Source and rely on their power to guide You towards the right direction. You must always maintain a great percentage of individualism yes, but everybody needs to be intra-dependent too. You have to be interdependent on God and the Universe and interdependent on the people around You to survive. Nobody can be a sole, independent individual and advance in life. You have to interact with people favorably and also help people too if You are able, and You will succeed. The way that You handle other people and situations will determine how You live Your life and how Your segments occur.

Some people are afraid of *unknown*, because in the change they *might* lose their stability and never get it back. That's their ego protecting them saying, *'You could lose everything if You do this, it happened to someone else. You will have to work harder or start over. You can lose Your friends or the people that You love right now. It will never be the same.'* During any change there is always a known and an unknown, and in that 'unknown part' is Your Source. Don't be unsure about a good outcome ever, because Your Source has Your back. You do need to ask the Universe for assistance and they will find the best alternative for You. Source will always be carrying You along, trying to get You every single thing that You need, protecting You and laughing with You if You wish. Just give Source a couple minutes a day to help calm Your mind, not to have Your dilemma completed and it will all work out better. You don't need to be in the same situation if it doesn't make You feel good anymore. It doesn't matter about the time line; it doesn't matter about that space in Your life that You have lived this, You have learned and You're ready to move on. It has to be You to do it and that does not mean by Yourself. You got this with Your Source by Your side no matter which path You choose. If You believe, and You know that it is always going to work out and be okay for You no matter what happens, that kind of calms it down a little bit and takes away some of that uncertainty. Again, in anything You are trying to accomplish just follow the right path, the one that makes You happy every time. Believe in Yourself and stand up with confidence knowing that Your Source is behind You with all Your power. You are always going to be taken care of while You're on this Earth and You are always going to be taken care of when You leave this Earth too. Have the courage to be in an alignment with the unknown, Our Source. *Fear of the unknown? Nope and nah, not Us, ever!!*

There are no Spiritual reasons to have 'fear' feelings or to have them for too long where they can affect Your physical body. Physically, fear increases the stress hormones which messes with Your physical body and mind. It is all connected. Remember, fear is person made, mind made, even if that fear is a true reality where You are right now. It is OK to be afraid, but not all the time, no. Continual fear will become chronic leading You to being overwhelmed, having anxiety and possibly becoming physically or mentally ill. You know what chronic diseases do to people, they don't get better and they multiply, and being persistent with fear, that could double some aspects in Your life. Those chronic diseases are partially due to people having that lasting fear attached, the uncertainty, that person made belief of whatever it is for You. If You've been in that deep rooted fear, that ingrained state for a long time, You have probably built up a whole list of things that You want to be different. A side effect of that releasing will be that You will be more Spiritually in tune with You and Your Source, and then Your physical body will show You the positive signs of health.

How do You release Your fears? I found that there are little steps to get out of this and to find something better. First, face Your worries and face Your fears because You made those fears somehow at some point. Second, stop thinking and talking about Your 'fears'. Find ways to change Your focus to something else. You must release those negative emotions of a person made fear from Your mind and body, releasing and filling it back up again with happy thoughts and creative actions. Use those fears inside You, ready to come out, to create something beautiful and wonderful, Your masterpiece. Music, art, a garden, the best foods, etc. It is so easy to get Your control back by taking in consideration everything around You in Your environment in the most positive ways. Open up a little bit more to Your Best Friend Energy who has been here with You for generations. You can start right here and now and decrease those feelings, because *You can revise Your conscious thoughts and You can add in positive emotions.* You also have to know and say, *'it is perfectly okay to change so I am happier'*. Once You start playing, if there's something that You fear, then look forward to it and be excited about the unknown, that mystery of Your life and then it will help to adjust Your mind about it. The choices are Yours every day and in every situation, and there are so many avenues to follow as You are letting go of something You probably never needed in the first place.

Some of You guys are going to say right now, *'it's hard'* and You know I'm going to say, *'it's easy'*. It is easy because when You get onto this side, which is just a step away, of knowing Yourself and being in love with **You, Yourself & Your Source,** You will say, *'wow, it really was easy and fun, not scary at all. Who can I help now?'*

Just know that in Your ==Play Shoppe Journey & Journal book== coming next, We break everything down, find the common denominators, or the basis of things, or the reference point for some people to get started. We can name all the 'fears' in a few little names and We can work on them individually, or We could just break them down, bundle them up again and deal with them all at the same time. Why not? It can be Quantum! You can do as many things that

You want to at a time with Your Energy, and if You do with Your Energy, Your Spirit, then Your mind has to listen. Your physical body is already there and will already be tuned in, Your mind is the only thing that You need to change and make it a little bit different, just a little bit. If You are afraid of something, You also have a mastery of it. Ask for help if You should and only You can answer that question. Make Your fears Your passions and You will be able to accomplish them better than anyone. Love them and they will benefit You… Believe in You and don't hesitate. Open up Your arms and have the joyful anticipation of what Your Universe, of what Your Source is gonna bring to You. Wipe that fear right off the dry erase board, because You will always figure it out and it will all work out, if You allow. If not, You will figure it out when You are automatically back with the other part of You, whole in Spirit.

It is always 'a self-imposed restriction'....

Man U faXured issuez,

Man U faXured scarcitiez or fearz

Man U faXured hurdlez,

CAN Be Changed...

Chapter 16
A Victim

Being a victim means You are around an environment that has a controlling factor in Your mind, whether those conditions are from a situation or secondary to a person or people. No matter what happens on Your path, when You let others in, You can end up with the energy of being a victim and it can show itself in any part of Your life that is not going well, or that is... You choose to be a recipient at least once, and it is usually unknowing and unconscious and now, it is present in Your life. Being a victim is a learned behavior and You can also become addicted to being a victim. The reality and the feelings You experience make You believe that You have less control or no control of those situations, or that You have all the control. The emotions that prolong this attitude affect You personally and basically make You a victim longer. If this stress happens with even a few aspects in Your life, You can become a victim in many parts of Your daily routines.

What about the person who believes that they are not enough so they keep on trying to achieve more and more and they are never satisfied? Those *overachievers.* I am not saying don't keep learning and moving up the ladder in Your career, but ask Yourself the question, *'how do I feel after the goal is completed and I am on to something else? Proud, fulfilled or excited, or is Your energy decreased and Your emotions are that You are less than and You need to do more?'* If You are trying to be a *perfectionist* You could also be a victim, hiding those accomplishments and celebrations from Yourself.

Judging and comparing Yourself to others makes You a victim. Being a target of Your own mindset with the things that You tell Yourself, or the way You look at Yourself, or the relationships You are associated with, or what You believe about the lifestyle You live, has a huge impact on All parts of You. If You are that casualty, *ask Yourself why are You trying to fit in?* When You compare Yourself to those individuals or communities that You think are better, You start believing that without them Your life would be terrible or even that the world won't continue to be. Critiquing Yourself is just an excuse for You not to take hold of Your own life, jump into the uncertainties that You have and live. Don't fret about living like someone else, because the life You want is Not Unknown to some, so it can happen for anyone, including You. There is plenty of Energy to go around.

Sometimes We put *people on a pedestal* and come to think of it, when I first learned about God, He was high up on a pedestal, very powerful, with Me trying to prove My worthiness. This is what I was taught; *'do this, don't do that, otherwise You will be in trouble with Him, You will not go to heaven and You will stay in purgatory'*. Now I know very differently. God is My #1 (and still on a little pedestal absolutely), but I also know that I am closer to Them and Their Energy is with Me constantly, giving Me all that power. You too have that resource, everybody does, but do not put Yourself on a pedestal either, You are only 'All That' because of Your Source. People You know that are in a higher form, also have a lower one too. If there is an aspect that You can see in someone, there is also one that You cannot and maybe should not realize, even from a higher mind. You don't need to be a sacrifice to anything or anyone, We are all equal in energy. No human should ever be put on a pedestal by You. No body! And it doesn't matter what *they* think. Your World should rotate around You, just like Your Source revolves Their worlds around You.

What about the feelings of *inadequacy* that You can have about Yourself, whether You are unsure if You can do something or not. You are craving more happiness in Your life and wish to make Your situations better for You. Then You start thinking, *'How many times have I tried this, done that or not even attempt it, and then the outcome was as expected?'* The feelings of guilt, regret and self-disgust come on in, all because You want different. You cannot do anything about the past except to bring in the good parts about it along with positive emotions for this new endeavor. Then and only then, can You change Your circumstances and life.

You don't need to be a *victim of the future either. Scarcity, or the fear of possibility losing this, that or the other, the what ifs.* The future is what You make it from right here and now, don't even go there.

There will be people that try to keep You down and make You a victim, even in Your own family or 'close friend network'. They will try to make You feel like there is something wrong with what You're doing, with what You're saying, or with You Yourself. They try to make You believe that You don't deserve it, that You're not good enough or that they're better than You. All they are thinking is that they want You to be on their side, and to understand You they must reduce Your Energy to be at their level to comprehend. Not in a bad way necessarily in a coping way. Remember, every person has their own burdens and dilemmas, just like You have Yours. Don't let them bring You back down again. *Your Source would not put it or anything in Your path if You could not handle it.* You just work on Yourself and let them take care of their own crap. Live Your life and include them if You want to. Don't let them make You feel guilty or victimize You into helping them if it doesn't make You feel good about it 100% either. You can say, *'no or not right now, You can do it Yourself; I believe in You'.* You can agree or disagree and then think Your Own thoughts, and You don't need to discuss it if You don't want to. Change the subject and if they don't want to, then those are the ones that You kind of step aside from for a little while until You can say with confidence, *'I don't agree, or I'm not talking about it anymore. Thank You for Your opinion, I appreciate You.'* By stepping away from their energy it doesn't mean that You don't love them, and it doesn't mean that You won't help them if they really need it, and it certainly does not mean that You hate them either, because We don't hate anyone,

We just don't appreciate their actions or words. You know how You feel, and if they want to follow You because they know that You're headed on the right path, then it is up to them. They have to follow their own journey. If You do not want to ever be around them, then don't, no and nope! At least it is for right now until You can get Yourself out of the energy of being some kind of victim. The only one that You're responsible for is You. If You have children and animals of course they are included, otherwise everybody else is an adult. They can make their own decisions without dragging You with them.

How many times have We heard, *'why do bad things happen to good people?'* The only answer We came up with is, *'because of the environments We live in'.* Like I have said many times before, You create Your reality of right here and now every time, but it is also 100% of the time *'what is in the environment around You and in Your mind'* how Your life is. If You are a victim for whatever reasons, 100% of it has to do with how You react in that segment and what choices You made to be there. A victim mentality is choosing not to see what is right in front of Your face within Your environments. It is Your choice not to admit it and most people don't want to because they want to feel better in that right now. It's like a cycle, 'for the attention or for not the attention'. When You look right in front of You with an open heart to Your Source, You will realize and acknowledge that the person right in front of You, is You, and Your mind is the only thing that You need to change. Sometimes at that moment You don't have a choice to be a victim or not, but just know that it is only for a little while if You choose, and YOU never have to go back to that ever again. Concentrate on that and the perfect resources, people, and situations are going to come to You to help get You out of the circumstances that You do not need to be in or that You do not want to be involved in anymore.

Can I say that I have lived some of the things that people have gone through? No, and I Thank God because some of those scenarios are unimaginable to Me. But I can say with honesty and love, being on the front lines of Emergency Medicine for 35 years, I Have Seen, Heard, Smelled, Touched and felt those emotions from My patients, their families, My coworkers and friends. I have held many a hand, cried with them, prayed their prayers with them and I did not care what their religion was either. I have felt that anger build up inside Me to where I wanted to scream out loud. *'How could this happen; I just don't get it'?* I learned that sometimes You just shouldn't try to understand it. Empathy is a good thing sometimes but I believe that compassion is better, because You can see things as an observer, filled with love and the want to help someone.

Nobody's with You a 100% of the time, because there are Your physical, mental and spiritual sides. No situation is with You 100% of the time either, because when You sleep that puts *it* on the back burner. The only entity that is with You a 100% of the time is Your BFE, Your Source and You have that power that nobody can get in between, no matter what. Now that You know how much power You have with Your Energiez, You just need to believe it and You will never have to be a victim again ever, anywhere. Be happy and joyful and if You are not, then You need to make the decision to do something else.

You can create the life You want, if You modify Yourself first. *The 'I can't must be swapped out for 'I can'. Say Thank You to Your stress and the fact that You are handling it a little bit better every day.* You do have the opportunity to change something that is not making You feel good, because it is Your mind that is making You a victim. Despite what has happened to You in Your past, You can keep moving forward now with Your Best Friend Energy. Don't look back if it was not self-serving for You, and if it wasn't at that time, then it's probably not going to be now either. Some things You just can't change and learn how to make better, no matter what You think. And if You need to forgive somebody and forget, just know that the people who need to be forgiven the most, are the ones who You would want to give it to the least. To forgive, You do not need to reconnect but it Must begin and end with You Changing Your Mind about it. You have to hit start with Your heart to heal and move forward, releasing and filling it back up again with things that make You happy. Some people forgive and this makes them happy and then they don't think about it again. It is done! Sometimes You do not find the positives in things, especially as soon as they happen or even a little bit later, but You can always find the calmness and peace within You. You pick out the pieces that make You and Your life feel good. It is Your choice, Your Sovereign choice to do and be so. You deserve the serenity in Your life from any situations, We All Do.

CAN'T >>>>>>>>>>>>>>>>>CAN

Your Power & Your Confidence can only be a Benefit for You when You make every decision with Your Best Friend Energy & You Own It!

Chapter 17

The Past

The past is meaningful just so You can see where You were, what You liked or didn't like about it, and the way that You want it to be in the future. Most things You start now and everything that challenges You in the now of Your life, is based on a reality from the past with You escorting it into the present moment, whether it is a thought reflection or a physical memory. Everything in the past was a blessing in disguise, and the past as of now, is a stepping stone towards Your future. You can't change what You did in the past or what happened in the past, and if You can't make something right from those instances then don't try to change them. You do not necessarily have to forgive a person for what occurred, but You could forgive the event or the energy of it and then You can change the outcome of the experience, which means *how You've changed for the better because of it.* One idea You need to remember about the stuff that happened in Your past, is that it has opened up the doors to where You are right now. So yes, acknowledge it and now it is over, and do You really want to keep bring it back in? You did everything in the right way at that time, and You already know that You're going to do different the next time. Don't start Your future with a reference point to back then, You want to start fresh right here. *You were doing the best that You could and You are doing excellent right now. Any past segments do not have to define You now. Believe in this truth and it will benefit You forever.*

There are always 2 parts of You, Your spiritual part and then Your physical part and Both were there in those situations. Your spiritual part is stronger in every way compared to Your physical one. Your Spiritual side during those downtimes or the worst times was trying to make it easier and calmer for You, reminding You that *nothing lasts forever the same,* even though it can seem like a long time. That is another reason to change the way You perceive things from the past that are holding You back from Your great life. Right now, some people would start naming the hurdles and talking about all the bad parts, and then pretty soon they are bringing the past back into their now reality. There are many people that feel this way, and if it is really affecting You negatively then please learn to forgive Yourself, because regret and guilt will bring in so many negative aspects to Your physical and mental bodies. *In the court of God, nothing is held against You*. Energy keeps on moving and so do You and You don't ever have to go back to those old conditions. You do however have to compromise with Yourself and forgive, release and relax.

You could forget all about Your future if You keep living in the past. Actually no, You could lose Your future if You keep living in the past. Some people stay in the past so much that their memories are all that they live in. This is when You kind of forget about Your reality right now. They only talk about the past and they don't take care of themselves in certain aspects of their lives now. Ask Yourself, *'why am I living in the past'? Are You missing something in Your present time that You had previously, wishing it could be the same? Do You believe that 'back then' was the happiest time of Your life and that happiness can't happen again? Are You afraid, guilty or angry from previous segments in Your life that You just can't release in Your here and now? If it's something that keeps bothering You over and over then ask Yourself how many times are You dealing with this?* Living in the past is good in little happy spurts, but not if it makes You afraid, not if it makes You cry, and not if it makes You have that longing or wanting to be in solitude with You and Your memories. Staying within a happy or a bad past will leave You weary, stagnant, suppressed and sometimes fearful. You can't live in history, *unless You keep talking about it, relieving it and bringing it into Your reality now.* Past memories can only bring You short term gratification, so keep the best ones and start making new stories to tell and smile about. Your life to the world, to Me and to the Universe is very important and since You live here now, We need Your light. Don't give away any of Your freedom, put Your troubles on ice or put them to the side for a minute and rest Your mind. Calm those thoughts, the past is done, even from a milli-second ago.

Some people ask, '*So why does it keep coming back into My life'?* Well, who keeps reminding You of it? You, Your family, Your friends, Your doctors, Your job, or is it that society tells You, *'this is what happens, everybody's talking about it'*. Or does it keep on coming back up from what You've learned? Your mental body is what holds You back from the life You want, because We have been programmed from society and We have been unintentionally brainwashed from generations of Our family's sayings, actions, traditions, mannerisms, habits or comforts. I have heard many times, *'It's just the way that We've done things for years.'* The hiccup is, *'which part of Your family's history are You bringing into the now?' Are any of Your worries and stresses about something that was inherited to You?* Talk to Your Ancestors and Thank them for all of their help and wisdom. Let Your Soul know that anything which happened in the past that was negative or not supporting You in Your life now, You are not accepting anymore. *'I am breaking this generational pattern of any restricting boundaries or thoughts of scarcity, fear or doubt. I do not need to endure anything that does not make Me feel good.*

How do You subconsciously remind Yourself daily of the hurdles and setbacks from Your reality and from the past? What thoughts do You tell Yourself consciously or unconsciously, without knowing what You are doing to Your psyche? What are You showing Yourself and reliving over and over again that is not positive for Your body? What about clothes that do not fit anymore or those items You leave out on the counter that remind You that You have something to be fixed? Your medications are all lined up, Your sugar checking diabetic machine is out,

Your breathing treatment machine is sitting there. You don't use those for the whole 24 hours and You are reminding Yourself that You have something not functioning with Your body systems every time You notice them. Even if You really do not see them fully. Yes take Your medicine, but put them away until the next time. You know that several times a day, usually around breakfast, lunch, dinner or bedtime, that You need to take something. Do not remind Your mind or Your ego about Your limitations, and in the meantime think about how healthy the other aspects of Your body are. Think about everything that is right. Keep asking Your Best Friend Energy along with Your practitioners, *'what else?'* You will know what's good for You when the resources come, because Your body and Your Source will let You know. Then, You just have to follow Your heart, and only after that do You take action.

To add to everyday life, You probably have a lot of s*** to keep up with and things to stress about now. You can't do everything at one time, but You could focus on one or two things right here and now. If You are supplementing in and thinking about what happened in the past or the what ifs for the future, that even makes more stress on Your body. Your past or Your future have no power over You right now in this moment, unless You let them. Don't let Your *mind* take You to places that You do not want to go anymore, the ones that will not benefit You right now.

If You keep thinking that You've missed something from Your past, guess what, there's nothing that You missed out on. That path is done. There is nothing that has been stolen from You and if there was, then You are going to find it again in several places, if You let Your new Best Friend handle it for You. When You learn a little bit more, grow and find Yourself or when You die, then You'll understand, '*Oh, that's why I didn't get it*'. If something is for You, it will not be missed unless You are truly not ready for it yet. Continue on with Your individual purpose, practice and play and then what comes along is going to be even better than You anticipated.

How many times have You or someone else brought up things from the past when You were arguing or better yet discussing an event from right now? Stop it, that only escalates the little discussion. We are talking about a right now situation, and actually that '*now*' is also in the past. If it is the same things over and over again, then I believe that something needs to change, and It is up to You to begin it, not them. Don't wait for someone else to start Your modification, that is giving away some of Your Sovereign Power.

Don't try to run away from anything past, present or future, because the more You do that, the more You are going to be running. Admit it, accept it whether it's 'good' or bad', it doesn't matter. '*I admit this, I accept it and it **was** a part of Me. Even though I know I could have done better or different in that situation, that is not what happened. As of right now, I feel fine about it. There's nothing I can do except to change My thoughts, emotions and actions about it presently.*' Don't run from a potential failure either, because it happened to somebody else or it has happened to You before. Pretty much any segment in Your life is a potential failure, but You are also an innocent, which means You could start again at any time that You want to. Your true self and Source with good feelings, honest beliefs and Your clarity of knowing Who You Are, will always show You the better way.

Now, changing Your thoughts about the past, there are a lot of ways to do it. Most things from the past You can just kind of let go of so You can live right here in the now. You don't want to bring up the past unless it's something that makes You smile to reminisce about, and there are some in every situation if You are opened up to seeing them. You just need to be selfishly focused on You, and the focusing point should always be something that's Happy. You can make that choice every single time, with every single segment, with every single person, in every single aspect of Your life. Your Job, play time, hobbies, church, going to the market, meeting Your friends out, taking Your children to school, picking them up, going to the bathroom, working with Your physical body, calming Your powerful energy, anything that You do. You know that everything that You do it is Your choice on how You respond to or react to it. All of the beautiful things that worked, absolutely bring those with You, because they are happy times, but the things that You didn't get, the things that didn't work out the way that You wanted them to, or those failed ideas and unfulfilled desires, let them go. You can transform slowly or quickly. You can completely change Yourself away from it or You can keep it there for a little while, as long as it makes You feel good. If it is not good for *You only*, then it might mean starting a whole new path with some people or those situations not being around You until You're able to handle it and see it with different options. In other words, *it just doesn't bother You anymore, it's whatever!* Use those negative emotions and thoughts or anything that makes You feel bad about what happened back then, to make right now and Your future better. To build a fire, what do You need? You need oxygen, a spark and a fuel right? For You to fuel that fire, You need little bits and pieces, Your kindling, the contrasts, to know how to make it warmer and warmer, yes towards that perfect path. Use all of Your elements to make Your life joyful, absolutely. *But what if I let it go and it really stays gone?* That just means that something even better is going to happen for You. There's always a positive to every negative story and You know what?, that will fuel Your fire and add in momentum in a different way. Think more about the positives and the ways that You are growing forward with Your Source. If You ask for something, Your Universe is on it, so don't give up. Are You opened up to finding it? Are You really ready? And You can say 'yes' to that question all You want, but Your Source knows when You are actually ready. So fast or slow, cut it off or keep it around for a little while. The question that You are asking will always be the same, *'Do I feel good about this, or do I not feel good in My heart and gut?'*

You can also help past thoughts diminish when You meditate or quiet Your mind and be closer to Your Source. Some people concentrate on a candle's flickering flame and that kind of puts You in an area where You are not thinking about life, but You are thinking about the cleansing fire ready at Your disposal. Say, *'it is released'.* If You say it's released, it will be forever, unless You bring it back in. Do Your breathing exercises and work on Your core daily and that will help You to release those unhappy energies, thoughts and feelings about those things that happened in the past away from You. It is a cycle that You will always win if You let it and pretty soon, You won't need the fire at all.

Your Source is here to help You and to play with You *All The Time* and nobody can ever take that away from You. *Nobody can ever take that away, even if they are with You 100% of the physical time.* They are not ever with You and Your Spirit in any percentage no matter who it is. You are never alone Spiritually or in that case, ever. Your Source is right there saying, *'yep, We agree with You because You feel good about it, let's do this!'* If You want to change, then Just Believe. Your Source knows it is going to be ok and Your Source will show You the resources. You have the control and You do have it within You to change the things that You think, and then to believe them. You have the ability to live a happy, joyful, fun, a holy c*** kind of life, every single one of You. Your Physical body, Your Human body is here to Play with You All The Time too. All those little itches, the electricity of goosebumps that You have, absolutely. That is Your human body filled with Your energy saying, *'Hey, laugh with Me'*. I'm telling You that Your energy and human body want You to be happy. Stop blocking it with Your human mind, stop holding Yourself back in the past, because Your life can change like You would not believe in the now. Join Us and show Your Energy to the world, show Your specific blessed Energy to the world and remember, You are not just portraying Your physical and spiritual bodies, You are representing all the Energies that are around You in every single segment. That is a lot of power, which means a lot more fun, which also is a lot better for the whole wide world. If You're focusing on Yourself and making

You really, really good, it's going to affect the world to also be really, really good too. That is how strong You are. Let Your sun shine, let Your light shine, let Your Soul, Your Source shine through You. And how do You let Your light shine? Do the things that You love and be grateful for the things around You. It is so important to do the things that You love every single day and it can be different every single day too, multiple different things. Do the things that make You happy all the time and then the things around You that bother You, those contrasts that make You uneasy or that make You start thinking and reminiscing about the past, will be turned around. Be positive about most things during Your day and You know by now that there are positives to every negative. Make it fun or make it amusing, that helps tremendously. Let Your inner child out, laugh and joke and giggle and play, that helps like You would not believe. In Your daily activities play a lot of games with Your Source, it really, really helps You move forward faster. Learn about Your physical body, because You need to take care of it. Even knowing that Your body is Organic, it is alive and it is directly linked to Source makes it simpler. It's Your mind that You have to play with and alter a bit. There are many questions and answers for Your mind to figure out and now You have trained Your human mind to also think about the other side to that story. If You can remember a happy glimmer of something that happened, the rest of it will be positive, positive, positive.

IN THE NOW there are no dilemmas, because worries are what You bring up from Your history. Leave most of the past in the past. You have grown, lived and You are not the same as even a minute ago, and that is awesome. Be appreciative of everything that happened for You, and actually it was and always is because of You. A positive way to think about Your past from where You are right now, is that it is done and as of now, it probably turned out okay, and sometimes even better. What happened in the past could be a beautiful kind of love, a beautiful kind of Energy to put forth in this world now, if You have made it positive. Me, I'm just here to help You get on that path and show You the way that I do the things to grow up, all out of Love. This is what I have learned from many people and of course, from Source. I wish I knew then, in the past, what I am learning and what I know now, because I could have helped even more people. Yet even I do not want to live in the past, so I can just start now, looking ahead and kick ass even better with My Best Friend Energy in My heart.

There is a fine line between putting Your past behind You or pretending that it never happened. Which is better for Your Happiness? Your past always shows You, 100% of the time, that there will always be something New, now.

Chapter 18

Ego, Your Protection

& Perspective

Everyone is born with a Spirit, a Soul, a Source or with Our subconscious mind. Our ego consciousness of self is here for Our well-being, for Our safety and security, for Our comfort and for the mental basics for Us to live on Mother Father Earth. Our egos are the weigher of consequences, and it usually goes by what is wrong or the contrast of the situation. Your ego grows and gets stronger from the places that You are the weakest. Your memories are stored in Your subconscious mind and Your ego can bring any stuff back up again for You to relive. Our ego is what sees fear as real and Our ego will get bigger from the judgements and comparisons We have about others, with fear or doubt, or from any thoughts that add in uncertainty or possible failure. Your ego will put all that information in Your mind for Your trial and Your survival.

Our conscious mind evolves as We learn. Thoughts and acknowledgements start in Our mind and the messages come from the environment through Our senses, supposedly making Us smarter. As this came about so came Our ego, Our 'I / Me' definition. Your thinking mind can talk You out of things, it can make You worry, have doubt, feel unworthy, and Your thinking mind can also put any thoughts into Your heart from Your egos past perspective. Our Ego is the one that reminds Us of what happened in the past. After the doubt settles in, Your ego will kick in pretty quickly and remind You of all the sayings from past generations. All those absolutes that happened with Your ancestors that are stuck inside Your subconscious mind, because You have been trained consciously as You have grown. When You ask for something and then You doubt it or You worry about how or when it is going to happen, You are being counterproductive to what You've just asked for and You are slowing down the Universe from bringing it to You. What You are unconsciously doing is giving Yourself a protective space, from Your ego, in case it doesn't happen. This should definitely tell You to get out of Your own mind's past and stay up here in the here and now, where anything can happen.

Self-sabotage is also a kind of protection mechanism from Your ego, to keep You in a comfort zone where You know that You are safe, where You know You can handle little bits of change at a time. Remember You can handle anything, otherwise Your Source would not have brought it into Your reality.

There are big and strong egos and there are calm and knowing egos, and all of Us have one or the other or both depending on the situation. For Your protection if somebody messes with You, Your ego jumps in and defends You. It does not always need to be that way, because most of the time it is not life threatening. At times Our ego resists the truth and keeps Us from accepting help from others.

In Your relationships, Your ego is a huge part of it. Your ego just wants to play, have it easy, and it tells You, *'We don't like that, because of this….* If You are complaining or being mean to somebody then You are not using Your heart, You are just spontaneously using Your ego words or actions. If You can't stop reacting in a quick, harsh, negative way to something or someone, which is also a type of protection, then You have to change Your awareness of the situation, alter the environment or just stay away from it. There are always at least two perspectives to any situation and many choices in between. Everything that is negative, is also positive from a higher perspective. Everything that is bad, is also good in higher perspective. Everything that is sad, is also happy and enlightening from a higher perspective.

A varied perspective definitely happens when You add in 'the chemicals' that are man-made, hormonal made or brain invented. If Your inhibitions are lowered because You're drinking alcohol, doing other things, staying stressed out, lacking sleep, addicted to all kinds of sugars, or even pumping Yourself up making You more and more of something, Your words probably aren't going to be what You really feel and want to say. Words can hurt the both of You, especially when You didn't mean it. What frame of mind were You in when You said those words, made those actions or added in Your excuses? Where was Your Ego hiding, behind something alternative?

A weakened spirit, easily influenced, could be inside of You. This is when You don't talk very good about Yourself or You don't like Yourself very much. To move forward to a better day, You have to like Yourself a little, at least in some aspects, even if it's silly, '*My toenails are beautiful, everything else I hate right now, but My toenails, let Me tell You, gorgeous.*' There are so many positive elements about You, just look, and please do not wait to receive the compliments from somebody else either, You have to start with what You think and believe first. Focus on Your strengths and be glad You know Your weaknesses. Be persistent, have fun with Your Source every single day and start with You. Your Source will never waver, They are always going to be on the positive side of anything and great things are always going to happen according to Your Source. On a positive note, a weak ego or a weakened person or spirit, timid and shy, can also learn a lot faster, because they are usually looking and ready to accept and emerge into something better.

Boosting Your confidence and self-esteem also boosts Your ego. A strong ego or a strong-willed person will be competitive and play harder and be ready to win. The bigger the ego that You have, the easier it's going to be to change Your mind or to change Your attitude, because once it gets started in that positive, happy way, *'Oh My goodness'*.

There are several ways that I found to calm Your ego. One of the first ways is, *'if it's not Your business, then mind Your Own'*. Second, *'if there's nothing that You can do about it except to talk about it, then shut the* *f*** up'.* And third, *'if it does affect You, then take a step back and see it from a different perspective before You act'.* Shift to Your positives and change Your reactive words. Try to see it from the positive parts of it, use Your heart and then all of Your questions and all Your little dilemmas about it are going to be answered in exactly the way they are supposed to be. When You are Spiritually here with Your Best Friend Energy, what You say is what You do because it is what You believe. You do not need to be programmed any more.

If You find Yourself getting overwhelmed, frustrated, anxious, irritated or perturbed, all Your spirit is trying to tell You is to slow down. Your Spirit shows You by the emotions that You feel, and '*This is a protective mechanism for You from Source, not Your ego'.* Even if there is a specific time that something is due, take a deep breath, do Your little pauses and slow down for a minute, or slow down for a day. If You feel emotions of anything less than satisfied, ease up, think about something positive, relax, do something that You love for a couple of minutes and then see what happens. That's what I always say, *'whatever We do today, whatever contrasts come Our way, let's have fun, let's make it fun'.* We all want to laugh and have a great day every day, You know. Even if it is Me making Myself laugh, I don't care. *'Am I kidding Me?'* I do that a lot and why not? And then I realize again, that it's not just Me, it is always, **Me, Myself & Us** every single time. And Us, They just want the funnest path and the one that makes Me/Us feel the best.

If You don't listen to Your Spirit and Your body, You could eventually have to slow down, without a choice. Protection is also listening to Your physical body. If You are tired and You feel like You need to take a nap, that's Your body's way of saying, *'Hey, lay down for a second, lay down for a couple of minutes or meditate'*. You know, 20 minutes goes by really quickly and it will be a huge benefit for You and if You can't take a nap or go within, then do what I call are, *My pauses*. I do them throughout the day to bring Me around into the right here and now and to say, *'Thank You, is everyone (My Source and Energiez) having a good time?'* Close Your eyes, ground to Mother Father Earth, take some deep slow breaths and do a little bit of the core exercises. (Chapter 35) You can do this anywhere absolutely and it takes nano seconds. See how refreshed that You feel and then see how many pauses You can actually achieve in a day. Please don't ask me what that number should be, it's all on how You are feeling. Are You a little overwhelmed, anxious, or do You feel stressed? Or, do You feel great and You want to share it with Your BFE? Well then, take a pause. No one even needs to know that You are taking a bit of time out for You and Your Source.

The ego gets such a bad rap, because using Your ego You are going to have to find the positives about situations. In Our cycles with the Law of Attraction and with the Law of Momentum, bigger upward cycles are going to have bigger downward cycles. The way Your life will be lived will depend on which side of Your ego You are going to see things from as You evolve from Your ups and downs every single day. The timeline which is diverse and distinct for everyone, moves in a cycle that We All go through. During Our life stages, there is a process for grieving, different phases of marriage, a cycle when people have children, when somebody goes to school or gets a new job. In those processes that We all go through to move forward, Our ego will be involved every time, it is just how much of it and which part will be the dominant one. Our purposes in this lifetime are to have fun and have everything We desire. If You want that lifestyle, then

You kind of have to release Your ego, because You cannot be happy and having fun while Your ego is up there and in charge. If You rely mostly on Your ego, You will have a great attachment to an outcome that You are desiring. With Your ego running the show, You will feel unworthy or a failure if You don't succeed. Our ego is Our individuality so it can't be labeled as bad. I believe Our ego just reminds Us that We didn't like something, which is a positive to Me. In its own way, Our Ego adds in fear, the doubt and the what ifs to Our daily segments, because it wants Us to learn and possibly go the other way.

I believe that Our egos are closer to Spirit than Our thinking mind is. Your ego just wants some attention or a recognition letting it know that it is important in Your purpose. Your ego, since it's part of Your Spirit, can only follow the Laws of the Universe, so what a benefit that can only be positive for You. Don't just listen to Your ego though, because the egos information is very limited compared to the quality and quantity of answers from Your Spirit or Your Subconscious. Collaboration and human connections co-create something that is already started between You and Your BFE. Think of the differences in the types of information that You can get from Your human mind, from what You have learned and been programmed with, compared to Your Sources library. Being One with Your BFE, the information that You could gain from the Universe and Your ancestors' generation's back is unlimited and exponential! These other perspectives are all Free from Your BFE, all You gotta do is Love Yourself to receive it.

Play the ego game and keep *it* to the side, because with the Law of Attraction, the more You let Your ego ride, the less You are going to see the other half of You, that other part of You, Your Spiritual side. Stay more in tune with Yourself instead of Your ego. Your ego can dominate while You are here physically on Earth and with a lot of people it does. It is not ever going to go away, because You need it. You require what the ego gives You, that safety feature, but it does not need to be dominant. Shouldn't the controlling part in Your life be the biggest part of You anyway? It is Your heart, it is Your Spirit that will help You to be able to be around and handle any situations, with the best things happening to You, with all the right answers, all the right people, and in all the right places with Your Best Friend beside You. Your ego is always there and ready just in case, to protect You.

If You work with Your Spirit, or Your Source, You're gonna be more at peace with what happens. Wake up every day and say Your thanks and hello's, brush Your teeth, make Your bed, everything that You normally do and then do Your meditation as soon as You can. Set Your day up with the Universe, with Your BFE at the helm and with You allowing it all to flow in. Calm Your ego and then try for the 1st half of the day to only find the positives and happiness, and then You'll say, *'oh shoot, it's been 8 hours'; then it's, 'My gosh, I did a whole day finding positives, what can We do tomorrow to find more happiness?'* Do not react to Your environmental situations, respond calmly and be careful of Your words and really, really speak from Your heart, because that's what You truly believe anyway. It will lead You with a new perspective in a better direction. Get out of Your little comfort zone and do what is right for You. Do what makes You feel good and that comfort zone will change and You'll love it even more, because it's going to be what You want, not what You are just satisfied with. You should only be satisfied and content for a moment because it is going to change anyway, and that's the beauty of life. That is the expansion of Medicine and that is the ability of Science and Technology too. Life is always going to change and move towards the better if You let it.

You have egoic power and You have divine power, which one do You choose to be dominant? Your Source, Your Energy always speaks first. Listen! Make it positive and move forward faster using Your Source as a confidant, using Your Divine Energy as a top influencer and Your day will be better, I promise.

The way to become the most Powerful is to play more...

Don't settle for less than what You want & deserve. Which means, be True to Yourself & know Your worth.

Chapter 19

Live in the Now

for Your Future

During Your whole lifetime then and now, You have been adding up the way that You want to live in Your future daily by playing with Your manifestations both consciously and unknowingly. Every single day, You make changes secondary to Your little contrasts: *'I don't really like that, this would be better, wouldn't that be nice and nope, that makes Me feel bad, or heck yeah, Let's do it'*.

There are several reasons to live in the right here and right now. First, Your heart only lives in the here and now. Second, Your confidence, words and actions are more powerful in the now. Third, Your physical body is available only in the here and now on Our Mother Father Earth. Fourth, a person who lives in the now will be a more stable, emotionally balanced and levelheaded person. An emotionally sound person will overcome any fears, doubts, judgements and setbacks from a calmer place, with what seems to others like luck, ease and a nonchalant attitude. Fifth, Your Source, Your support team is only living *currently* for You. The best reason to live in the here and now is that Your Source shows You which path to go on through different signs, to communicate with You using Your intuition only in this immediate space. To let You know that Your Source, Your BFE is here the signs can be anything that You think of to see, hear, smell, taste or touch. With My hints I always say, '*make it funny and 'Yes, Oh, My God, make Me laugh or smile and They do, so often'.* They won't predict which way or on which path that You're going to go either, that is a choice You have to make. *And how do You know if it is the right way?* Along the journey You will know which way, because it is always going to be a path that makes You feel good. *'Do I feel OK doing this or not'?* If You are not playing and living here and now, if You are thinking or dwelling about the past or the future, You are going to miss that instant to cocreate with Your Source.

Also to help You, stop working too hard at the wrong times and adding hurdles in. These are the things that We *worry* about and *wonder* 'when or how'. You know, those *future potentials*. Oh, My goodness! The Universe doesn't think about all the little details that Our minds come up with, so don't stress about them. If You think about the future *too much* with everything that needs to be accomplished and all those what ifs, You could have a fear of the future, an uncertainty that You are making up in Your mind. With these feelings of worry, You might be afraid to step forward and You might be hesitant to start moving to where You really want to live. Worry is just an unconscious excuse that You are using not to live a full life right here and now! What about having to pay Your bills? Even if Your reality is that You are cutting it close, paying the bills is in the future. Yes work towards that goal daily, but if You bring in that anxiety now, You could be stopping something perfect from coming in and changing the scenario. I heard somebody talking about anxiety the other day and they just said, *'think of it as excitement'. What if Your anxiety is actually excitement?* Go with that aspect of it. The bigger part of You is working with You, so just go about living Your life, doing what You *need* to do, all while having fun in Your here and now.

Do You feel bad for not accomplishing or even starting 'that thing You want to do' and then You bring in the other 'not so Happy parts' of Your life into Your reality and then

You feel bad about those too? Those are regret and guilt, two aspects of the past that You don't need to carry here. The number one regret researchers found out after talking to Our elders, was that they were saddened about not having done what they wanted to do during their lives, and because of that they didn't live the full life that they wanted. If they could just go back 20 years and do what they really wanted to do without uncertainty, doubt or fear, *'who knows the life I could have had'.* They felt like they really missed out, and if they could just have a little more time to play with or really love the people in their lives or the ones that they wanted to know, it all could have been different. They reminisced about the dreams that they did not complete because of the choices that they made. They didn't believe in their courage to live their true life so they just lived the life that others expected of them. It's not necessarily the great things that You did in Your life that people remember You for, it is also the things that You didn't do when You could have. The procrastinations, the excuses, or whatever else You do unconsciously, all slow You down. Take that leap at any point in Your life and then go slow, so You enjoy Your journey and

You learn more to share. Really, what do You have to lose?

I was listening to a woman talking about some of the last discussions with her mother before she passed. She asked her *'what is one thing that You regret'?* Her Mom replied, 'worrying about that last 10 pounds that I needed to lose, what I wouldn't give now for those 10 pounds to be on My body.' Oh, My goodness, did I resonate with that and bust out crying. How many times, and I can't even begin to know that number, have I said that? Well, I won't think that way anymore, not now, not ever. Thank You Ma'am.

The only time I can think of not to live in the here and now, is when You are in pain either physically or mentally. Sometimes it is good to step aside, be with Your BFE and imagine a place of serendipity, a space where You feel happy and have no discomfort anywhere. Know that the pain will decrease as You calm Your mind and body. You could still have some residual, but it is not the same as the initial feeling. It can seem like a long time if You have chronic discomfort, especially if You think about having it for the rest of Your life, but it does change. Is it exactly the same every time? No, it Is not. *If You think about it, everything is forever being recycled, but nothing lasts forever the same, even if You try and make it that way.*

Some say that the end is near and it could be any time. (fear of the future and regrets from the past) If You've been living in Your past or if You've been living too much in Your future and not right here and now, You are going to have that uncertainty, and You will be missing SO MUCH. Nobody knows their time limit, but if You want to stay longer, then You say so, act so and feel so, and because You are going to be living in the here and now with glimpses of the future the way that You want it to be, You'll get more of the good stuff happening. You need to make some room in Your life for something bigger and better. *If You don't want to leave something behind You don't have to, as long as it is for the good of You.* Never a sacrifice, only a surrendering of what does not serve You. Jim, a good friend and mentor of mine said yesterday even the word surrender is a little iffy, so from surrendering to accepting. Yes, I like that better too. Thank You for all Your wisdom every week.

Everything happens because of You, for You and it absolutely works out every single time. You just might not see it that way at first. The more You are with Your Spirit, the more bits and pieces will fall into place. Your intuition will show You the best path. *'Oh wow, I was thinking about this or I didn't even think about that, and then it comes for You to try, at the perfect time that You needed the information'.* Listen to Your Source, listen to Your intuition, listen to Your Spirit and just practice and play in the right here and now, knowing with the upmost clarity, that it is going to be great and that You are going to have everything that You want in this life, if You really need it.

Nothing lasts forever the same.

To start playing the games to how You want to live, You have to stir the pot and get things going if You want change, and You must start by working on Yourself first. Love a little bit more, be a little bit kinder, be excited about life and life will be excited about You. Because of the Laws of the Universe, victory is going to bring in more victory. If You think negatively about the things that did not work out for You and You believe them to be that way, those thoughts are going to bring on more failures. That is why things from the past cannot be a failure, even if they did not turn out as expected. You have to learn to use Your positive mind in every situation, and that goes for when

You're able to, because sometimes right away, You can't see the positives. You need to go through Your little cycle, but then *if* You, no *when* You end up with the positives only, that downfall for that minute, can be a victory in Your future. Most people do try to find the positives in every situation. Some examples would be: *as You go in to a room You find the best place to sit and then You fix Your chair the way You want it. You make Your house a beautiful home by finding some way to make it a Happy space. Now You can add in another little space with Your BFE, where You do Your little workouts and Your meditations. Light Your candles and put plants there, make Your Paradise the way You want to. Have that little intimate place for You to rest, relax and reset. If You have children, no matter what age, let them help and decorate their special place too. Anything to make it positive for You and now, for them too. Find the positives in Your environments and within Yourself right now, or start with appreciation and gratitude for things about You or Your environment, whichever is easier and funner.*

Some of the quickest ways to a happier place are to know where You are right now, accept it and just concentrate on where You want to be, not '*where You don't want to be*'. You also need to have Your starting point, Your reference point right here and now where You are and not where You were. *If You feel apprehensive about missing something, then You are not ready for it to be concluded yet.* Because of Your acceptance of the now and those positive emotions, Your Source knows even more that 'there' is where You want to be and They will try to get You to that life in the best, funniest possible ways. If You want things to move quicker towards a goal, value them before they are here and brighter ideas will come to You. Be passionate about Your endeavor, celebrate it, and then reflect back on Your journey and all the value that it has for You in the now. Don't focus on the *whole* dream at once, because all You can work on is what needs to be done next. And of course, You need to be in a great space with Your BFE, finding the positives, joking around, laughing and playing, sensing the beauty and the wonder in Your environment, these are the quickest ways to get You in a happier place. So, start only in and live in the right now and make the rest of Your life everything that You want it to be. Hang out with Your BFE in the happiest and funnest of ways. It's up to You to follow the right path to the things You want now. Either way, it will always work out in the end. Have patience and see what the Universe has, just for You.

> As above, so below means that it has to happen in heaven first. That little vibration from Your Energy Source starts, then You get a thought, then You acknowledge that thought, start contemplating on it, begin practicing & playing, & then You start believing.

Chapter 20

Release & Refill Again

New Years resolutions should happen every day and in every segment, because every single second is a New Year, not just on the anniversary of Your birthdays or on the celebrated holidays. Since most of Us do make New Year's goals, next time add in some *'cleaning out too, a little releasing from Your space'.* You can hope and pray all the time for stuff, but are You clearing out the old to let in the refill? You have the right to live the way that You want to live in this life, and when You release things, that leaves so much more room for extra love, happiness, and material things to come into Your life. Everybody and every Organic deserves a refill with what they desire from the Universe.

How do You talk to Yourself about those things to release or to let go of and fill up again? Do You tell Yourself that You are happy, satisfied and content in Your reality right now, but You really wish for a better way? And like We say, 'it's different for everybody'. If You're not happy with every aspect of Your life, then what do You need to release, the thoughts about it or any physical aspects? Do You not want to let it go because You are afraid of what could take the place? Make sure You throw out fear of the unknown if You want to change Your constant or Your contentment for right now, because You do not just go straight there. Get rid of the fears and release the ones that aren't helping You. All those that are stunting Your growth. There will be many unknowns as You learn how and there will also be many resources behind You. If something arises then *We* will figure it out, *every step of the way*, because in the unknown, is Your Source.

By keeping things that You no longer use You are giving Yourself a negative connotation, and You can put this in for any aspect of Your life. What are You keeping and why? Are You getting sick from the storage? What if it is something that You love and You don't want to give up, but You know it is not for Your best interest to keep? What are You reminding Yourself of every day that will just cycle around again? Let's take clothes for example, because I just cleaned out mine for this reason. The apparel in Your drawers or closet, how long have they been sitting there? Do they fit? Are they a little bit tight, but yet You still save them for when You do lose the weight? How many years have passed and they are still hanging there? You basically have been telling Yourself, unconsciously, that You are overweight just by looking at those clothes over and over again. You keep reminding Yourself about something that You need to change, without You realizing it, even though You know it. Get rid of the clothes that don't fit and clear out the past. You can have a better wardrobe that fits You perfectly along Your individual, specific, happy journey to where You want to be. Go to the consignment shops and add in a few tops and pants that fit. That is where I do My shoppin', such a variety. When You change Your mind and start clearing out the clutter, say to Yourself, *'Yep, that's Me, I just purged My clothes and other things from My home that I don't need anymore. I can buy whatever, I want and someone else will love the clothes and material things that I donate or resell'.*

As You are cleaning and clearing, also go through Your books and donate them. Those books will be enjoyed by others and they might even help somebody else.

When You are releasing and cleaning out Your home, it might take You a couple of times, so don't be in a rush. When You go through the old pictures that You've had forever, You know, don't be in a hurry to release them. Just keep the special ones and if You want one back again, I am sure that Your friends and family all have the same pictures also.

Go through Your phone, social media and old emails too. If You think You will need the information later, then put it in a file and review it again in a few months. In Your contacts, if You don't remember them or haven't talked in ages, reach out if You wish, otherwise -*Delete with Love.* If on Your social media there are people who are rude, talking negatively or arguing, lovingly unfriend them. You are in a more positive refilling space now. Make sure that when You purge anything that Your positive thought processes are always present.

Saving things that You don't use because it was expensive, well, if You think that $100 for a shirt is expensive, how are You going to believe that millions of dollars is still not that much? Remember, You can't think of *it* as 'big', because it will make it harder for You to believe that *'yes, it can be Yours'.* Invest and release with a smile and the refilling of money automatically comes back to You.

What about things that are supposed to bring You good luck and money that You carry around with You. How do You speak about those trinkets? Are they working? Do You have a lot of money? Do You have good luck? What about crystals and tokens that people carry around for safety and security, but yet things happen to them. Do they really work? I say yes, if they believe and if they word the affirmations positively. *'I'll carry this around and I'm safe and protected', instead of, 'I'll carry this and I won't get hurt'. Say things in a more positive way.* Refill by asking and speaking about what You do want, not what You don't.

Make sure that You release other people's baggage too. It's not Yours. What about something You saved from an ex for whatever reason. Why are You holding on to that? What kind of memories does it bring back up? No regrets, no guilt, no remorse and no storage. Make sure when You release everything to the wayside, that You do it with love, joy and happiness for You and for them. If You can throw positive Energy out there in the world for them, then that is the best thing You can do for You too.

Release and Refill is a constant change and growth for You, just like Your physical body does. Your elimination systems work every single day for 24 hours, just for You. Hopefully You release Your bowels every day or even a couple times a day. Hopefully You urinate many times a day too and You refill with the best fluids. Hopefully You rinse off the toxins that release out of Your skin and sleep on clean sheets. Your body talks to You all the time. Those little aches and discomforts, or waking up during the night, or having an upset stomach or headache, or those tickling, prickling, itchy feelings, or the calmness and peace that You live when You are balanced and healthy. Release those energies every day that don't make You feel great. If You love something, it is going to love You back even more and You know Your physical body loves You, but do You really love it or is it just 'here'? The Answer should be, *'Yes, We Do!' Source, My BFE, let's get this going, help Me release the toxins that I've been storing in My body and mind'.* It is up to You to figure out what Your body is tickled about, or why it is unhappy.

In those thoughts of release and refill, there are all different kinds of diets too and You don't need them. Nope! You just need to stop the sticky, indigestible foods and drinks to decrease the inflammation in Your body. Keep Your body nice and cleaned out, don't store so You have to purge later. Getting the sticky stuff out is easy and it's fun. *Please watch on My You Tube channel under Cathy Copperthwaite, the sticky toxins that We put in Our bodies that We don't know about. I put many years of research into this so I could be healthier, and now it is there for You.*

To do this detox, first You have to accept and welcome the things that You want to change to be able to release them. If You have to go into the deepest darkest areas of Your mind and of Your memories, You just have to remember that You are not going by Yourself. You always have Your Source with You. An Energy that made this Universe that You are a part of and that also co-created with You to compose You. Release the negative ideas that You think about Your physical body as You are changing what You eat a little bit at a time. Concentrate on the things that are going right in Your life and don't keep reminding Yourself of things that make You feel bad or less than. Talk to Your body, help it out and nicely say, *'Now I know the truth about My nourishment and it's making Me feel so good not to put those things in My temple anymore. I'm so much more satisfied, the foods taste great and I am learning new recipes. Now I slow down when I eat and I enjoy it more'. This is the key, speaking positively about it makes YOU feel so good about Your choices and the outcomes.* You will learn new things and You will meet new people who eat a little better. Those resources will come to You because You are loving on Yourself first.

If You have any low frequency energiez or patterns, or basically negative feelings of anything less than satisfied, You can't keep them bottled up or push them to the side and just pretend like they aren't there. You need to get rid of what no longer serves You and that also includes energiez. These feelings are from Your past, living in Your junkyard of guilt, regrets, defeats and sadness that You have collected along the way. They will keep You on hold. It doesn't matter if it was a person, if it was a situation, if it was a whole bunch of people, or if it is You, it is all a memory that You can choose to release and refill with an improvement, or change Your perception of it. Every time You tell the story; it is all up to You on the amount of positivity You bring forth. There are 2 parts of You then and now. If You do have to relive it to release it, even for a minute, try to do it from the other part of You, where You can be objective and see it from a different point of view. You can turn the other cheek and realize it in a different light, through Your Source's perspective. If You feel uptight, tense or stressed or You are not in a good vibe, release it and make it better for You now. You can see it from a high or low. You can see it from a give or take, or You can see it as a loss or a win-win situation during Your refills. You do have control to release some of that energy and there are many ways to do that. You can make love in a happy way with Your person. You can do something that You enjoy. You can exercise and sweat it out. You can scream out loud or You can sing or dance. Don't let those lower energiez pinch You up. Another way to get rid of 'that' energy quickly is to ground. Walk barefooted on Mother Father Earth and say, *Thank You very much for balancing out My energy. I accept it. I love it'.* If there is not enough time, then take Your little pause. You are going to feel so much better. The best way I feel to release energiez or feelings is to *'quiet Your mind and spend a time with You, Yourself & Source'.* If You can balance out Your energies, it is going to help Your physical body 100% of the time.

When You release something that's sticky or no longer serving You, make sure that You are open and ready for the good stuff to come in and fill it back up again, and the time limit for that to happen is different in every situation and for every person. A lot of the stuff You really don't need and it can be freed only on Your time. Release the fears of the new, and the changes that will occur will open up so many new doors for You. Expand and ask positive questions to answer and affirm. If You imagine it, You are predicting it. If You dream about it in a positive manner enough and ask, You will get it. All of Your concerns moving on will be answered, no problem. Your life is going to keep on going, it is always a continuation, an open end, with no final part at all. It is healthy to release every day, so trade some *things* in and think about all the possibilities that You can refill it with. Do You always want to be flowing and filled up with happiness and joy? Yes? Then You need to change Your mind and free up some space first.

Don't challenge it, channel it from Your Source.

Chapter 21

Patience

Ahh patience, one of My more difficult things to grow and expand from. *Patience,* oh My goodness that word makes Me, a Leo, a Lioness, an alpha girl, kind of cringe, You know. Most of the time I want stuff done right now because I already know it's always going to work out for Me, so I want it pronto. Patience should be contently and calmly enduring, with no negativity, while waiting for something that is due. Patience is on the feminine side of life, the allowing part. Put that in Your thoughts and start with relaxing now. Be patient with Yourself and within all of Your environments, because that part of self-control gives You Your full potential.

I also know that having perseverance with consistency and a good-natured tolerance for My desires to unfold, will make what I have asked for even better when it comes. There's no such thing as a coincidence; everything happens for a reason. Abraham Hicks said that a 'coincidence', if You break the word up, is co-creative instances between You and Your Source. A lot of the time Your coincidences, Your serendipity and Your surprise moments are actually Your intuition right there working a manifestation. Get up higher on that happier frequency and go from there. You are never going to miss out on anything if it is for You.

Temptations that You follow through on could be positive for You and they can be negative. Don't make decisions quickly or take action unless it is absolutely necessary and You are in Your happier mind, because what happens with the Laws of Attraction and Momentum, that's the kind of Energy that You're going to get back to You, period, and there's nothing that You can do about it. Just think, if those negative one's kind of went on the wayside because You were practicing patience and not focusing right away on something that You think that You are possibly going to miss out on, or how the outcome could be better for You. If You are patient and higher up in the frequencies of happiness, Your urge to think negatively and act quickly about anything will decrease and more intuition will be acknowledged by You, and then that little bit of time can become very short to get what You need.

They say, *'don't do something for immediate gratification because in the long run, You probably won't appreciate it as much'*. Isn't a little bit of gratification from being happy, of being cheerful and finding the positives, instant? Aren't all fun situations in Your life instant gratification segments, even if they are just for that moment? And if that segment wasn't good, then isn't it instantly gratifying that it is now over?

Moving slowly to get things that You want, sometimes seems like forever, right? Well don't try to speed up Your journey, really. I have always heard that and now I know why, and You know what I am going to say, 'there's a reason for it'. First, there is a lot for You to learn and play with on Your journey. Slow down a bit and take in a little more of something that You wouldn't have even thought about learning. It is also because when You are here, Yes, You could be excited for something else, but You can have so much more fun in the now if You just relax and be patient for the future to come, because all of a sudden, You are going to be there.

If You find that You are not having enough time to get things done, then You need to think about that a little bit differently too. Patience also gives You the benefit of not going back and forth or continuing in the same cycles, flip flopping between this and that again and again. Also, while trying to speed things up, it will make You unsure and want to quit more often.

Patience also means listening. Yup Chatty Cathy, You have to be quiet sometimes and listen to what people are saying. I am a leader; I love to talk and make people laugh and I know that I should hesitate to speak and listen to their whole point of view. That was one of the hardest things for Me to do and I'm still practicing, because I truly want to help people and I do not want anyone feeling down for any amount of time. Now I do occasionally become the observer. I just sit back, relax and pause to watch the world, and I really can only focus on the people that are having a good time. These are the things that are attracted to Me now, because of Me. All those people that are laughing and joking or loving on everybody are so much better to follow.

If You are not patient it can weaken You, and eventually it's going to impair Your physical body too, because You won't be able to listen and hear that part of Your Intuition speaking. Your microbiome and cells will tell You energetically what is going on with them and then You will feel that physical part, which are those aching pains, nausea or tiredness, etc. Be patient and listen, Your body will tell You when to slow down.

If You're afraid to say what You really, really truly feel, then don't say anything, be patient and just know in Your mind that You are backed up no matter what happens. Believe in Yourself and in Your Source. Step back a second, wait to react, recharge and find Yourself again. Go from there and better things will happen for You. Just remember that everything is going to finish to a degree and pass, and then You can move forward with Your positive decisions. Tomorrow does not have to be like today. The next hour does not have to be like this hour. The last minute does not have to be the same as the minute before. Your heart knows that Your Spirit is here 24/7! Have that patience, because Your BFE and Your desires are waiting for You to move in that direction when it is the perfect time. If You are impatient, then happily go find something else to do.

I want My life to exceed from the thoughts and wishes that I have now and I want to teach people that their lives too can be greater, and I know that patience is a huge part of it. I have to tell Myself, 'Don't be in a rush, slow the heck down, have patience'.

Don't miss out on what is right here and now, Your wishes will come. Patience can be a long time or it can be a short amount of time, so just close Your eyes, take a long deep breath and there, *You have practiced Your patience.*

Even God himself tells You to be in the Feminine side most of the time.

♡ Be still & know, I am God..

Psalm 46.10

Chapter 22

Our Imaginations

Physically You cannot be in 2 places at 1 time and what is wonderful to realize is, *physically You can be in one place and mentally You can be in another.* This is when You are using Your imaginations in daydreaming during waking hours or dreaming at night. Imagination is a wonderful aspect of all the Organics, given to Us freely at birth. Our inner channel of knowingness. Imaginations are a state of consciousness that allow Us to explore other ideas and realities. It is a way for Us to visualize and then to receive what We want by exploring potentials from other timelines. Imaginations are like intuitions; they are little snippets here and there, from the messages between Us and Our Source that We need to put together along Our paths. While daydreaming or sleeping, it is You and Source in the 6th dimension, living how You want, with all of Your desires present. Our emotional journeys, daydreams or whatever You want to call them, are not just random things that You come up with either, they are inspirations from the past that We have collected along Our lifetimes. For Your benefit, imaginations should include Your inspirations. That is a beautiful kind of medicine to use. Your imagination can take You anywhere You wish to see. To other countries in the world, to other planets, civilizations, or timelines. When You are dreaming or imagining, You can bring back situations or You can envision the future. You can imagine anything that You want, good or scary, adventurous and exciting, and the best part is, You can make it anything that You wish for it to be. All Yours! Imaginations are ingenious expressions of something that You appreciate, and if You keep on valuing it, then You will like it, and if You keep on playing then You will love it and You will have added on something else that You love to do in this lifetime. Being able to use Our minds with Our BFE's for future play, can be and is available for every one of Us. Just think about where You can go, if You believe in Your imagination.

When You sleep at night Your Soul is there with Your Source in Your dreams, where ever You wish to be, and You receive information. Even in unconsciousness, You can still have conscious thoughts and be consciously in places, all in Your dream consciousness, because You are aware of it. Sometimes You can remember it when You wake up, because

Your memories are stored in Your subconscious and Your conscious ego can pull that up into Your awake time. Think of the direction You want to go and then go to bed smiling with that thought in Your mind. Your physical body is here, Your conscious mind is asleep and Your subconscious is keeping Your body alive. When You can really, really relax at night, oh the places that You and Your Energiez can go, You just never know. You can dream about it all night while You're sleeping and when You wake up in the morning, write it down, the story to tell will be worth it.

Since imagination is a very powerful occurrence, You should try to make it positive and You need to be happy and satisfied with Your right here and now. Basically, You need to be who You want to be in imagination or in theory and then You will get exactly what You deserve. *The Universe reflects back to You who You are.* If You can imagine it and get those happy anticipatory emotions going, You can become it. After You imagine it, *make it an expectation and try not to resist*, *'I expect to get a front parking place, I expect to meet the best people, I expect to drive with friendly people driving around Me. I imagine it, I know it is true to Me and I believe'.* This is what I do and it happens. So much fun.

Imagination is wonderful and what happens after imagination is fantasy. Your fantasy is kind of like that 'end goal'. Don't live in the fantasy world too much though and just be at that goal every once in a while. Your fantasy future it is not present in Your physical life yet, but it is in Your Spiritual existence. Know that it is where You are going, because it is what You desire. Live for Your life right now so You do not miss out on all the good stuff. Really start believing that anything can happen for You, but as of right now, it is just a figment of Your wonderful imagination.

Your imagination can either help You soar or it will give You Your limitations. For some people their visions are necessary for them to feel happy emotions. In their daydreams they can see smiling faces and feel the life that they want. For Your fantasy to have a good outcome, You need to get in alignment on that path. You cannot be complaining, judging, blaming other people or waiting for the result to be joyful. The Universe doesn't give You what You want, those gifts and desires, the Universe gives You who You are according to the way that You are acting and how Your emotions are. Use and accept Your imaginations in the right frame of mind, as a potential reality for the happy future of Your choice.

A lot of people live in a fantasy world but they don't move forward. Why? With some people this thing happens as soon as they are done imagining and asking, they judge or doubt it with an emotion that is less than satisfied or something on the lower scale. Being worried or trying to figure out how it is going to happen, makes You doubt it even more. Resistance! If You are negative or angry at what is happening in Your life right now or just in part of Your life and You start fantasizing, it's not going to be the best outcome and You could get stuck in that wishful thinking.

Imagination is also one way to get out of a reality that You don't want to be in right now. Your thoughts from past memories or from a reality happening presently are both true, and now, not here anymore, done! Try to decrease Your uneasiness, because fear is person made and person changed. If You want things to transform, then You have to be different. You are the VIP every single time in Your Spirits eyes and You have plenty of support. Bring Your power into Your body and heart, oh My goodness breathe in that new life and feel that love from Your Source. Imagination gives You the inspiration to be the observer, to find Your outside in the other part of You. Now it is up to You individually with Your Energiez to feel positive about All of it.

Don't feel like You are doing anything wrong if someone tells You 'imagination is bad', and what do some of them say? *'What are You doing, daydreaming?'* Haha, silly people. Everybody has an imagination and anybody can use it and they do whether it is admitted or not. Visualization is what gets Us going, You know. You have to use Your imagination to start anything, and it is great to play with every single day. Don't tell Your friends, family, the people at work, or the ones that You meet about Your imaginations, because only You can understand them anyway. If You tell others and they are negative in any way, it could lower Your confidence, which will close off the belief in Yourself. Most of them will wish the best for You, but still not believe until they see it happen. You don't have to explain how it feels either. All those emotions of joy from anticipation for the next thing, You know. They will see it in You while You are happily dreaming, living and doing what You want to, and by having so much fun without them. Only a few of Your family and friends will accept Your thoughts with love and have the belief in You, and there will be people that You'll connect with from all around the world too. Say hello to everybody and You will be amazed by the people that You meet in any kind of travel, carrying similar visions, even in Your Own communities. You just never know.

Have Your imaginative times anytime that You can. During Your meditations You can connect with the version of You living in Your desired life. I think one of the best times to use Your imagination is after a meditation, because You are so calm, You are so at peace and just full of love. Feel that love all around You, and it is all around You. Use the power of Your imagination to create the life that You want and do it while You are in the right frame of mind, which means in a good mood. *This is in alignment.* And how do You live in the best mindset? Spend Your time in the morning with Source, take Your little pauses, have fun the rest of the time and always find the positives in every situation You can. Use that wonderful imagination, add in all the desires You want about the way that You want to live, and Your loving fondness and happiness for Your life will become a reality in Your conscious mind and world. Picture how wonderful Your life would be if You just put in Your imagination practice and playtime?

Co-Creative imaginations have shaped the Universe for greater expansion and adaption, and have changed the world with science, literature, technology, music, medicine, movies, etc. Everyone is creative, especially with cocreation at its finest between *You, Yourself & Source.* So, join that club, meet Your other team, because Your first team is already here, Your Team Source, who has always been here with You, at every age, in every timeline, looking out for the best for You. If You need to see it to believe it, then imagine and dream about it. *Find Your Shangri la moment in Your daydream, 'a remote, beautiful, imaginary place; Utopia', where You would love to be.* Your imagination can take You far into the future if You want or it can also be as close as You wish. Now that You have accepted Your Best Friend, They will show You using Your little tid bits of fun and discovery. Talk to Yourself and Your Source and play those games. Your Source will make great things happen in Your life and it can all start right here and now. Let Your imaginations run crazy every once in a while and get those daydreams in, kids do it all the time and they are much closer to Source than most of Us are.

The reality of Our lives is like a game of catch. Back & forth, conscious & unconscious, 2 sides, opposite poles, a 180' difference, or 2 ends with infinite answers in between. There are only 2 things I could think of that do not Share an opposite, Your Source & the Laws of the Universe do not waiver. Follow Your Heart, one that associates All & be Happy…

Chapter 23

Who are You Today?

Who are You today, who are You every day? Are You living the cultural life where You are supposed to be this specific way to fit in, with the stereotypes of.. wives need to do this, husbands should do this, these people do it that way, mommies should act like this, children may be this way, a friend should be this way, teachers, this is what You will be required to teach, and You My employee will be this way every day? How do these obligations make You feel? Do You live for others daily? What about Your satisfaction of You in this world, how high up the ladder do You put Yourself? Do You complete tasks that need to be accomplished, so the recognition comes to You? Do You live life for society every day? Taking into account all that pressure to perform, what is Your value in this life and in Your positions, not by what society says, but by what You feel? Do You sleep well at night? How much do You do every single day with a mask on? Do You wear Your mask even when You are at home? Are You wearing a different mask for each segment of Your life instead of being You in every situation? I mean, don't most people love Halloween or like Halloween? Well, that party is only once a year. What about the responsibility to and for *You, Yourself & Source* to live Your purpose of Joy and Love? Are You having fun, smiling and at peace? Do You have Best Friends to help You when You need it, especially just to laugh? Are You healthy both in Your physical and mental bodies? And if You think that everything is great then ask Yourself, 'are You where You want to be right now or are You stagnant and just living every day to get through'? Are You Yourself today, or are You somebody for someone else to be Happy?

Think about the performances that You have to do daily for Your family, for Your work, friends, community or for Your life. In these roles, how are You playing, acting or living? Are You trying to be *'abnormal'* to fit in because You want to have friends or for people to like You? You could start or You can already have feelings like You have no value without them, and that's the lowest of the lows of those emotions at the bottom half of the *Happiness Scale*. It can get to a point where You give Your power away so much that You start believing in the character Yourself. When You are trying to be known or to be seen and You are not being Your true self, You are not going to feel very good inside. Your Source is putting in that little thing called intuition, letting You know that having to change the way You feel so You can fit in with '*these people*', that You probably don't really want to be there anyway. I did this in some chapters of My life. I wanted to be rich and live that lifestyle, so the way to do that is to hang out with people that have money, right? I thought that is what they meant about 'living the life of where You want to be'. It is good to start that way yes, but the people that I chose were in a specific group of wealth and I was changing to be like them. I was putting My mask on to fit in so that they would like Me. I get along with pretty much everybody and We had some great times, but I didn't feel good about some of the situations or about Me. Now I know why, because I was not supposed to be around them and now, oh My Goodness, just meet My family and team today. Mine I call, '*Our Soul Pride*', because I am a Lioness. The people that I hang out with these days are rich with so many other aspects of life that I was not even thinking about at all. '*Thank You Source for bringing in that contrast so that I could grow in a more beneficial way for the world and for Me*'.

If You feel that certain aspects in the roles of Your life have some negativity attached, or if You are just content, maybe a little satisfied but still want more, then You need to ask Yourself, '*What do I need to do to change My attitude'?* One of the first things to know for certain is when You're trying to get out of a situation, You always have **You, Yourself & Source**. You did the best that You could and now You are going to do better, because You lived the opposite and now You know different. Take things as they are, You know. You are not alone. Be grateful that You have choices and be grateful or better yet, be appreciative of the things that You have right now and the way it will be in the future. All Positive for You. Live Your life and keep adding more to that sentence. So be appreciative but don't be satisfied for too long, because everything keeps expanding and growing as You should. Nothing should have the label of a 'permanent satisfaction'. Only Our Spirit lasts forever.

For anyone to grow and move forward they must experience the side of life that they don't want, that opposite or close to the opposite part, the contrast, and You have to acknowledge and embrace those negative sides that You believe are bad about You too. But if You are constantly thinking about negative things, You are standing in the way of Your own life. Both sides are Your choice to stay in or not, and You must be satisfied and happy with both ends. You have to accept the dark part of You, that *SHADOW SIDE*, so You can let the light back in again. If You are happy and on the joyful side, Your light comes easy and so do the answers You seek. To Me, it's never totally black or white either. There are always different colors to make up black and different colors to make up white. I call it opalescent; A little bit of all of it. I love that shade. To help Yourself out of those unhappy feelings, make Your shadow side Your favorite color with a little bit grey added in. Doesn't that make it seem a little bit better and brighter? Your God, Your Source believes in You and adores You 100% of the time so don't have any struggles believing in Yourself as far as 'where You are', because You are exactly where and what You are supposed to be for right now. Make it easier on You, Your Source is providing that for You, just ask Them.

We are always doing the best We can, especially in front of other people. Most of Us say things to make Ourselves look better and to make Our psyche feel better. Some people embellish what happens in their lives so they can fit in, because We do want other people to believe in and look up to Us. We don't get away with the things that We're saying about Our lives if they are not honest because eventually, the truth will come out, always. Teach others how to treat You by Your actions and emotions, Your moral authority. Your life is really none of their concern anyway and You don't have to impress them with anything, because this is about You. Be strong, stand Your ground in a calm way, use Your respect and kindness for Yourself and Source, which will make them even more crazy to know what You are doing. My reaction now if someone is trying to act better or be greater than they are, is to give them a true genuine smile because I know that they're doing the best that they can and they are living how they believe it to be true. It is My decision for the next segment to stay or to walk away. If You really want to help that person, sometimes You have to turn the other cheek, which just means to walk away and let them be, leaving love and respect from Your heart to theirs.

Look and act Your age according to society or according to Your family's timelines and background. Ummmm! To live happily now You have to release Your attachment to Your false identities. For Me, if You look at the signs of living associated with an age of a 59-year-old woman, as far as society and medicine, most would or should be at that age physically and mentally too, not just the chronological label We are given. If I look at the statistics and stereotypes and those files that I have been put into, I'm like, *'really, I don't feel any of that stuff and I certainly don't act the part either'*. I basically play a lot and My Energy and Physical side show it. Glowing and being Happy will help You to be Your Younger self and that is definitely the way to play. Be that light, right! I have that on My Facebook page, I am a light and nobody has commented on that either. Ha! But then when they meet Me, they are like, *oh yeah, she does kind of light up the room and she laughs a lot, and she talks a lot too, oh My*! To Me, that is a great way to have people think about Me, and if there is anything different that people think about Me that doesn't make Me feel good, it is not My problem, it is theirs. **NMP!** *Right Zanny, right Claudine?* I Love You Guyz so much.

Some people feel because of certain conditions that things need to change for them to be Happy. That is *never* the case, it is always about You being happy in the first place, which means being True to Yourself. Remember, You make the conditions the way they are by observing what is going on and then responding. You can only live and do anything in the here and now and whichever way makes You feel good, is the best choice. Living true to Yourself, You might have to let go of the identity traps that You've used for Your benefit along the way. And also, don't listen to what anybody tags You with either. You can label Yourself if You wish to and You do not need to even acknowledge their comparison. Take the time and brand Yourself with all positive highlights. I chose My descriptions from the top of My *Happiness Scale*. *'I am happiness, I am joy, I am love and I am peaceful about it. I know who I am. I am, I feel. It is Me that I am today, it must always be Me'.* Ask Yourself, *'how well do You love You? How much confidence do You have in Yourself so that You don't really need this, or that, or them to be happy and feel important? Your uncertainty is really whether You answer it according to You or is it for someone else?'* If You want praise or recognition for something it's better to hear it from a person because it makes it more personal and You kind of feel more appreciative when You hear it in Your mind rather than just to read it in an email, or to get a plaque or a piece of paper with the CEO's signature. Well, if You don't get that praise, because You cannot control people, My gosh, anything that You learn even if it is the minutest little thing, anything that You accomplish, any change of habit to make Yourself happier and to make Your life better, the Universe is right here celebrating with You every single time. Your Source is right here saying, *'oh My, that was great. What do You want to learn, celebrate and move towards next'?*

There are 2 sides to Your mind, an introvert (concerned with inner thoughts and feelings) and an extrovert (concerned with social and physical environment). We all have a little bit of both, but which one is dominant about You? There is always that little part of You hiding or that little part of You shining and laughing, with every little segment in between. I believe You need both to live during specific times in Your life. So don't label Yourself with just one aspect, because there are 2 sides to Your emotions at one time. If We put sad and happy on one scale at opposite ends, there are all those emotions and feelings that We could put into words and actions in between, right? There are 2 components that make You whole, Your Spiritual and Physical portions, and there are 2 parts of Your psyche with everything in between.

Here are some *Don'ts,* a word that could be negative if You want it that way. For Me, it is in a positive position now.

Don't be guilty or have regrets about a decision You have made, and don't let anybody else guilt You with anything or make You have doubt or fear. If something makes You hesitate and say no, then acknowledge it, *'Yes that's Me, those are My thoughts and My mind is made up for this moment'.*

Don't argue, it could get worse. Whenever You're in an argument with somebody, You are also arguing with Yourself. Make the outcome better than You expect and step back. It doesn't ever mean take abuse, it doesn't ever mean feeling bad for a while or even hurting someone else. It is all about You coming out on top with Your Source at Your side. There is no need to argue, You are both correct in Your own way and if not, the answer will come out during a calmer time.

Don't be afraid to edit Your commitment sometimes, You are allowed to. Yep, You made that obligation back there in the past, but things change, and I'm not saying don't do what You say, that has nothing to do with this at all. Just because You made that engagement doesn't mean that it is right for

You now. This is how You grow to a better place, otherwise You will stay in the same cycle, doing the same kinds of things, with the same people all the time. There are myriads of ways for You to alternate Your initial commitment for the positive of You and everybody involved if You need to, and when it comes around again, You'll know when to say, 'No Thank You'.

Don't fight against change and don't try to stop it either because You are afraid of the unknown. You can't. You will be fighting against a force that is so powerful. You can resist varieties in Your lifetime, but it will only hold *YOU* back. You cannot control changes from occurring, but You can ride along that pathway with ease and flow and fun. Reshaping of life is going to happen and the main thing about *now* is, in every moment You can actually pick what You want to happen as You're going through Your journey, not just what You want to happen at the end with Your goals. If You live and play during Your journey, You're going to have such love for life, You're going to have excitement and optimism every single day and for every single segment. You will have power and self-assuredness knowing that You can handle any situation that comes along, because now You are adaptive in a positive way to Your environment. The most adaptive it's not the strongest, it's not the smartest, it is just that, the most adaptive to changes in life. These are the ones who survive and have the most fun.

If You want something to happen in Your life, it's better to hear the positive things about it first. If You ask somebody for advice, it is their perspective of the truth as they are comparing themselves to You, as they are putting themselves into Your shoes, and as they are thinking of how 'they' would feel being beside You as You are being You. Think first, are You asking somebody who's been there done that, or has heard about it from somebody else? If You want to be rich, are You talking to rich people? If You want to be really, really healthy, are You talking to a really, really healthy person about suggestions, and does that include Your unhealthy doctor? Are they following their own protocols and following the timeline of society and disease? They have learned protocols on how to treat sickness, just like I learned how to treat emergencies in a one, two, three step manner and filling in other treatments as they came up. In those situations, following protocols and specific guidelines are essential for the survival of Our patients. How do You feel about what

You are desiring after You speak with these people? There are 3 sides to every question: what You are asking for, what You don't want and what You really need. There are 4 sides to every answer: Your truth, their truth, the truth and what everybody else is talking about. So then, how many answers can there possibly be? If You consider asking every person, it is Infinite! Every person has their Own opinions and truths and You get to choose the ultimate answer, *'Do I feel good about this or nope?'*. Everyone will have a blind spot when it comes to You and I don't care if it is Your parents or Your best human friend, it doesn't matter. It's good to hear some of them, but look and see who You are talking to. The only One who is really going to tell You the truth for You and show You which way to get everything You want, is Your Best Friend Energy, Your Source. *With 'Them' it really, really all is for You, and yes, they have been there and done that*.

You continue through life with contrasts in tow, with the expectations from living with Your family, Your community or the people that You hang out with. Why? Because You want to fit in or You need to fit in. But if something doesn't really make You feel good about a situation, I am sure that there is something that can make You feel better, and if You can think or say that, then maybe it is time to move on.

When You start changing to take care of Yourself and Love Yourself 1st, You might lose a few people and it is just because they are definitely not ready for You yet. If they are, then great, there won't be any break ups or standbys, but remember that they still have to follow their Own path. If You are living with them or have to assist with their needs, then that is a different situation, but You should always have a choice. You have to take care of Yourself and that's what You tell them, *'I need to take some time for Myself right now'*. If You want Your environment to change, You need to let some things go for a little while every single day. Your significant other, Your children or the people around You, which is usually what adds to the conditions in Your environment. Just gradually step away for Your Time daily. Take Your 15 minutes every single day and then suggest, maybe if You can, that they take theirs too, and if they don't wish to then You at least get Yours in. Your family should all also have their 15 minutes a-day too. Some things should be a family affair, actually a lot of things should be a family affair, then picture how Your environment would be, and who cares about the neighbors, this is between You and Your family. The more that You practice this, the more that You play in Your new life, the easier it becomes and then You look forward to doing Your 15 minutes a-day and seeing what happens because of it. Imagine if You did this for Yourself, Your kids and spouse would want to come to family dinners, they will want to be around Your Energies. So awesome, so awesome. Be glad for that time alone, without 'some' Energiez for a little while. By stepping aside, You learn and You experience the strength of creating strong boundaries for You to live the Life You desire.

How do You feel when You are alone? Do You like to hang out with Yourself? Can You hug Yourself and honestly smile at Your face in the mirror? When You find things to do, is it watching TV or reading a book? Both are educational, so it depends on what You're watching or what You're reading for You to get positive benefits. Do You at least give Yourself Your 15 minutes to meditate every day or twice a day? Do you play video games all the time or browse Your phone for hours? Do take Yourself far, far away from You? Every moment on this Earth is about You, but it's not about the persona that You give forth in Your environments for whatever reason. Are You just acting in a play to write

Your book or are You living Your True Self story? You can meet people when You are Yourself or You can meet them when You're trying to be somebody else or trying to impress somebody else, when really the only person that You have to impress is Yourself. *Me, Myself & Us.* When You are sporting Your mask the Soul Pride ready to be Your community and possibly Your person, will miss Your true light or Your inner beauty and walk right by without a second glance. Find out what Your True Self is like and spend more time alone. Learn the things that You like. Find things that make You smile and make You excited for more. Have a great time, work on Your physical body and play with Your mind. Learn from Your past and Your present and especially find wisdom during the times where there is fun and laughter.

Again, think about all the roles in Your life. These aspects are what You focus on in the physical world. Now that You have named all of Your roles in this lifetime, quadruple that a million times over. You are all that, but You are a lot more than those things, people or ideas. Don't think of Yourself only on this physical plane, because We are so much more. Be curious about Your True Nature. If You add in the vastness of You, the bigger part of You, that is who You really are. You are a huge, powerful Energy not just deep down but all over the place. This information of just how big and powerful that You actually are, if You set Your spiritual mind to it and not just Your conscious mind too much of the time, is what has been hidden from society, from Us for a very long time. You are Pure Positive Energy, a wonderful Soul and a lot more unique than You originally thought or that You have been trained to believe. This is what Source lets Me know, *'You are not just an ex-wife, a friend, a tutor, a comic, a piano player, a momma, a horticulturist, a dancer, a nutritionist, a smart ass, a singer, a painter, a sister, a leader; Cathy, You are so much more'*.

So, ask Yourself, *'is it OK for You to be Yourself right now'?* The answer should be Yes every single time, without hesitation. Yes! And to Me, the only time You have to think about is right here and now, but You can however think about some upcoming situations. *Do I have permission to be Myself tonight when I'm making dinner? Yes! Do I have permission to be Myself tonight when I am out with friends? Yes! Can I have joy right now? Yes!* Have a positive thought before You go to bed and as soon as You wake up in the morning, it will benefit You so much and the rest of the day, You can happily do whatever You want. You will find Your Soulmates or Your team, but only if You start being Yourself. To be successful in Your story, it always has to be You first. Take Your time out and look for Your inner light and Your Source will help You find it. When You are in a crowd just remember, *You see Yourself as many,* so You pick and choose the best qualities You would love to be. You do not need anybody else for You to be happy. You can accept all the love You could possibly hold in from All of the Organics around You. Enjoy Your life right now just the way it is and the Universe will help You move forward and give You more things to be joyful about. There is no question or doubt about it at all. I, We believe in You! So, who are You today for that much love to flow in?

Even if nothing physically changes, if You switch the way that You perceive things, You have changed Your life.

Your consciousness moves energy, which means that what You have emotions about becomes Your reality. Whether You believe it or not, Your reality is Your point of focus & attraction, which is the way You are living right now.

Chapter 24

The Highest Alignment

Choosing You

Ok, right from the start, *'The highest alignment **is** choosing You'.* You do need Your self-care and I am not just talking about the physical and mental aspects of You. What should also be included, even before the other two, is Your Spiritual side because it is related to every part of Your life. *Spirituality is 'You & Your Source, with no one in between'.* Realize the power that You have, because You are mostly Energy, and the power is not power as in 'thinking' or 'strong', I am talking about the Spiritual part, Your Best Friend, Your Source, You; that strength. Your power is knowing that You actually have the choice of which way to go when any situation comes along and having the clarity to recognize it is Your right path. You can choose to feel positive and this is something that nobody can take away from You. Listen to all of Your brains, but look for the guidance and the answers with Your Source, Your Best Friend every single time. You do need to pay attention to what Your mind tells You, but most importantly the One that will get You through everything is what Your Source is going to show You. The more You resist changing Your relationship with Source, things just aren't going to work out as easily as they could. 'Well, *If I do this, what am I going to get out of it'?* Umm, You can have more fun with Your family, You can live the life You wish and You can meet different people on that higher frequency, all because You are thinking about how important You are to the world. Select You and Your emotions first, second and third and be there for Yourself. The more You take care of You, which also means to do things that You like or love to do in the physical world, the higher Your vibrations, Your positive emotions, are going to be. Feed Your passions with a good attitude and love, and You will be in the highest alignments. In chapter 29, We go over the Happiness Scale that I received part of from Abraham Hicks. Since I first heard about this, I have added many more positive emotions to the list and it will keep on going! It is all positive emotions on the top half of the Happiness Scale and they can change daily per an individual's mood, and You want to be way up there on that scale so You can feel good or great every day choosing You. As of today, for Me the top emotions are Joy,

Happiness, love, peace, alignment and clarity, and at the top of '*My Emotional scale*' is where I try to stay most of the time.

You build sentences all day every day to get Your point across. You set patterns and routines for the comforts of Your life. We all find different ways to laugh and have a good time and We try to devise a plan to get the things that We desire while here on Mother Father Earth. Because of all the comparisons, judgments, opinions and thoughts from You or others, some of You have forgotten Yourself. When You compare Yourself or judge, You experience Yourself outside of Your world as if You were limited, separate, different or needing to be fixed. You are doing the best You can and You are growing all the time, even if You don't see it. Turn the corner to what else is going on. Think the way Your Best Friend thinks about You. Your Source is never cutting You off or attacking You or anyone else, so please do not do that to Yourself or to anyone either. Be a creator with Your Best Friend doing most of the leg work. If You can't speak up for some reason, then try to show Your emotions in a positive way just to Yourself. *Is Your doubt because You fear criticism or somebody saying something that doesn't agree with You? Is that why You don't speak up or is it something else?* There are a lot of reasons and You know what, everyone has their own truths and You have Yours. If You really believe it, then most of the time You should speak up because You are probably not the only one who thinks that way. Be true to Yourself and say what You will in a positive note, and sometimes that means only in Your mind with Your BFE, or just smiling and walking away. This is also speaking up for Yourself. During this time, You might feel like You are on the outs, but You are going to be free and You are going to be feeling good, all because You made Yourself come first in Your life in the most loving way that You could.

Are You complaining, condescending, unkind, or giving excuses because You are basically afraid to come out of Your comfort zone? When You are criticizing and talking down to Yourself or feeling guilty about things or even saying 'what if', You are kind of attacking You. If You feel that You are unworthy, then You are just going to be settling for the rest of Your life. Turn up the light that is in You. Make that light brighter than ever before. Even a light bulb that You can turn on and off, if it goes out You just change it, right? The same goes with a candle. You can relight it over and over again and get that little spark going no problem.

Eventually the candle is going to burn out and You can't light it anymore, so what do You do? You go find something new to spark Your life. A continuation of what is going on, yet something fresh, and then You light up that new candle, grow and have more fun. You can change to something new too. Yes it's safer to stay the same person, but if You really want Your life the way You want it, You have to build that relationship just a little bit at a time with You and a little differently with Your Source and then see what happens. Don't hide, just be in Your truth and let no person hold You back from Your desires and dreams. You are never wrong to want to change for the better of You, no matter who tells You it is or could be. Don't keep procrastinating and not begin, Your true life could start right now with infinite possibilities to choose from. Be glad that We have this God given, this Universe given right. Just realize and be happy that all those people that complain, critique or criticize other people that You are not going to be that way anymore. You are going to be looking and living for the positive situations and people, and for the beauty and the Love in everything that surrounds You now. Keep companions who will inspire or reinforce those beautiful qualities in You. Ahh Yes, enjoyment and inspiration, You want to stay around that positive company.

To make it easier to take care of Yourself, first You have to give Yourself permission. You deserve not to watch certain shows or look at the things or talk about the things that You don't want to. Just because Your friends are saying it, and the world is saying it, and Your government is saying it, and Your insurance companies are saying it, and Your medical field is saying it, or Your Mother is saying it; if it doesn't make *You feel good* then give Yourself permission to say, *'no, I don't really like to look at that and I don't need to think too much about it either'.* Stop hanging out with the people that make You feel bad when You say what is on Your mind, or that make You feel obligated to follow the pack. Again, give Yourself permission to turn the other cheek for right now. You are not abandoning them; You are just being with Yourself and Source alone for a little while. You are not leaving them forever, actually You are inviting them to come with You on a happier journey. You can say to them or in Your mind, *'You can come with Me, because this is what I'm going to do for Me and My life, or You can stay back there'.* They have that choice themselves also, and the people that You're leaving behind, You don't need to give an excuse to either. Sometimes You just can't explain it to them, because they're going to give You what they think and their excuses of 'why' to keep You around in their energy. The things We give excuses for are usually not for the most obvious of reasons, the majority of time it is going to be about Our fears. Excuses are Our fears popping up quickly, to hold Us back from what We think We need, *protection.* Like I've said before, if You need to say 'nope' and put up Your boundaries, then construct that wall. When You start being Your true self and realizing that You are never alone, that Your' Energiez always have Your back and that You are a great creator with Them, You will notice that You don't need all the other people to be around anymore, just the special ones. If You do realize *it is that negative* with the people You hang out with, then go somewhere else and find the people who say 'oh yeah, I agree with You and this is My idea'. You just might be in the wrong crowd right now and You do not have to go back to that situation ever again, and somehow You won't have to. If You do not want to do something, then don't do it, and if You absolutely have to, then make it fun! The more passionate and the more excited and in love with what You are doing You are, the better success it is going to be.

Choosing You also means to allow in gifts and compliments, right? Just accept, Love them and say, 'Thank You'. Don't feel obligated to give one also or return the favor, unless of course You want to, but think, *did You accept that love fully first?* Let the Universe show You just how important You are with appreciations and love from other people and Your family. Those praises are coming from Your Universe. Give Yourself compliments and laugh a lot with You, Yourself & Source. Love and appreciate Yourself and say, 'I did that' and give Yourself a big hug. You would not believe the rewards and the fun that You will have for the rest of Your life.

The movies and shows that We watched when We were younger and even now has people, all people, adults and children alike, believing that We need to have a struggle before We can get to the Happy ending, *'this is the way Your life should flow'.* Do You really need to have a hardship first to get through to the next chapter? Or for some people, they have a lot of hardships to get through and then in the end, it should be good. Which one are You, what is Your answer? To live, You do need every part of a segment and the contrasts too, just don't focus on the contrasts. Be glad it's there for You, acknowledge it and then switch them to be better for You and let Us see Your beautiful story unfold. You don't ever have to watch a movie that You don't like and You don't have to stay in a story line for too long either. You can make Your own movie and make it fun along the way to the dreams that You have asked for. You should be the producer, director and the only audience with a voice that matters in Your movie. Yes listen and learn, but the Happy Journey and the endings are All up to *You, Yourself & Source*. I love watching Disney movies, documentaries, comedies, and even scary movies, (sometimes). I mean, most movies have a Happy ending, right? Well, so do a lot of people's biographies in the world, We just aren't privy to that good information. We hear mostly about the doom and gloom of life. Everybody should be living happily ever after and they do, even if and especially after 'the end'. You don't have to have bad difficulties anymore before You get to the happily ever after, because this is not Disney or a love story movie, this is real life and You could have that dream or desire at any time that You want it, easily. You ask for it, it's there for You and it will be a part of Your life no matter what, You just have to accept it and be ready. The easiest way to live Your fairy tale story is just to be Happy, find the positives in anything and be satisfied but not content where You are. It is supposed to be as it is right now, so just be excited for the rest. Live deliberately for the magic in Your life to unfold, it is so awesome! Make Your Own movie, tell Your Own story, play the part and yes, get it going now, You know how to do it, We got this, absolutely.

Happiness or chaos in Your life all at one time, just means that something great is coming. Chaos makes You feel a little overwhelmed and that could bring in uncertainty, but chaos is temporary and that discord in Your life makes You more creative. If it makes You upset, it just means that it is 'really important to You', that is all. If it makes You cryingly Happy, it too is 'really, really important.' This is about You so You need to be concentrating on the happy parts of Your life, not the fears. Don't focus on worries, aim for Your desires and know that they are coming. Nurture all of Your dreams, not Your uneasiness. Try to find the good things every single day, because in the Laws of the Universe, and this is not made up it is already proven by science, if You feel good most of the time, You are going to attract those *'feel good things most of the time'*. You are going to draw in nicer people, a great job, a better environment, anything and everything that means something to You. You are going to step into the other zone that You could have been missing for so long, and when You get to that other side, which isn't really that far away, You are going to say or at least I said, *'holy crappness, how fun was that, why didn't I learn this earlier in My life?'* That was one of the 1st things I said, *'why did I have to wait until the 3rd chapter of My life to learn this stuff'*? Well, I know there's a reason for it and why it didn't happen in the past, and I know now it does not matter about the past anymore, because where I live, right here and now is so great and easy flowin. *You have got this, believe it, because it's true. Focus on what matters most*, **You**. OOowwhaa, a rhyme!

To help, here are some thoughts when You are choosing You. Try to look in the mirror to increase Your self-esteem, and if You don't want to look at Your whole body then look for the best parts and search for Your Soul. Sit in front of the mirror, put Your hair back, look into Your eyes and see into Your Spirit. Speak and feel only positive affirmations towards You, Yourself & Source. Today is when You are going to see Your Soul in the most beautifulest of ways. You actually expand outwards, because You are going inward finding Yourself, and that is Huge. This is 'the who' You want to look at and see every time. The more You rehearse and play, the more comfortable You get and the more excited You become about practicing it every day. Yes that saaweet anticipation! Within an hour, Save Space for Source. Find Your special time to just sit there and close Your eyes, even if You can only start with 5 minutes a day, that's fine. Build that time up, You will want to because of all the great things that will be happening for You and the calmness and confidence You will feel the rest of the day. If You are crunched for time, You can use John Campbell's habit stacking if You want to. What is stacking habits? Combining two routines or habits saves time, because You multi task. You can only think of one thing at a time, but You can multi task by doing 2 or 3 things at once, like while You're brushing Your teeth, You can also see the positives in Your scene, be thankful, do squats or core play at the same time. Be joyful for everything that You have within the environment around You now, and there are lots of ways to make it 'Happier' for that positive atmosphere. Paint the house the way that You want to, have good lighting, create Your paradise and make Your mood wonderful on all levels, and please make sure You put plants in there too. Make Your thoughts positive as well as Your actions. Smile at somebody, do a good deed, be creative, play music, or dance. Anything at all that makes You happy, because Your fun will anonymously change the world. Existing in the ways You feel it should be, You will be meeting the right people, the human co-creators of Your life. Anything that You think of doing in Your life it should always start with a smile. Actually, it will make it so much better if You can make that smile a little giggle too. Oh, My goodness the fun that You could have. Create a positive life because through You, it does build positivity everywhere, and yeah, We can help the world and heck yeah, We can save society. Period! Isn't it so wonderful to know that You can really, really change the world when You start living within Your moral authority and choosing You?

For Me now Life is so exciting because all along the way to My goals and desires it is so much fun and I meet the best people that I might not have met otherwise, or at least not in the same capacity. I am so glad I found *Me, Myself & Us* at Source's perfect time for Me. You too should be having the time of Your life, a happy time of life, living in Your highest alignment.

Society should never hold You hostage. Age should never give You limitations.

Chapter 25

Relationships

On this paradise, Our Mother Father Earth You can select *Your Queendom or Your Kingdom of Relationships. So which ones are You choosing during Your lifetime or better yet, in Your here and now?* Our relationships can be with material things, people, situations, addictions, plants, animals, communities, Mother Father Earth, the Universe or Your body and there are more, but the most important one for Your life here is Your bond with You and Your Source. Our Source does not know a separation or being alone, They are with You always. Your relationships in the Universe should flow in this order. First, always start and end with Your Source and You, Your BFE, Your Energy family which also includes Mother Father Earth. Then it goes on to Your physical body, Your 2nd Best Friend. Once these are recognized, established and appreciated every day, then We have Our family dynamics. You and You, then You have Your kids and pets, Your blood family, Your person, the Soulmates that You pick out from the billions of people in the world to be in Your life and to be a part of Your family, and then You have friends, acquaintances, Your community, Your state, Your country and then other the countries can come into play, and the orders can be switched around in priority according to situations unfolding. The strongest and most supportive of family that You have on this Earth however, is Your Energy Family from Your Spiritual World. They were here with You from the very beginning and are continuously with You, forever and ever. We are all one in the same energy. We are intertwined and connected. Our Interstitial Matrix is Our biggest organ system and it connects everything that is alive or Organic. It is energy that flows through You, Me and everyone. Our matrix also helps others around You feel the emotions that You feel. This Energy Family relates You to every ancestor, to the Universe and to every Organic, which means the foliage, the animals, the insects and every human. This Energy relation also associates Your human mind to every past thought, every past life and to all the knowledge in the Universe too, whether You believe it to be true or not. This relationship will not and cannot ever let You down, They are here for YOU! This partner for life must also follow the Laws of the Universe, for We All made them together. Ahh! Our extended family is so much bigger than You thought it was, hu?

Environmental care is so, so, important in the relationship between Us and Our lives. Our environments and the relationships associated should include safety, security, nurturing, love, joy, and expansion with happiness and fun. When You are in any relationship make sure that You feel good about You and this includes in Your family relationships. Families should work and play together. Make sure that You do not feel like You have to perform for anybody to be deserving of their attention and please do not put Yourself in Your shadow side making You smaller than them. *While trying to find Yourself or seeking Your true identity in this space according to the world and according to people, don't ever feel unworthy no matter the circumstance.* Being worthy for people, ha! No one is that important for You to hide You, ever. Nobody is equal to You because You are You and nobody else can compare, but they can complement You. If You are a people pleaser, You've learned it from Your environment and society. Trying to people please will eventually deplete You in some way. Do not be afraid to release it and do not be afraid to change who You *were*. Consciously choose to be the way that You want to be. Try that for a little while in Your home. Feel the way the Energiez are towards You and then You'll know if this is where You want to stay or not. The energy that is coming from them should make You smile; it should make You wanna giggle and play and have fun. You should feel all of those words at the top of the Happiness Scale most of the time in Your surroundings. This is the way all of Your relationships should be, even if You have been with them for 50 years. Start now, from the very beginning in this current timeframe with, *'I am worth it, I am the best person in My life',* kinda attitude. Be Yourself and never cover up the *True You*.

Have humility, but never hide Your True Self.

As far as any relationship, You can pretty much get along with any person if You are with Your Source. Healthy connections should not make You feel negativity about You at all. With any Organic, You have to learn them by loving their energy always, and listening to their actions. Just like I tell people, *'You cannot really learn from reading a book, or going to a lecture, or studying, You have to experience it in Your life and then You'll say, "oh yea I got it now".* A lot of people have to encounter the idea many,

many times in their lives to finally get it, but that is ok, it is just perfect. Take a couple times absolutely, and hopefully You will grow and expand from all the adventures.

If You are working with Yourself trying to find the positives and becoming friends with Your Best Friend Energy, just be aware that as You grow in that upbeat direction, with some of Your friends and even Your family, You might relive their same stories over and over again. Those things that they talk about and the way that they act keep replaying. Some of them are Our Elders reminiscing about the past with fond memories, and some just cannot help it because they are forgetful and those are the great stories from their lives that they recall and could be living in within their minds. While others, they have not grown and that is ok, this is their life to live. Let the Energiez in only if it serves You, follow their lives for Your benefit. When You start to shift and make Your life Your Own, if people do not understand what You are doing and they try to bring You down (to their level), that means they are threatened by You, especially if You are already Spiritually higher than where they are. Now, I did not say better than them either, there is a huge difference. They are trying to stop anything that would upset *their* balance and they would rather try to hold You down unconsciously or consciously; it doesn't matter, than to try to understand or let You go. The main thing is that they are afraid for some reason of You being better than them or possibly You leaving them behind. Some people just don't want to change and grow, so they try to coax You back to where You were or where they think that You should be, which is with them. They are not the only ones to love, Your true person and Soulmates will be coming closer and closer the more You raise and live in Your higher frequency, which just means feeling good about every aspect of Your life. Again, it's Your choice and they can come with You or not.

If We want any questions answered of why things happened with this person or people as We went through Our life, because We want closure on it, especially in relationships, We might not get the answers. Most people want that resolution to satisfy any unknowns left in Our mind and heart. Some people feel that if they don't get closure from what transpired, then something is missing. *'I didn't get why that happened, has something been hidden from me? Am I not supposed to know this?'* Well, My Soul Family, there is never really a total ending. You do not really complete all of Your goals, because You can always find something more after that mission is accomplished to keep it going. Sometimes it is on the same road and some of the time it is somewhere brand new. Yes, there are little paradigm shifts at times, but it is still a continuation of Your life. So, with a closure, if You can't find it, just keep on movin along. Know for sure that things are always going to work out for You the way they are supposed to, and it could be fun, if You let it.

If someone tries to come back into Your life and You know better, ... then... If You say yes and start the same habits again, they will know that they really have a majority of Your power at their disposal. The easiest way to get through things that have happened from situations or people in the past and to move on is, not taking them back. If something is bothering You about someone, it is not necessarily the person that You need to think about and change Your opinion of, a lot of the time it is the obligations to that situation. Commitments to people are individually made and should be individually changed according to You. To make it a little easier, remember You are forgiving somebody from something that has happened in the past. *It's in the past*. Forget it, release it, and forgive it. You are here and now and hopefully You are safe and better, or *great* if You want to be, if You let it be. It is up to You, so maybe... do not let it begin or better yet, don't let it continue once more.

When You start from the very, very beginning in new relationships, most people are going to think about and compare the past ones. Don't base every relationship that You have in Your life now from the attachments that You had in previous partnerships or when You were a child growing up, especially if it wasn't happy. If You do this, You will tend to lean towards and attract the people that *will be* the same. With this new person, You were probably not born or raised around them so nothing has to be the same unless You let it be. You made choices back in the day, but don't worry about them now, it is history, and if You are going to bring something back up from Your past, make it be a positive scenario.

When You are encountering a new person they say *'first impressions really matter'.* You have to start from the outside in when You meet someone, using Your senses. It takes around 3-5 seconds to judge a person or a situation, and this is really how We initially form an opinion of them. With this first occurrence Our thoughts can determine whether We keep this person in Our lives or We don't. People will show You who they are and how they are going to treat You pretty soon after You meet them. They will tell You all about themselves consciously, but it still might take a few rendezvous for them to really open up or sometimes years, because people will be on their best behavior for a while. At any time, Your connection should be depended upon how they treat Your divinity and how they behave towards other Organics. This is why I always say, *'first, second and third impressions matter'*. Pay attention to their actions with other people and then listen to what Your intuition says. Using Your intuition with Your Source by Your side, You can start educating Yourself about their energy simultaneously with Your senses. You can start learning what they are unconsciously telling You and You will know right off the bat that something is off. Then You will have the choice to stop it early in the game. My good friend *Stephanie wrote the book. 'Red Flags',* look for it on Amazon and learn to look for the signs to get away sooner if You should. Such an awesome Soul Pride Sissy, so happy to have met her. We are so glad She is on the Team. :)

If You really want to be in a community and hang out with them because they are the top group in the community, You have blocked Your intuition and You could bypass what they are actually showing You. If You think 'this person is the bomb' and You want to be with them, You have put them at a higher point than You already and You could miss all those little but important hints. Please do not settle for anything that You do not fully appreciate. There is better waiting for You to step away and forward to. Knowing what You know now, what skills are You going to use so the environment You pick is perfect for You? You will know the answers by communicating with Your Source using Your intuition, whether it is positive or negative. Using the quieter side of communication of just listening and observing, will show You exactly what is going on and which way to go.

If You want to be in a relationship with someone and You want to know how this person feels about You, then don't ask. Because if they have to come up with words to try to explain their emotions, things may get fumbled up. *If I could only find the right words to say'.* You're never going to really know that what they tell You is even the whole truth anyway, so You must use all of

Your senses to feel their actions and energy, then You can get a little inkling. Do not disregard what You are feeling about somebody no matter what they are *saying* to You and no matter what other people are saying to You about them. Asking others opinions is just gathering up information so *You can make the decision*. Listen to Your BFE. Remember, communication starts as soon as You notice somebody's presence. Their facial expressions, body language, eye contact, gestures and their actions are all nonverbal communication. Tap into their Energy. Only the person in question knows exactly what they think about You or the situation, so don't ask what anyone else thinks. The whole world is a 'book of opinions' and Yours about You and Your life, *is the most important one.*

If You think You don't like somebody, it's because You have put Yourself in that position with them agreeing that You don't like it for Yourself. It might not be the person You dislike and it usually isn't, it is the way they acted or what they said. They are not in the same energy space as You are, that is why You feel that discord. They will find their resources and they will move up the ladder if that is what they choose to do. Again, do not listen to the words for true answers, notice the actions from an objective stand point, away from the situation with Source by Your side. If You can't understand them, then don't try, and keep movin' along. The easiest way to get through this, is forgiveness for You and them. To Me this is one of the highest forms of love, pardoning a person or a situation. To make it easier when You are trying to handle others, You should look for their divinity, because every person has some good in them somewhere. *Look for their divinity, that's what God would do, that's what Jesus would do, this is what Your Source does, no matter who You talk to.* **And now You are thinking about the worst person in the whole world and the terrible things done, right? You don't know them a 100% of the time, even if You live with them. You don't even know them 50% really. What if they are going through trauma or generational trauma for many lifetimes or in this one and they don't even know it? It is not Your responsibility to point that out or to help them change. What You can do though is to find the positives in them, which will definitely be the similarities in You, and if You really cannot find a positive at this time, then walk away or turn the other cheek towards something happier.**

If You want to break up a cycle or a pattern with somebody, guess who has to shake things up? YOU! And who tells You that You can't? YOU and Your Ego! You have to start working on Yourself and thinking about Yourself first. And yes, You might have kids, a marriage, taking care of someone and other responsibilities, but You need to work on Yourself first, and if the other halves are not willing to work on themselves, then that is their life and You might not end up with them. That is Your choice. If that cycle can't be broken on their side, it is solely because they want it that way. You cannot change somebody else and You cannot make them change their mind, but You can influence their Spirit with Your light. Sometimes that means it will work out and You stay together, or You don't. Either way, it should always be about the best for You, and if they can't get over it, that is still up to them. If You are ready to be happy most of the time, and You wish for Your family and kids to be laughing and playful and having the best life, then that is Your choice to make, starting with You first.

I believe that every human in Your life should have boundaries. When it comes to Me, I believe that every person is living their life, doing the best they can for themselves, and the only way for them to know My limitations in situations is for Me to tell them verbally, emotionally and energetically, but not physically. Being aggressive to Me means to put up Your boundaries and learn when to say 'maybe or no', and also to know when to back up or walk away. If they don't comply then they do not respect Me and they won't be in My life. It is always My choice. The only partnership in this Universe that has no boundaries with Me is My Source. I cannot even think of one or half of a reason why. There is no time, place, or situation where My Source needs to withdraw and give Me space ever, but They do occasionally step back on their Own terms though. What a great Best Friend that I have, that We all have. I know that They are living life through Me on Mother Father Earth, so I acknowledge Source throughout most of the day. If I see something gorgeous, I say. *'Oh My gosh, that is beautiful. You guys did that for Me?* Anything that makes Me smile or wonder over, I always talk to My Best Friend Energy about it.

If You've been alone for a while finding Yourself and getting to know Your higher Source, and You believe that You are ready for that new relationship but You feel like nothing's happening? Ask Yourself, *'Am I still doing most of the same things? Am I going to the same places, seeing the same people'?* This is the time when You want to use one of the 80/20 rules I have heard of. 80% of the time go do something different, something new that excites You or interest You and 20% of the time, continue to do the activities that make You happy and let the Universe do the rest. Know the way You want to feel and live in that lifestyle, even if You just start imagining it within Your mind. Your Source knows the perfect timing for Your relationships to occur. Find Your respect, balance and beauty inside. Be a little selfish, a little selfishly focused. This is about You finding Your light and then You can do whatever the heck You want and be able to handle it. You want to be with Your Source and to feel Your Energy around You most of the time, not with Your Energy scattered all over the place. This is not up to or about anyone else, it is all and always about the One We Love the Most, YOU. You My love are the most important question and answer in any of Your relationships.

Start with Your bigger character in any interactions, to keep or purge the things, those thoughts, beliefs or people that need to go. Your Source has been waiting for You to be Your Best Friend. If You want Your

Source to come more into Your life, then You have to let them in. You just have to allow in an Energy that wants to spoil You with everything that You want and desire. This is why You've got to practice every single day quieting Your mind for several minutes. Meditation, described in Chapter 33, is a conscious way of reconnecting with Your BFE, and then the rest of the day consciously have fun. Find the positives, giggle and laugh having a great time. Also, throughout Your day, several times a day, take a deep breath and ground to Mother Father Earth. There are many ways to Ground too, all with the same basis. (Chapter 34) Be open and happy while You connect with Our Earth's powerful Energiez. You also need to be like Source too. You have to look at people the way God looks at people. You have to treat the Earth the way God would treat Mother Father Earth. You need to love Yourself and take care of Yourself the way God or Your Source would take care of themselves, period! Even if You are unhealthy, You still have to start happy, satisfied and self-assured that You're going to move into the direction that You want to, a little bit healthier than yesterday. You know You are strong enough. Have that belief, because You will receive all the clarity that You need when

You talk about it with Your Best Friend. If You focus on this, You will find out that it's so much fun to learn about Yourself. You have to have that special relationship with You first and then You can love everybody in the whole wide world. All those people that You don't even know and everything that is Organic, which means all the plants and all the animals, all the insects and of course, Mother Father Earth too. Send them All Your love, because everybody deserves to be happy, healthy, and to receive this special Energy from You. When You are ready, You definitely can help others, but for right now, in the beginning of Your journey it should be about You and Your relationship with Source. Once You start to play the games with Your BFE along Your quest to bliss, ecstasy, love, peace and more cocreation, it's going to be so fun, informative and joyful, and people that You would never even think of meeting, You will find, all because of You and Your Source's connection. I know for a fact that the most important relationship should be between You and Source. Start and end with the bigger part of You, Your Energy and then move on down to the smaller part. That little piece of You, a *fracktol* compared to the whole, Our physical part which also includes Your mind. Be with Your BFE always in every situation and in every segment. Teaming up with people to cocreate will sometimes get You to where You want to be easily, but collaborating Spiritually will get You there with ease every single time. Spiritually is always between You and Your Source only and it must be first on all of Your to do lists.

If You really want a relationship with somebody, then work on Yourself first. Don't plan things between You and them, work on Yourself first and let You shine. Play with the associations between You and Your intentions. To do this You need to have some confidence and You must be self-assured. You have to know that You are never alone and that Your Source is always here. It's never ever going to be only between You and them, it is always going to be between You, Your Source and them. It needs to be that way, because if it's not, Your experiences might not flow as well between You two, because You could lose Yourself along *their pathway*. This is what happens at work too, You are on the CEO's tract. Your job will be better if You really concentrate on Yourself first and then those relations that could really be meaningful will welcome You without You even looking. Once You start believing in and loving Yourself a little bit more, the people who will believe in You and that are going to uplift You, will come to Your side even more, and the ones who won't, You will be able to pick up on it right away. The closer You are to Your Best Friend; You will be able to use Your intuition better and You will just know things. If You want others to be there for YOU, then YOU need to be there, happy and positive about You first. Love is better in any aspect of Your life if You start with You, because You can only truly love someone else as much as You love Yourself. One of the best ways to show love to Yourself and others, is just to be Yourself and shine Your light. If You are shining Your light on the world or if You are silently observing it with Your Source, Your essence is still there, and please absolutely be that way! BE YOU. This is the best way to achieve Your happiness in any relationships. This is the year to fall in love with You! It just has to be.

The best way to give what You wish & want for others, is to be that Yourself..

Your potential, how long have You been waiting for someone else to help You move forward? Everyone should have the chance to take the Lead. You should be Leading Your Life, not following.

Chapter 26

Parent'ing & Kid'ing

As far as the performance of a lifetime….. Parenting. This is what I believe to be true to and for Me. I am just speaking My mind, so take this chapter as You will. I love You no matter what, and I hope You love Me too.

My life period and then Your life period. Parenting, teaching, learning and finding the time for Yourself is so important for the balance in Your family life. The only Organics in the world that You really need to take care of because they cannot yet, are Your children, Your pets and of course Our elders, if We are able. Our kids do take care of Us too in the best ways possible. They help Us to grow yet be childlike, they make Us smile and laugh and they are very wise if We just listen.

Your time, with kids, ha, yeah right! Well, Your kids are not awake for 24 hours. Yes, that's when You need to do some work. Yes, that's when the house keeping needs to be done. Yes, that's when the food needs to be prepared for the next meal and yes You need Your sleep too, but just to relax for a minute at sometime during the day, You are going to be smiling from ear to ear or at least on the inside, calmer, knowing that Your children are little angels and You took their gift to You and spent that time, that little bit of time for Yourself and Your Source. They give You that space to be in Your happy, positive reality between You and Your Spirit when they are in their happy places, and just for a moment when they rest. Even if it is just 15 minutes, it's still 15 minutes for You to sit down, ground, talk to Your BFE and not think about what You need to do next. This is one of the reasons I can think of why the Universe has children to take naps, so We can have Our Time. You will think, *'oh My gosh, My children are the best kids in the whole wide world. I can't wait to see their smiling faces and hear their giggles again, oh and the chaos that will ensue when they wake up'.*

Know that Your children sleep for another reason too. As their little physical bodies rest they are growing, healing and being closer to Source. That goes for You too when You are sleeping, and what a benefit it is for the whole world. If they don't take a nap it could be because they are excited or they feel like they are going to miss out on something. I could be that they are overtired, or now a days, usually and unconsciously on Our part, it is from the foods that they are eating and drinking. The crap doesn't give their little minds or bodies time to rest. They will be restless and irritable, so be careful of what You are feeding You, Your children and Your pets.

There shall be NO Favorites out of the bunch either, even if they participate more in the family, or are new to Your family. Let Your kids know this too. You are equal and loved by Us (You caregivers) and loved by Source, so play the games fairly.

If somebody else is able to help You with the household or yard jobs, then don't be the only one, and I don't care if they're out of the house working either. 1 or 2 days a week they can help with the things around the home also. They are living there and participating in making the messes too. Then You can rest together knowing everything is taken care of. Why not do the necessary things to be done for the home to run smoothly as a family most of the time? How exciting would that be to make Your list of chores with them and then lists of the things that could make the world a better place somehow too? This would of course include Y'allz meditation time. Imagine the bond that You would form with Your family.

In trying to find a positive way to tell Your kids that they are going to do something and being polite about it, instead of saying, *'Would You mind sweeping before You leave, please?'* It is a question and a polite one, but they can still answer 'no or not right now'. Make sure You ask in plenty of time for it to be completed. Since I already know that it is going to be done, I make it fun. I just kind of say. *'I love it when You sweep the floors, I totally appreciate it because it always looks so good and it helps out so much. Could You help Me out with that today?'* Doesn't that change the way that You take it? Now I get asked, *'would You like Me to do the floors before I go?'* Shut the front door, *whaaawhoooo!* Now this doesn't happen every time, but it does most often. At certain times it has to be their choice of when they're going do it, but they still should be able to tell You a timeframe.

If it is 'they' who made the disarray, no matter who or how, then really, there is no exception they must clean it up, but don't complain or get mad, mess happens. Take a second to be calm, smile, it is just a little bit of unplanned time to use up. Unexpected things will happen especially as You help others live, grow and learn. You can still help out and make it a positive family affair.

Unfavorable mishaps are blessings in disguise and they don't last for long. So, change what You say and how You speak to Your children, and they will want to do more with a better job done and be around more often.

What all parents should do and hopefully they try, is to make sure that a child is nurtured, safe and fed as best that they can. When You are doing the things together that You guys have so much fun with, just watch them playing and interacting with siblings, friends or the family pets. Look for their unique abilities and their ideas of what they like, then expand their horizons and go with it. Observe them as they work by themselves and then go in that direction. Most of the time when they are younger they will follow Your lead, but as they get older and meet society, that expansion is inevitable and they will remember and add in what You have shown them. Try not to stay within the regiment of school and sports only, because children can only sop up so much stuff You know, and what You have to teach them is so much more important, in a special, life living way. How many languages could they learn as a child, how many hobbies can one have and how much play time, not TV time, to open up their minds? There are so many varieties to choose from. Look for their talents and the things that make them glow when they show You, and in the beginning there will be a lot. Praise all of their ideas and trials, show them the way and let them show You too. You will both learn, grow, adapt and be happy to be around each other. Do this, and at any age Your kids will be so much more excited and willing to talk to You about what is happening in their life. To me, this is a great parenting aspect to do and don't fret, You will still get to put in Your two cents.

Your child's going to see the way You treat Yourself, how You relate to different people and the way You let others treat You. First of all, and as always, You must accept and love Yourself initially. For You and the world, have self-respect and be connected to Source like Your children already are. Remember Our younger kids are more associated to Source than most adults because they haven't learned the rituals, traditions and programming yet. If You gossip about other people and get into other people's business, You are actually decreasing Your own self-respect. Honor for Yourself is also minding Your own business and Your kids will learn it from You and Your actions. Your friends can do whatever they want. What is important for You and Your family should always start with You and Your integrity, compassion, reciprocity and Your dignity.

For the Kids, what about that domineering parent that seems to not let You do anything? A lot of it has to do with the fact that they do not ever want You to suffer or get hurt. They want You to be healthy. They are trying to protect You by keeping You from the things that could happen to You that they have heard of on the news, or of the incidents that have actually happened to them, or to the people that they knew growing up. There is a point to it and sometimes it depends on how sensible You are **and** about the friends that You hang out with, not about Your age. *How responsible are You and what are Your actions towards situations? What do You show them?* Your caregivers actually want You to be okay and they want You to have a full life with many positive choices. Just remember, they don't want to lose You. Sometimes the best for them is doing whatever they can to make sure that You stay with them and don't ever leave. You, who is so important to them in this life, just look at it from their standpoint and You will not be angry for very long. Put Yourself in anybody's spot if there is a disagreement, especially if it is Your parents, and that will calm Your mind. They are doing the best that they can and they are having to live their life too, under more demands and stress, and also taking care of You. For most parents, they do love You and for most people, they do care and want the best for You. You might not like their methods because they don't make You feel good, (and at this age You Know Everything, I know), but *You* can always make things funner with the activities that You have to do, and feel ok with not doing the things that are not allowed. It is not forever, although it seems that way. Pretty soon You will be on Your own, doing some of the things You couldn't do before and realizing that, 'hey, My parents were right, this isn't that great.' As You are growing up they try to give You structure in the ways that they were taught. Give Us a Lil break, We actually do it for You a lot more than You know.

Programming comes from society on how You should look, how You should act, things You should believe and say to fit in, and if You don't, then……! Your parents, grandparents and the greats on back, all were taught, 'how to be.' The most important lesson to most is about 'making money'. There are lots of conditionings about money that has come down from generations that I have mentioned in previous chapters. You need money for most things in life and We achieve it through Our jobs and careers. We are taught that You have to go to school to get a good job so You can make money. You need to work for most of Your life, live and save at the same time. But don't cha want to play around and do the things that You love to do and then get ideas from there to expand? Because everybody starts at the same part, everyone begins as an innocent, We all start at the bottom so wouldn't it be fun just to play Your way up? Make what You are doing right now positive and fun somehow. Yes, go to school, get Your degree, but not only what Your parents think You should do. Move to the top levels in Your job and in school by doing what Your heart and gut say. Learn the things that interest You, discover something that sparks that excitement in Your heart, but not because it's going to make You a lot of money. I am not saying that it won't, it might, but You will be working harder to get it if You focus on the moolah. A journey with something to look forward to every day and adding new adventures is a better way to expand and move up in Your job. Do things that You love to do to make extra money with a side job from a hobby. Spend time with Your Source, listen to Your intuition and the Universe will bring You the perfect resources to cocreate ideas with for You to move further along in life doing something that You love. Really, the best benefit from it is that as You are doing something that You love, You are raising the frequency of the communities around You. Enjoy Your life on the outside of work and school, and help others to enjoy life that hang around You. This is Your Dharma. Please read Chapter 11, Careers and Chapters, for more tid-bits of information if You wish.

If when You were growing up they were terrible parents, know that You cannot change that past, but You can find the few or more positives from then and start Your reference point from right here and right now bringing forth the good encounters.
Were all of the adults in Your life a-holes? Probably not, so pick and choose Your memories. You have to change Your attitude, know Your confidence and then if You wish to, when You are ready, You can show them that they also have a Best Friend to talk to and then see how Your relationship goes. If You do want any kind of connections with them now, don't think that they're going to change, You cannot change anyone, but they could surprise You. This can be with

anybody, a boss, a sibling, or any person, it doesn't matter. Know who You are, and if some friends or people from Your life go to the wayside, that sucks, but it is for Your happiness.

Some adults do say things and are pretty controlling. Do You at least get to speak? If You feel alone, *'how much time do You give to Yourself daily'? How close are You to Your Source'?* Become better friends with Your Source through meditation, finding the positives and looking for the things that make You feel better in Your everyday life. These time frames are between You and Your Source in private, You are not with Your caretakers 24/7. You do not need to tell anybody at all in this world that You have a new Best Friend either, because Your human best friend will not appreciate that and some people will not understand it unless they also know that it should always be You and Your Source first. The closer that You are to Your Source, the less control that anybody is going to have on You and it doesn't matter who it is. They just won't feel like they have to, but do not try to control it. This does not ever mean that You do not listen to Your parents either, You do not always know best. With Your BFE at Your side, You will better handle any requests, demands or boundaries. If You do need to 'escape' for a little while, that does not mean to do drugs, even if Your parents do, because these agents are temporary satisfactions that will always have to be replenished, and will usually be at the detriment of You. So please take Your time for You in a conscious way. If You are not safe, please let someone that is out of the picture know. You can always talk to Your Source and the perfect people for Your life will show up. Source's Love and assistance is free for everyone, it is always available, so easy to obtain and retain, and all just for You.

This is how I tried to live when My son was younger and I did the best that I could. To this day, I am still learning and growing up with him even at My age. He teaches Me so much also with what He is absorbing in life. Of course, it will forever flow with Source always at the forefront of Our lives. I Love You More Devin, to the Moon and Back and to infinity and beyond.

We All have Mastery in Many Things, & if You Love to do it, it will change the World for the Better.

Chapter 27

Your Desires

If You want something to happen for You, don't depend on fate or luck or miracles, make the magic happen by asking Your BFE and preparing for it. You have Your Source, Your Angels and the Energies all around You in this lifetime and that have been with You for generations, to help. You can absorb Your perfect life from Your desires, You just need to follow the Laws of the Universe and they will also help You to succeed. After You have asked, what Your Source does is accumulate all of the things that You've been requesting, from Your whole collection of everything that You have asked for in Your lifetime and set them along Your pathway for You to find, say Yes to, and accept fully. Expectations are Your desires, plus the knowing and the belief that it will happen on the physical earth, because it is already there in Your Spiritual world due to You asking for it at some point.

Really, the way the Universe works is that You and Source think of something You need. You cocreate an idea, then You acknowledge and ask for it (1). Source gets it ready to hand to You, but how many times have You changed Your mind? They start over with each wish (2), and then You have to allow to receive (3). Allowing has many phases. The main approach is You just have to believe in You and in possessing Your request. After You ask, make 'it' in Your reality, starting in Your mind first. *If* You keep it to Yourself, it will be all about You. Once You tell someone else, it is not just You anymore. If You are attempting to figure out the who, what, when, where or how it's going to happen, or trying to take action too soon, You are actually unconsciously telling Yourself, Your Subconscious that You don't have it. This time frame is not forever. It does not mean it is going to take long, and it does not mean a short time either. It will be just perfect for You.

They say go within when You want something or pray to the heavens. You don't need to look up to speak to Your Source, They are a part of You on this Earth and You are a part of that Energy too. This is about You and only You, so keep it between You and Your BFE in the beginning or forever if You wish. If You want to look up that's fine, but it doesn't have to be that way. Heaven could be on Mother Father Earth, if You let it. Mine is. Heaven on Earth, just feel around You, it is here.

If You really, really love something, it is probably part of Your destiny.

For You to know what Your dreams are, You also have to realize what You don't want. A contrast, usually the opposite of Our wish. During Our emotions of regret, sadness, guilt, fear or powerlessness is usually when We ask for assistance and a change. It is especially hard if it is something that You've been praying for a while or that You want so much. One true thought is, You shouldn't really be asking for things if You are less than satisfied, which is actually when You need them the most. *Is the wish for You not to lose something or someone, or is the request for someone else's benefit?* In asking for both of these scenarios Our mind frames need to be the same, happiness with an emotion of it already happening. So, with no sadness or fear attached, ask with a feeling of peace and knowing that it is here waiting for You already. Know this, They will always listen to Your requests, but sometimes those wishes just cannot possibly happen.

I have heard in several different places that the number one blockage of You getting what You ask for, is out of definite programming from somewhere in Your life. At this point though, it doesn't matter who, or how, or when, because the conditioning is from the past and You can change it right now and keep on moving in Your current space to Your chosen future.

If You think about how to achieve Your desires too much, a little bit of hesitation could creep in and mess things up. If You have any doubts on how this could happen, You are unconsciously telling Yourself that it might not be possible. If You are completely absorbed with the want and the why, those emotions on the bottom half of the Happiness Scale, those negative thoughts could slip into Your mind and into Your heart. If You worry or think about all those what ifs, which is the future and then add in uncertainties, You are bringing in that negativity and it is not usually just once. Every time You think about it, discuss it, or ask for other's opinions, it all adds up. Uncertainties go along with anything new or basically with any segment, because We do start over again in any moment.

If You do become overly consumed, You are probably not going to get Your wish for a very long time or it's not going to be as great as it could be when it does show up. If You think that You need to work hard to get something that You desire, that is also You telling You that it is not Yours. You cannot try and figure it out to make it happen faster, You just have to know and believe it will happen because You asked for it. The truth is, if You are too attached to what You've asked for, You are kind of afraid that it's not really going to happen. It did, so feel that way now. You ask for it and it is readily available for You to accept into Your reality.

If You have wanted something intensely for a long time, You could also become obsessed with it, I know I would and did. Obsessing, the more You talk about it, the more You need it and the more You want it. Then the farther away it actually goes from You, it takes longer to show up. Obsession is not positive and if it doesn't happen sooner than later, then You start thinking that it is not going to happen, and then those negative emotions start to override Your confidence. Over obsessing could also lead to an infatuation or an addiction. If You are bound to Your wish, Your infatuation could keep You from enjoying the path to the life You want. *If You are too fixated on it, those feelings make You forget about where You are right here and now and the fun that You could be having.* Think about the broader aspects of how You are going to feel as this comes into Your life, because You already know what they are going to do. They are going to change Your life for the better. That perfect love or partner for You, great friends, prosperity and abundance where You don't have to worry about any kind of financial discords anymore, or with health for You, Your family and for others that are suffering around the world. Yes, more peace and ease in Our whole lives and We want safety and Freedom too! These are the things that people want the most and of course, they also want to be happy. This is why We ask in the first place.

Some people might say, *'well, I'm asking for a bigger house or a better car, because what I'm believing is that what I have right now is not good enough'.* That sounds like guilt to Me. Also, Your Source would never say that it can only go to certain people and not to You either. Change what You are saying because there's so much more out there to explore and to upgrade to. *'Yeah, My house is wonderful and it provides so much for Me, but everybody and all materials eventually need a refreshing enrichment'.* There is plenty of everything to go around for All of Us in this lifetime.

Another hurdle is that some people do not really feel like they deserve their wish.

'Somebody else could do better with that, or I'm sending My health to somebody else; it is ok, I am strong'. Don't ever sacrifice Yourself from what You need, unconsciously or consciously. No sacrifice, no surrender, just alignment. At no time ever does Source say that You are not worthy to ask for and get what You want. It is a birthright for everybody to have whatever they want in this life and to live in their desired fashion. *'I know that I am worthy because I am part of You, My Source. Thank You for reminding Me how whole I am with You by My sides.'*

One more idea if You are not receiving the life You wish for, 'What are you holding on to'? Material things, emotions, thoughts, longings, memories… You only have so much space for things. There is only enough room in Your belly, in Your closet or in Your tolerance, and then You require more space. Ask, Yourself, *'How much have You released, let go with Love for the new to come in?' 'How well have You prepared and adjusted the areas for the new and better to come forth'?* For the things that You want, the desires that You are asking for, there is a place that You need to be first. You need to accept where You are in life, in Your reality, and love it or at least like both the good aspects and the parts that You wish to change. You cannot make Your happiness dependent upon the outcome from a desire that You want. You have to be Happy on the way there, for any and every reason. One action to add in more energy to Your heart space is to acknowledge, love and be appreciative of the things that are in Your situations and in Your environments right now. They are there and it might not have anything to do with what You are focusing on. They are specific for You, because You choose what makes You smile. Practice Love, being thankful and live for the most important components in this world and the Universe, *You, Yourself & Source*.

Another way to be in a 'happy asking mood', is doing the things that You love to do. If You think that You shouldn't start doing things that You love right now or to ask for what You want because You have to wait for something else first, that is not a pleasurable way to live. Change Your scenes around to where You are happy most of the time doing things that You love to play, and continuously ask for what You want. You will be joyful and Your Energy will make other people happy too, even if it is not people that You are around. Your happiness does affect the whole world. It will make somebody happy and those somebody's could be a whole freaking community. They will grab on to the joy and then it will spread like a wild flame of Love and fun all over the planet.

To help You even more consider this. When You are with Your Source, You feel great about every aspect of You, both mentally and physically no matter what is going on in Your world. Your physical body is with Your Spirit, ready to be healthy and functioning so You can live the happy life that You wish for. When You are with Your Source, You Love Your physical body more and You love all the animals and greenery of the world more passionately too. If You love You, the trees even sway towards You when You approach. If You love You and You love Your life, that is going to boost Your immune systems and then who knows what can happen or how You will feel. When You are with Your Source, You can only feel those positive emotions, nothing less. *This is the best way to stay delighted and self-assured.* You will know how great You are, You will know Your goodness and You will find Your individual purpose to be here, Your Darma to the world. These support systems are with You all the time, Your body, mind, other individuals and Spirit. In some cases, ask Your human team. In every case, always rely on Your Source first and they will show You the resources and who to receive advice from. Just imagine having the right answer to every single question that comes along and responding calmly with confidence and ease every single time. The more You pay attention to Your Source, it will be 100% positive for You. It is Your choice to stay on top of the positivity scale. All of Your emotions are in Your control, eventually.

You have a choice every day and with every segment if You want to be with Your Source, Your Inner being or where Your heart is. In Your heart is all the Energiez of the Universe, everything that You desire in life and all that You love. Your heart can only live in the here and now and Your Source that is working with You can only live in the here and now, so this is where You need to live also. Again, the most important partnership is between You and Your Source. Remember who You are and most of all, the one that Source knows. Your Source already believes in You and in Your desires and they are waiting for Your asking, so they can put them together. If You do start feeling any of those other emotions lower down the Happiness scale, that just means that You are not in alignment with Your Source anymore. That's it, just try not to break apart from Your wholeness and if You do, don't stay away for too long. You don't really have to think about 'how' to be with Source all the time either, because They are already here and want to experience life with You in a positive, happy, playful, joyful, loving way, with many learning experiences. This is what I started saying along My path, as I have learned and adapted. *'I am so glad that I know I have this huge powerful energy that surrounds Me and loves Me, and every single person here can say that without any kind of negative thought at all. It is what You/We are supposed to have. A lot of the time, they make it funny, because Me being Myself is usually joking around and trying to make people laugh too. They love to laugh with Me and I have such a good time with Them. This is just what I want with Source, because then that brings My inner child out and the more fun that I could have.., and then the more fun that I will have again..., and the more fun that everybody else around Me can have too. This is one of My jobs, to help everybody have a great time. I create their amusement for Me and they make Me smile even more. I just get so amazed with My life now and I know that it is all for Me'.* If You are playing with Your Best Friend, They are playing with You. This will make a huge difference in Your life. You will be ready for anything and You will always be in a good place.

This is the way the Laws of the Universe work, the way that everything operates and with these Laws Your desires will expand exponentially. Using the Laws of Attraction and Momentum, You can pick any aspects to be happy about, and then more things to be Happy about will come to You and Your desires will show up in front of You along Your journey. If You love Your life, life will give You more things to love on. If You start being healthier, the Universe will bring You more segments and approaches for a healthier You. If You want positivity in Your life, start finding that good attitude within You and around Your situations. Thinking about the future and the present in a positive light, brings *it* in for You.

Eventually We will get everything We desire, but sometimes it is only when We pass on to be closer to Source that We realize they were right there in front of Us all along. While You are moving happily along Your journey to Your wishes, if You have patience, live Your life to the fullest and live Your purpose of joy, happiness and love, the outcomes will be even better than what You imagined, anticipated or even prayed for in the first place. Once You get down all the little play points to the game of life that I am sharing with You down pat, You are not going to have any dilemmas at all in manifesting Your desires. Yes, there are consequences to the ideas that You request and achieve, and consequence is not really the word to use either. There is a reaction to every action and wish You create, so just make it a positive one. Listen to Your intuition from Your Source and to Your brain prompts too. Listen to what You are saying to Yourself, no matter how much You have wanted it or how long You have waited. Your Universe knows which pathway to send You towards because of what You want, and They will help You out any ways possible. Play and Practice with Your BFE and continue in Your now life, always asking and dreaming of more.

You can't possibly know all Your desires and dreams, because You change Your mind all the time adding in something that You believe is better. We continue to grow and so should Our wishes, because Your life is going to continue to go on. Our wishes and desires are gifts from the Universe. Yes, they are actually not from the people in Our lives although they are the ones giving and sharing. They still all come from Your

Source. The same material things are not going to satisfy You forever because those ideas of things right now will change. What makes You happy today, or what is going to make You happy for this hour, might not be the same tomorrow, and it is ok. Nothing is permanent unless You want it that way and choose it every day.

Let's practice telling Our Energiez how We want to live. If You can't think of anything, think general. Tell Your Own Energy how much You want to live and do not just use words, remember emotions work a lot better and a lot faster because You're not just saying the words, You are also feeling them. With emotions, Our Energy believes in what We are asking for even more. You also need to be satisfied with the way it is, even though You want it changed and be grateful that You're able to make that conscious choice to revise it. When You start with Your Spiritual self, this also tells Your physical body that, *'Yes, I want to get up and live, absolutely! My body loves Me and I love it. I am healthy. I want to eat more nutritious foods and drinks, and now the food that I'm craving is so tasty and yummiee that My microbiome is wanting the good stuff too. I am not going to rehash what the doctors say to Me when I'm on My Own. I am not going to think about it because I am with Me and My Source right now. I'm not going to think about the things to do tomorrow to prove something else, I'm right here now. I'm going to be grateful to do the things that I love. I'm so happy that I have this opportunity for Myself. I want to live a great life and I am already here living a good one. I have added in My Meditations daily too, and every day is better than the previous one. I am so excited for what is unfolding next.'* Even with Me just saying these things, My body's saying *'yes, I know You want to live'.* You do not have to wait for anyone for Your wishes and dreams to come into Your reality, You do not have to beg, or try to be worthy or worthier, or to sacrifice anything or anyone, it is rightfully Yours already, because You asked for it with a positive, *'Thank You', at the beginning.*

Now get up and do what You have said, and be grateful that You have Your Energy and willpower. Your dreams, wishes and desires should be the size of Your Soul, and because We are energy, that is huge and infinite. Once You make that decision, just start playing Your games and living Your life having fun! Your desires will happen when You need them, which means when You are truly ready, not when You think You are, because Your Source knows when You are available to handle it. Concentrate on You and Your BFE's friendship, use Your logic along with Your intuition and all of it will work out better, far better than You have ever dreamed of.

From My life to Yours I am adding in, *'To make it better for the whole wide world, make sure that You put at the top of Your list of desires or that one of Your goals is to be the funnest person that You can be in that day or in that segment and see how much more Your life will be. All that positivity will come rushing in to You.'*

Everything is just a moment in time & the moment in time is here for a reason. There are no such things as coincidences, only co-incidences. Everything happens divinely guided from Your Source.

Chapter 28
Manifesting

Magical Manifesationz, ohhhh yes, the funnest part of the games. Your requests and the proof are a combination of all Your emotions, thoughts and desires put together from Our environments, from Our imaginations or from Our dreams. For Your comfort on Earth, You can ask for anything that You want, and We usually get the ideas from the events happening in Our surroundings, because when You know what You desire, You also know what You do not want. When We wish for something or We suddenly ask, how long it will take before Our wishes come true is dependent on where We are in Our alignments in association with our Best Friend Energy and towards Our environment. For You to manifest Your best life, Your thoughts and Your feelings have to be in a happy harmony with right now, You must make some space for new and You must believe in You!

Actually, You manifest all the time without full belief of Your power. Your desire to laugh can come at any moment and from any occurrence if You let it. What about Your desires to be smart and to be able to learn things? We are all geniuses and have the ability to absorb and utilize ideas without asking first. Manifestations of knowledge and fun! A lot of desires are happening that You don't even think about, like hopefully Your desire to be present and alive. It is not only about the material things that You're looking to touch, taste or whatever, '*Boy My heart beat all night without Me even doing anything, and I took a breath whenever My body needed nutrients. My body heals itself at night, so when I was sleeping I know My body repaired itself. And oh yea, the earth kept on spinnin, all for Me'.* So whaaawhoooo! You have manifested them, *all these gifts from 'Yours Truly' -Source.*

Everything initially starts from a thought, even Your emotions because You have learned the words associated with the reactions from people, whether they were angry, sad, or if they were really, really, happy, even if We do not let them surface. *Your emotions are manifestations.* Emotions are attitudes from Your 1st and 2nd brains, (heart and gut), and those interpretations can come out quickly and initially. As You have lived Your life, Your Own emotions prevailed and they come in now as a reflex to what is going on in Your surroundings.

As We live and learn, it can be an emotion and then a thought, or vice versa, a thought with an emotion attached. Thoughts and emotions are the first conscious manifestations that We have and then momentum builds and it goes from there. Your very first emotional manifestation was probably a sensation called love when You were an infant. That love emanated from Us with the sounds, the smells or from the energy around Our caregivers close by. We did not need to see them to feel their love. Our very first hunger feeling from Our stomach to Our brain was a physical emotion of not feeling right and the need for something to soothe Us, so cry We did and then Our manifestations came to be and We learned one of Our 1st lessons, a method of 'how to get nutrition and some lovin'. Our emotions go way beyond Our five senses as far as Our power, even though We can use all of them at once to know what is going on in Our worlds. Emotions add in Our higher senses beyond the 3D, allowing in that bigger part of Us and Our intuitions.

A thought cocreated with Source is also a manifestation. Again, Your thoughts are the words that You have heard or that You have learned from Your environment. We create Our sentences with words and feelings every day and that is how We communicate to the World, to Ourselves and to Our Energiez. The spoken word gets things started and words are magic, but You cannot learn from just words, You need to take in that knowledge and then apply it to Your situations to grow. New Technologies, Science and Medicine begin with an idea, then the observations, and then the words flow with the answers to the questions that came up along the way. So, it all starts with a thought, which stimulate a vibration also, but then if You really think about it, that cocreation and everything You think about, comes from Your Source, from the bigger part of You. In being a little separated, that means the vibration or the little nudge from Your Source comes first and then that thought comes into Your mind, and it depends on what You do with the idea, where Your life goes.

You mostly manifest because of the seeds that You sew and when using the Law of Attraction, it is more difficult to attract something that You are not already feeling. Feelings have a greater power over words when playing with Your Source. *Talking is the physical side and feeling it while You speak is the Spiritual side.* Your emotions, thoughts and actions actually tell You what Your manifestations are going to be.

Manifestation begins at the number 3. Between You and Your Source is #1, an acknowledgement of a desire and an ask is #2, and the allowance and presentation of… is #3. Your job is just to get prepared for what You are asking for, and to get what You want, try to make Your emotions about Your desire's positive ones. If You add in the right and best emotions, Your life will happen as You wish.

Don't You want to be in that really, really, good space, so You find that really, really, good person? What else do You want in that scenario? It is not just the Love You want; You also want to be nurtured and to feel safe, and You want to be excited and have fun with them being in Your life too. There are too many definitions of Love to count and so many people with many, many, many true perceptions, but it all boils down to this: if You want the love of Your life to come in, You should be the love of Your life to Yourself and to Your BFE first. If You want love and a great partnership in Your life, then You need to start playing and practicing Love. To Me what matters about Love, is the true connection between any Organics and Source.

Do You want to meet the best people and have wonderful moments together? If You want good, happy relationships around You to travel, grow and laugh with, You better be happy most of the time to attract them. You need to be a better friend to Yourself and to Your BFE and to other people, and be kind to the Organics in Your environment, including Mother Father Earth. You should be kind to everybody anyway, because You never know if the person You just walked by, that You didn't notice because You were thinking something negative or about the past or what You have to do in a minute, could have become Your next Best Friend on Earth. If You were just living in that moment and not somewhere else... Living on Earth, the common denominator is *'People'-* 'Us', 'You', and 'Me'. People to people, people to animals, people to the greenery and people to Mother Father Earth. Make joy and unconditional love more prevalent in Your life, then those great relationships are going to come to You.

If You want to live a life of luxury and freedom as far as finances, think happy thoughts when money is involved, even if it is a penny or You are paying the bills. Luxury is also different for everybody, it could be a house, cars, clothes, travel, the best food, it could be anything. If You wish for a bigger home then You should make the place that You live now, a well-loved, comfy, balanced, well cleaned area in Your Own way and as best You can. Talk good about where You live and start living that way too. What about money luxury? There are so many people that are manifesting money and it can come from many different sources, so why not let it be You if it is going to make You feel better? The only reason most people feel in a negative way about money, is because most of Us are programmed to think that money is not good. It's not good to have too much money, that is greed. Do you think people who have money aren't good people? There were mostly negative connotations when I looked up someone who 'likes to spend money' in the dictionary. Careless, a spendthrift, compulsive, excessive and reckless to name a few. The definitions in the dictionary of *some* words were made negative for Us to believe that it is so. I loved the word, 'fritterer' so I adopted it. My new job is a *Fraktol Fritterer*. Fraktol is how much of a part that I am, compared to My Better Half, My Source, and Fritterer is someone who loves to spend money. I am a Fraktol Fritterer and anyone else can be too. If You continue to feel like You do not deserve to have money or accept a lot of money but it's something that You enjoy, then at least go out and make a lot of money and donate it to the right causes. Many people need Your light.

If You want to be healthy, know that Your body doesn't wait for You to start healing itself. If it's something physical that You want changed, You are going to have to do a little bit to help out. Most of Us have to catch up, right? But it can be done easily with the help of Your BFE. Start talking to Your body like the God or Goddess that it is, full of life and vitality, no matter what Your diagnosis's are. Don't frown when You are looking at Yourself in the mirror and if You do, then look at a part that You think is beautiful. Smile and talk good about Yourself to everyone. Learn a little about nutrition and how to decrease inflammation in Your body. You know, deep down, that out of the many thoughts about newest fad diets, that fresh is always better, no matter what the processed food labels say on the boxes and jars. Discover the many ways to get Your circulatory and elimination systems working great. Get up, feel Your body and make the best choices for You, not for others, and go with it.

If You want a great job and an exciting career, You have to like where You are right now and make it better somehow, even knowing that You want different. You will have more fun along Your journey if You are doing stuff on the side of Your normal every day, 9 to 5 whatever job, that You love to do, like hobbies to make Yourself feel better. When You are happy doing what You love, it will make the world a better place, whether it is the Earth, the Energiez, the people or the other Organics, it doesn't matter. Bring out that 'side hustle' that You love to do, and it could move into a possible career that will help to fill up Your bank accounts in an exponential way.

If You want to be more abundant, know what You already have, appreciate them and even add them up because it can come from many, many things. The definition of abundance is different for everyone and We all do have some aspects of it. As My good friend Marian said, *'just say 'Wealth', because that covers all of the abundance from material things on the Earth like money, a place to stay, a great career, healthy food, to personal ideas of how Our health should be and who the good people around You are'.* To change or add anything into Our lives because We wish for more, We must first look around, acknowledge and love how much that We actually do have, and then happily just practice and play being abundant.

Then You have Your Spiritual Wealth which encompasses ALL OF IT, which to Me should be utilized 1st, 2nd & 3rd in My book of a happy life. Without Your Spiritual side, everything else will be more difficult with less fun. You have to get Your Spiritual Wealth closer to You. You are already a part of it, so that gives You a head start. The *Laws of the Universe* will give You a big boost also. So that is *two* things in Your favor, just waiting on Your requests.

The things that You ask or wish for are like 'a plan for Your future', right? That preliminary plan, that 1st rough draft and then You add things to it along the way so the Universe can put it together for You. You can only calculate so far ahead in Your life. Yes, plan this and yes, plan that, but do not fret about it at all. It will all come together when it should. Manifest for the future absolutely yes, but it is funner to manifest for the day and sometimes only for the segment. *'I would love to see, hear, smell, taste or touch ….. or I am so grateful for front parking again, yes please, or I love and accept the rewards and gifts I receive, Thank You again. I am so happy to meet the perfect people tonight, Thank You, I love new friends, right Teresa B, the best people every time! I love You so much'!* When You ask for things, You do receive the treasures and gifts from Your Universe on a segment-by-segment basis. Try it this way for a week, play with it, manifest it. So much fun could happen in every single minute of Your life.

Everybody pretty much has the same 5-7 wishes, each specialized for the uniqueness of You. Number one for any part of this life, is always working on You and Your Whole being. Yes, it is true and this will be in a different way. I know You've heard 'to work on Your mind, body and spirit', absolutely, it has to be all of those **and** it has to be worked on together and integrated. This is what I love to call it *'My Negativity detox'*. It is alternative and it also uses historical protocols. You need Your Practitioners and medicine, but Your Spiritual side must be in the forefront. You will live a longer, happier, more functional life because You changed Your thoughts. *I only live and be in the way that brings Me the most joy, and that helps Me have the most fun with My families and My Best Friends. Involving My BFEs helps Me* *be the happiest that I can ever be, every single day.*

What about, *'why it seems to take a lot of time for Your manifestations to come in'*. One reason is because it's not usually just one single thought. The desire, *'I want a million dollars'* is never just that because then You add in other things. It is not just the thought of those millions of dollars either, it is also what You would do with it, how much fun You would have, the ease of life, or the people that You would meet that You might not have met in the 1st place. As Your Universe works on those millions, remember, They are probably working on thoughts from a long time ago too, because how many times have You asked for a million dollars in Your lifetime?? Trust the Universe and don't keep asking over and over again. They heard You the first million times.

When You asked for something, how did You leave it, on the negative side or in the positive contrast area? What is the last thing You thought about it, a complaint, a doubt, or a fear? Is Your mind ready to argue about everything that is challenging or being changed? Is the thought of ending up in a different place rather than where You are right now causing stress about the future?

When You asked and when You are thinking about Your desires, was there giggling or are You thinking the opposite? Are You giddy and excited about meeting Your person or are You thinking about the things that happened with Your past relationships? If You are anxious about something You have asked for, You are just telling the Universe and Yourself that You don't have it yet, although it is here Energetically waiting for You to accept it fully. Another 80/20 rule I heard was to live through Your heart 80% of the time and use Your mind 20% of the time. It doesn't sound very smart to do it that way sometimes, but Your Source is supporting You 100%. You must ask for help if You need it and use Your conscious, thinking brain 5 to 10%, and leave the rest to Source. You are taken care of and this works. Make what You think about an even smaller percentage and just allow what You desire to come in. This is when You don't think about the 'who, what, when, or how'. When You start believing in something, You can put Your emotions into it, and Your true emotions are what the Universe reads more of. You have to be 'You', the true You, for that particular desire to come.

Another reason it seems like forever for some wishes is when You ask for something, it actually has to go through Your Whole self. You, Your physical body and mind, and because We are humans, You have to ask Your Source, Your Soul, Your Subconscious what You want and also let them know how much You want it by how You act, what You say and what You believe, and then that idea has to get to the Universe, the bigger part of You, the huge Energy part that We are all made of. The Entity that gets everything done, the Ones who manifest and get all of the little pieces together in perfect harmony for You to get at Your perfect time. The hardest aspect of all of this is to believe it to be true in Your mind first. What You wish for and what You believe could be, are both aspects that You need to consider also. Two different connotations about what You say and what You really believe can actually happen to You. You have to speak from Your 1st and 2nd brains (heart and gut), believe it to be true, trust in Your decisions and not use Your 3rd brain (the thinking one) too much of the time. If You think about it too much using Your 3rd brain, You try to set Your Own path. After You ask for Your wishes to come true, all those beautiful things that You desire, do not think about it too much again, really! And when I say, '*don't think about it*', You say, '*that is hard, I am so excited for it, I dream about it'.* Well, that is perfect, think about it yes, but You must release the need for it. *'I am good right now'.*

Out of all the things that can hold Us back, the biggest one is *Us*. We are Our greatest critics, talking Ourselves out of things and especially if We listen to other people's ideas and comparisons. For You to manifest You have to basically, ultimately step back and away from the specific outcome even though that is the main goal, because if You think about it too much, You could put a hold on it with all the 'what ifs' that can come up. Your Source knows when You are ready, and when You are ready, You will have no questions or what 'if's' left to think about.

For some people, if You feel like You are not in control and You mess things up as far as achieving Your desires and living the life You want and deserve so You don't even ask. Just know that You have control of every aspect of Your life, either before it happens, during, or after the situation. At one of those points, You can exert Your control and change Your thought process. Can You change Your mind around to be happy for the rest of the life that You have left? If You want something changed in Your life, You are the one who has to 'change Your mind'. *This is the one part that You have to do that affects all of the other segments and cycles in Your life.* Believe and play with Your heart, gut and Soul and Your mind will follow. This is not for You to try to figure out how. Work on the positive realities of what You have right now. You are not powerless, find the positives. Take a deep breath, think of situations when You feel relaxed and when You are Happy. You have back up for a 100% of Your life and now You just need to have fun with it and see what happens.

So, We have gone over some of the reasons Our manifestations don't come true. One is that We are not in the happy mindset to receive or when We asked. Because We are not living as a Whole Entity, using All the Parts of Us. Another is that We don't really believe it could happen or that We don't believe We deserve it. Basically, We don't believe in Us. Think about the way that You are living today. Are any parts of Your life really worth Your time to be negative or angry, or to hate the world or hate this person or dislike this situation? Think about now and live happily in the right now where Your Source is, because You can only manifest in the present time. If You have thought of it, then *Yes It Can Be Yours.* If someone else has done it, even throughout all of the ages, so can You. If You have done it before, You can do it again even better now. If no one has manifested it yet, You Can!! I am so excited and happy for You.

If You can think about Energy and Quantum for Your desires to come true, basically the minute that You ask, is the minute that it is there. The Universe adjusts to what You're talking about, to what You're thinking about and to what Your emotions are. So, when You ask for that *thing*, Your Universe, Your Angels, Your Source or God, whatever You want to call Us, and I'm including Me with Them now because by now We know that We are all part of the same Energy, They are trying to set You on the right path to get there. This powerful masculine side, all in Your favor, showing You which pathway to go and answering all Your questions along the way. On the timeline in between, is Your doubt, Your lack of faith, the belief that it really can happen or that You deserve it. Your emotions kick in pretty quickly after a thought, within seconds and it's different for everybody. If it's the same scenarios that You're going through, You think about it and get the emotions started beforehand. What emotions or vibrations are You putting out there in the world? Your potential fears about the situation, those 'what ifs', or All the positive stuff. Don't You want life easy and fun and flowing with passion and clarity along the way? Accept Your wishes without hesitation, because it is Yours. Don't try to figure out anything else and let Your intuition lead You right to it or it right to YOU. Let Your intuition and Source be the masculine side, that action part. Be in the feminine role which means, *'sit back and let Your masculine side do it for You.'* You requested it and it is being taken care of by Your Spirit. The action for You to take, is to talk about it and Your life positively, believe it and live as though it were completed and release the past issues to make room for the new. To get ready and prepared, You need to start playing the role of that person that You want to be, because the Universe brings You 'Who You Are', by what You say, do, and believe about Yourself and about the situations every day. For all the things that You want to happen in Your life, You should start practicing and playing more in the way that You want to feel, and be in that wish any way that You want to. Always keep an open mind, get more data if You are not sure, take Your time if You can and change Your mind if You need to. Revise what You think and say, and care about Your emotions, not just the facts. Act out the life You desire with Love and live Your purpose. Play and practice.

The most powerful part of manifestation is not asking for what You wish for and not feeling guilty about it, or all the little steps that You need to take, or the games that You should play to do it. The most important aspect is 'believing and knowing that it is clarified this is going to happen'. Then it goes from belief and clarity to Alignment. In alignment, Your association will be unquestionable to Your ego and Your mind, because those are the only ones that can separate You from Your wishes. Being in harmony with Your Universe lets You relax and be peaceful about it, and during all of this manifestation fun, I am telling You ahead of time that You get one desire for free. You get the best relationship with Source, Your new BFE. For Me, that was the best wish that came through for Me that I didn't even ask for. I guess maybe I did ask for a Best Friend, yeah, someone that I could talk to and be loved from no matter what. What a special outcome for Me and soon for You. Now all My wishes have come true, so I need to keep thinking about new ones. Humm, what now? Oh, My goodness: More people to love, a growing community, an evolving and expanding second career with workspaces all over the world. And Yes more freedom, that ease of choice in the decisions that I have to make daily. And then of course, the way that I want to feel in My life with My physical body, My vitality. All of My wishes go together and they all work for the betterment of Me. My Spirit showed Me the way and I listened and played. I make sure *I Save Space for Source every day to let Them know how much I love and appreciate Their presence in My Life. When You're hanging out with Your Best Friend nothing in Your life really needs to change for You to have a good time or to be happy, or for You to be satisfied in the moment, except for Your mind.* If it was just up to Your Source, You would already be there.

I wish for You to start opening up and saying, *'okay, let's do this, I can feel it with My heart that it is right and it is something that I want to do, so I am going to ask. I am happy and excited for this.......'* Yes, You are going to expand Your life more than You've ever thought, so go for it. If it ends up being something that You do not want, and You are still satisfied and glad for the opportunity even if You have to start again, I guarantee Source is going to show You another better path. Then You will say, *'Oh wow, I didn't even think about it this way, it is so much better'.* How can the Universe know what You want unless You present it to Them? Talk to Your Universe about it and if They don't give You that little happy gut feeling now, You probably shouldn't do it then. Go with the pause, have that patience We talked about, sit there and think about it 20% of the time, and the rest of the time, 80%, continue living Your positive, happy life and let Your Universe show You which way to have the most fun and which way to go towards next. That's how simple it is, do the things that You love, do the things that You want to do, that You know would make You happy and follow those paths along the way. Your expansion is going to be exponential. Be more here in the now, finding the positives in Your environment and always asking for more. You have asked for it and it's going to happen in ways that You are not sure of, which is so awesome. *'I Love surprises and I know that it's going to be fun along My journey, if I make it that way, and it's probably going to be better than what I thought of or asked for in the 1st place. I look forward to that anticipation and excitement of the "little and big' things every day now'.* Remember, if You only concentrate on the 'big' goals, You will miss out on All the Celebrations and Successes along the way from the 'lil manifestations' You have received. Oh, my goodness, You know! Come on, just let Your Source do the job. They love it and They want You to join in, *You, Yourself and You.* Find the Happiness living with Your Energy and do not wait for the weekend to have Your fun, nope, every single day, even Monday is a holiday.

Manifestation of Your wishes are what happens beyond Your imagination & dreams, because whatever You imagine & believe, will happen.

The Universe doesn't always give You what You ask for. They give You the things that You need & They will base it on the way that You are living, from Your reactions & Your emotions in Your everyday life. This is what They hear, not the excuses or Your arguments. The Universe gives You 'who You believe You are', with a view of the way that You behave showing up in Your reality. A 'view' because You are able to change it. You need to be Who You want to be in theory, in imagination & consciously, & then You will get exactly what You have desired & wished for. Again, because of the way that You are thinking, speaking, or acting, it reflects back to You what You receive. Change the direction of Your thoughts, believe in Your situations, live the way that You want Your life to be with Source & then all of a sudden, Your life will be everything You have wanted plus more.

Chapter 29

Our Happiness Scale

Our Happiness Scale has the ultimate goal of Wellbeing for Our lives. The Happy scale is a Self-control scale and it helps You figure out where You are and where You want to be. This Emotional Scale has the most powerful words ascending all the way up to the Pure Positives of Joy and Happiness from the lower frequencies or negative thoughts of hopelessness and powerlessness. Imagine or not, feeling that way. Maybe I should change the paragraph to start higher and then go to the lowest because We should always start in positive manner. I know I don't want to start any segment at the bottom or less than satisfied ever again and guess what? I don't have to and You do not have too either. On this emotional scale to Wellbeing or Alignment be a little selfish and just know that it is natural to want to feel good most of the time. I read this scale from Abraham Hicks and then added more words along My Journey. Make Your Own Happiness Scale and please share it with Us and *You, Yourself & Source.*

Society names certain words and label them as bad or cuss words, or file them as a good word. I've looked up some words to see their definitions and if society has said they are bad words, then those were the predominant definitions I found. To Me, it is really all about the emotions that You have with the words You speak and Your nonverbal communication. Emotions are like an adjective to Your request, just like cuss words are to My sentences, and it shows a higher Energy to Your Source. In the ==Play Shoppe Journey & Journal,== there will be a whole chapter on 'Words' to play with. That will be the next book in the series, **'Our Energiez Your Power.'**

To use the Happiness Scale, the object of the game is to climb up to be in a happier place in each aspect of Your life, then Your emotions help to change Your thoughts and then the Energy about it updates. On the Happiness Scale, each word has emotions attached to it and they have different meanings for everybody. Each term has infinite power in any direction that You choose and all of those words or feelings can be interchanged and moved up or moved down to Your specific flow. From any word on the lower scale that You actually feel now, try to obtain better control of the emotion and just pick 2 that are higher up and practice those. Replace those negative feelings with something else higher on the Happiness Scale and there are plenty to choose from. Switch *that word* for *this word* or this emotion for a happier one. Say the word, think of a positive relation to Your life right now and bask in that happier emotion. Then You can see Yourself rising up and up and up, to be at that Joyful and Happy state most of the time. One of the first things some will think is, *'I can't do it or I can't do it by Myself'*. You always have help, always! You have a lot of power and You do not have to do it alone. Your Source loves You, adores You and cherishes You. **You**, My Love are the only human for Them on Earth. Realize that You will feel better and know that You do always have control over how You feel. Carry the list with You everywhere, *absolutely, l*ook at where You are on the scale and move up if You need to and when You are in a good mood more of the time, Your desires will happen sooner. This is the way You should be all the time, most of the time and it can work for You fast or slow, it's all up to You.

Being in a higher frequency means that on Our Happiness Scale You are happier than satisfied. High frequencies are all those positive words, and also are Your desires,

Your dreams and Your imagination. If You can be positive all or most of the time, that's a great way to stay in the high frequency areas. If You do things that You love to do and enjoy the things that are less than satisfactory to You, then You can stay at a higher frequency more. If You can be grateful and appreciative of what You have and about the things that You see around You, and it doesn't matter what it is, that also keeps You in a higher frequency or in a happier mood inside Your mind and then Your body feels that way too. Because of the Law of Attraction, if You choose higher emotions, then the more joyful You will be. *'Happiness is being in tune with Your Whole self'. Yep, it is being in harmony with You, Your Soul or Your Energy and following the Laws of the Universe.*

You are not going to have to give up anything that You love or like to do, but You do have to give up some things like: guilt, worry, frustration, anger, criticism, sadness and the judging of others or Yourself. At times those emotions will be prevalent, but there's no reason to *stay* in those feelings, they do not get You any closer to happiness, it only keeps You with more of those same emotions and happenings in Your life. *In any of the emotions on the Happiness Scale, if*

You stay there for too long it's always going to lead to more of the same. Fear is an emotion on the very lower scale and there are many definitions associated with fear. These feelings are usually because You feel powerless at that moment. Being fearful, nothing will seem to be happening right for You and then it keeps building up and up, or do I mean 'down'. Can You build down, I guess so? If You are afraid, You could power down and stay away from society or You can move up and go out and play, it is Your choice. When You consciously choose the lower frequencies then lower You could stay. You do not want to stay in those negative feelings. Joy is the focus that You should have no matter what's going on in Your life. In the lower frequencies of less than satisfied on the Happiness Scale, the lower that You go the less energy that You actually have. Your energy slows down and if You keep headed down, all of a sudden, especially if there are other things involved, You could lose it, You could blow up, or You could hurt Yourself or others. It is a bondage to be less than satisfied and it really is easy just to turn around and know that You have everything on the upper scale just waiting for You to accept it. Anything less than satisfaction on the Happiness Scale, You basically need to stop living it or bringing it into Your life. Even if You have to stop for a second and let the emotions filter through, *'oh no, this is sad, or this makes Me feel bad'.* It is what is supposed to happen, so grieve, cry, scream, save time for Yourself and Safe Space for Source, and then move on back up to Your true life. *Say, 'thank You so much for the lesson, I love You, or Thank You for the life I had with them, I know They are happy and safe with You now'.*

Everybody in life ultimately wants to be Happy and not to suffer, and happy is the way Your life is actually supposed to be. If We are not living within those higher, happier emotions then We simply are not Ourselves. If something that happened to You in Your past experiences that was less than satisfied ask Yourself, *'is My life still the same way now or has it become a bit better? What did You learn and change about Yourself after each episode'?* Living in the past or trying to guess what could happen in the future, a potential, makes for more work in Your mind. Leave it be, make it easier on Yourself and live now. Any questions I think about that might happen in My future; I will have the answers when it happens. My BFE takes really good care of Me, please allow Yours to care for You also. Update Your limitations and open up Your boundaries. Look at the other sides and open up Your mind. Focus on the positives, don't isolate Yourself, because You always have *You, Yourself & Source.* Believe that You can have it, feel happier and know that You are worthy. No matter what path You take, it will always lead You to the same place in the end, partying with Your Source.

Everyone has the same purposes in life with Source of having joy, happiness and love in every segment of the day. If We live that way, You and I are very, very powerful. Again, if You want something out of Your life for whatever reason, in whatever section that it is, then You need to change *Your thoughts about It* period. When You add in Your individual purpose, and it's for the good of You and for the good of all, which it's just means You are happy and passionate about it and You're not being greedy, selfish or judgmental of others, that Personal Power is beyond what so many can visualize. Add up all Your Source's purposes for You and Your personal Dharma for this world and yes, yes, You can manifest all the Happiness You desire in this lifetime. Play little games and say sentences like, *'oh, wouldn't it be great if.., wouldn't it be nice if.., I can't wait for this to….* Name a whole bunch of things and then get Your imagination going. You might as well feel great about them now before they happen, yep getting prepared. That is what it is All about, feel great about them now because they're going to happen, just believe it. *Right now, for this moment I am satisfied finding the positives in all of the roles of My life.*

All of Our cycles and progressions in life should be Happy, at least a little bit. That is what You are striving for and this is what Your Source, Your Subconscious, Your Soul wants for You. They want You to be Happy like They are. All You can do is move forward in life, not backwards. So how do You move forward? Flowing and Happy or fighting and stressed? Think of new ideas and rise up that Happiness Scale. It's so easy to get in a positive mode, just think of something else or new that makes You happy. Those Happy pathways lead You to Pure Bliss. There are many ways to think differently and more pleasantly about anything; a person or a setting and this is what the ==Play Shoppe Journey & Journal== are going to be for, helping You find the positives in every situation, and You actually already know many ways to stay up in those higher emotional states. What are Your emotions when You smile, or when You see kids playing, animals playing, people laughing, or people having a good time, or doing something that You love? Doesn't that just make You warm and fuzzy all over? Oh My gosh, a higher frequency. You can always make anything funner. You can always find something happier to concentrate on. Have unconditional Love for Yourself and unconditional Love for others, there are so many benefits. You are only going to be here for split second and then You move on to something else, both in life or when We die. Have an unconditional belief that everything is really good if separated out and then when put back together. If You are in love with life and Your environment, You can find more and more love for life, Yourself, Your Best Friends, Your family around You and Your world. Acknowledge and Accept now, be glad about now and change Your mind towards the future with positive feelings about situations.

I look at My list all the time and add more words as I hear them. I use it to know where I am in life according to My emotions. I am always, well for most of the time, on that first page of Positives, thank goodness. If We can just be nicer to Ourselves, We can help get people up to the next level in their frequency too. We can help anybody out of anything just by being Our True Selves. Show others, when You can, how to move on up beyond satisfaction to Happiness. Just Imagine, Everyone in the world on their way up the ladder of Love and Joy, just a smidge Happier, one step at a time. It's a start, right?

Your Perspectives determine Your Experiences.

Your Perspectives are Your life.

Perspective is everything & only You have control of Yours.

Happiness Scale / I AM / I FEEL

Me · Glowing · Self Assured · Desire · Fun
Joy · Warm Fuzzy · Delighted · Passion · Goosebumpy
Happiness · Radiant · Empowered · Amazing · Sweet · My
Alignment · Comfy · Inspired · Indulgence · positive · Space
Peace · Hello · Ready · Enthusiastic · Intuitive
Love · Enchantment · Playful · Embraceable · Flexible · Yes
Bliss · Deserving · Pristine · Eager
Magic · GALOR · Safe & Sound · Thriving · Progressive
Unconditional · Interesting · Elated · Nirvana · Gracefull
Natural · Sublime · Receptive · Choices... The
Appreciation · Motivated · Optimistic · Soothing · Best
Clarity · Balanced · Sure · Exhilarated · Knowledge · NOW
Ease · Anticipation · Giddy · Excited · Vitality · Truth
Freedom · Sanctuary · Fullfilled · Paradise · Faith · Compassion
Joyful · Willing · Magnificent · Allowing · Able
Life · Advanced · Expanding · Orgasmic · Luxury
Organic · Excellent · Confident · Glee
Unlimited · Powerful · Adoring · Vibrant · Invinsible
Flowing · Forever · Pleasure · Certain · Joyful Expectations
Blessed · Exhaltation · Harmony · Open · Advancement
Guided · Beauty · Solid · Ecstasy · Liberated
Whole · Trust · Calm · Motivated · Wonderment
Serenity · Gratefull · Success
Infinite · Capable
Dynamic · Euphoric · Belief
Welcome
Awe

Hope ShadowSide   JustAMisUnderstanding
Neutral   Overwhelmed   I feel
                   Lost   You/us!
Settling   Stressed
Contentment   Pressure   What if?
Satisfied   Insecure   If Only?
Boredom
Disappointment   Guilt
Unhappy   Shame
Blah   Fear
Tolerating   Unworthy
                   Stuck
Worry   Judgemental
Doubt   Resentful
Bitter   Self disgust   Limited
Inpatient   Jealous   Depressed
Pessimism   Blame   No control
Complaining   Hatred   Bound
Irritated   Anger   Dispair
Anxious   Revenge   Powerlessness
Discouraged   Devalued   Helplessness
Struggling   Broken
                   No purpose

HEART EARTH

Chapter 30

Changing the Situations Using Your Power

Everybody deserves to be happy, Every One, and don't start thinking about those people who You believe do not deserve to be happy. *'They don't deserve s*** in Your book'.* For You to live the life that You wish, mind Your Own business even if they were or are involved with You in some way. As for right now We are focusing on Your happy, positive, evolving, fulfilled world. This is all about Your relationships with You and Source, with Your Inner Self and Your Outer Self, with Your feminine sides and with Your masculine sides. The Whole You!

Before You're ready to make a change, make sure that You are actually ready. Make sure that You are Spiritually there, physically ready and make sure that Your mind is prepared to play. Start from a good place and be excited to learn something new and to possibly continue on a different journey than You expected to travel. All to the same goal, with so many different routes to choose from, allowing Your Best Friend Energy to take the lead. With Source and the Laws of the Universe, if You focus on the building up, the recreating and the cocreating with Source about the things that You can do for Yourself or the things that You could do for the world, it will be fun, easy, and a definite success. You must acknowledge and accept what You wish to change, but don't try figure out who, what, when, or where. They know how urgent it needs to be and then guess what? *A new environment in any aspect of Your life.*

There are only 2 things You really have to work on about changing Your physical aspects. Your physical body is already rejuvenating and You can most definitely change Your mind. Your body will help You and the Laws of the Universe must help You, and Your BFE will be at the lead. Your ego, Your mind, Your attitude, Your programming and Your cycles, these are the parts that You have to modify and You are the Only One that can do it. You just have to change what Your perception of the past was and how Your now is, and possibly adjust Your environment a lot or a little bit to Your satisfaction or bliss. It is Your choice. Just let Your Source know that, *'I would love to live in a better environment where it's cheerful and safe.'* You know how You like to feel,

You know how You want to live, and You know that if what You are doing right now, makes You feel better inside and outside or not. You have to love Yourself first and know it can be better for You. Believe in Yourself and say *'heck Yes, let Us go live the life that I really want to live'.* And I can't say this enough and I will keep pushing the fact that 'it really all revolves around You'. Now You just have to figure out what You want better and different.

One of the first things You have to tell Yourself when You're starting to fall back in love with You, is that, *'Yes, I deserve the best. This is something that I am supposed to have, it is My way now for the rest of My life. Thank goodness I can start today. I have the right to My life. We all have the Love and potential from Spirit and I am aligned with it. I've asked for what I want and now I'm allowing it in'.* The thoughts must be positive emotions about it and You. Pick out Your favorite happy words from the Happiness Scale, add in Your Own and play. If You can't find positives in Yourself right now, look for things, situations, hobbies, music or whatever makes You Happy and bring them into Your focus. And if You don't feel good about anything, that's the moment to let it go and think about nothing else. As soon as You can, change the subject in Your thought process, take a pause and a deep breath, be thankful for Your body breathing and Your heart beating and all the things Your body does without You even thinking about it. This pause can work for anybody to reset.

On Your path You will have questions to answer. Is Your response at this time, *'a maybe or I don't know?* Well then, it's perfectly okay to say, *'No or not right now'.* It doesn't mean forever unless You want it that way and You don't need to make that known either, but when You say 'no', make sure it makes You feel better, calm or relieved. Don't feel rushed from anything or any person at all. Remember, hardly any circumstance is a fight or flight or save Your life now kind of segment. You can wait, contemplate and when You are ready to say, 'Yes', smile because it is going to be something that You really wanted to say yes to and then the best will happen for You.

Some people want to understand or want to know why *it* happened so they have the power move forward. Well, one little part of You let things occur and then with the Laws of Attraction and Momentum it just kind of progressed and kept going in that way. Some people are saying, *'I would never let that happen'*, but think about it, it was Your choice to be in that way at least twice and You can try to put the blame on whomever or whatever You want to, and some probably are guilty, but…. *'Well, My parents did this, or this is what God let happen to Me, or My job, My coworkers, My kids, My health issues, My ancestors, I don't have a choice.'* You are living right here and now and most of these excuses are from the past. Even yesterday is the past, an hour ago was too. Whatever the excuses are that You are telling Yourself, if You are not happy in all aspects of Your existence, then You can choose better even just starting in Your mind. There were and are many reasons for what is going on and *fear* is in the title. *Was it because You were afraid for You or someone that You have to take care of? Was the fear there because You have to start again somewhere new, but where? Is it because You say and now believe, 'Oh, it'll be ok, it's all right, they are trying or they will be alone if I leave. They are My family, they need My help, they need Me'. Do You tell Yourself or hear that there's probably nothing better out there for You? Do You say, 'but I can't afford it, I don't have the time, I don't know how make the very next sentence, I have too many responsibilities, I can't do it by myself, or who will help Me? Or is it because You are content, satisfied or comfortable, yet unhappy??'* Did I tap on something for You to resonate with? If You don't speak up then there is a definite fear in You of some kind. You might have residual from instances, and I say residual because it can go away, but fear doesn't need to be with You now. Think about the way that someone treated You and the feelings that You had. There are always 2 sides of You. One side of You could have said what You were thinking, 'that is enough, I'm not happy, or I am not helpless', while the other side gave some of Your powers away. It was the other part of You, Your mirror image, so if there needs to be a blame, that's the part of You that was allowing somehow, for some reason, to let a smidgin of You be suppressed. No one should define or control who You are at all, except for Your True Self. Now, it's up to You what You do about it presently. And it doesn't matter what anybody else says either, they are on the outside. *The way You are treated by people is the way that You treat Yourself unconsciously or consciously.* Please, I love You so much and I am certainly not disregarding anybody's life or sufferings, if

You are being talked down to, if You are being abused in any way, if You're being forced to do things or feel persuaded in any way that You don't like, and You know if You like it or not, and it doesn't matter the reasons why, I'm just saying, *'You treat Yourself that way somehow too'.* Even if it is just by believing the things that You hear that aren't true to You even a little bit, or by hiding the ways that You feel when certain things happen, or by the things You tell Yourself, or the excuses and the *'it's oks'* You give. Hopefully everybody's safe and if not, then here is Your choice and chance. Concentrate on adaption, Your growth and the building up of Your life by starting with Your Own attitude. People in Your life are around You for a reason, whether it is for a change or for a continuation. Please, You and Yours be safe. I am crying as I write this paragraph, please get help so *blame* can be taken out of Your story.

Sometimes You do have to bide Your time for something better to happen if You are not satisfied with what is presenting right now. Patience! You will know when the time is right. If You want to start telling people right away, *'this is what I'm doing'. How much negativity and how many steps back are You possibly going to take because Your confidence is not here yet?'* **You are still probably going to want to tell Your closest friends or Your family, but ask Yourself first,** *'How are they living? Is it in a way that You want to be too?'* *If not then shush!* **Don't let them take some of Your power away or make You feel bad. They are only saying things because it is a part of their conscious and they are looking out for themselves. Which is perfect for them. Their life story is for them to figure out. It is up to them, not up to You. The people on the wayside from Your past environments, or from Your present ones, if they're the ones that are judging You, talking about You and saying 'You can't do it' or giving You negative ideas and thoughts to hold You back, it is all on how You take it what happens next. This is between You and You, and then when You are ready You can speak up, or not. Eventually, they'll say,** *'what are You doing differently, show Me',* **and then You have that choice to tell them or not.** *'Oh, I'm just kind of working on Myself. I am making Myself healthier and happier.'* **That's all You gotta say, because health covers Your body, Your mind and Your Spirit. If You don't know who to trust, then You are thinking about humans and We do need those companions absolutely, but for right now, who cares about the others at this** point when You're trying to find Yourself. Not that *people* can get You out of a funk anyway, it is ultimately Your responsibility. The people around You will start to treat You differently, but it won't be that long before the Universe divinely guides You to those special others to help You start moving Yourself up that Happiness Scale.

As You're moving through Your journey of becoming healthier and happier with Your Source, You will have the right words and the perfect situations will appear. You will find some new friends and family that fit with Your path better. Those special people will start coming to You and You'll know just who they are. The good ones, the better ones, the ones that will move You further in the way that You want to go. Because You are rising on Your Happiness Scale, You are getting closer to Your Source, and with Your practiced communication with Your Source, Your intuition, You're going to be able to read people's energy. All that means is, You are gonna be able to interpret better their true emotions and actions. You will know right away certain things or You will find out sooner than later. Your intuition is what tells You more about a person than what they are saying anyway and with Your new found power, sometimes You will be able to feel emotions when You come into a room. Again, it does not have to be between anybody else in the beginning.

So how do You get out of situations? You don't work against it; You play with it. You do not fight it; You love it and You do not lie and hide it from Yourself, You stand with clarity and confidence. If You work against anything then that's what You will focus on and the Laws of the Universe will bring in more 'fights to work with'. It's not an argument that You are not happy or that You don't want to be there anymore and You want a positive change in a certain segment of Your life.

It is always self-imposed restrictions....

It is so cool when You are ready to move on with *You, Yourself & Source.* No matter what You believe, no matter who You are, You are great in some aspect. As for Every One else, it is not their business. Listen to Yourself, listen to Your Guidance System, They will help to remind You how great You are and assist You in creating an idea that You want. Do not talk about the negatives and don't feel guilty about moving on, just cocreate and build something better for Your life. Don't bring Your dissatisfaction, fear, guilt or Your disempowerment with You on this new journey. Dream about and feel the happy emotions about what You want. Talk about the positives, live the positives and change the whole world around You, even if You're just smiling to Yourself inside Your mind where nobody can be with You. You have Your Source and Your protective 'wingmen' beside You. Body guards and wingmen are actually Our Angels, Our literal 'Winged Men'. I thought of that after a meditation one day. So much fun, so awesome to play.

Again, the more You know You and live in Your true purpose of joy, happiness and love in Your life, the more You will attract the same. So, what can You say nice about You for You? For Me, I would say, *'I'm the kindest, most tender-hearted, funniest person in the whole wide world. Mostly happy, that's Me. How would You describe Yourself?* What about moving forward in Your life, what can You say differently now? Try these, *'I'd love to do that, We'd love to do that, Me and My Source can find a way. I'll be happier than I am right now and My situations will be better. Oh, yeah, all for Me, because of Me.*

If it's something that You really want to do and it makes You have that smile, then come on… Now that You've changed Your mindset, changed Your attitude about Yourself just a little bit, the Laws of Attraction and Momentum are going to kick in and push that forward a little bit more. This is My main idea; I want You guys to know the power that You have to use when You wish. Your Spirit, Your Best Friend, God, Your Source, They just want You to hang out more on that other side, on Their side and realize Your power. Your hidden, God given power. Make Your time for Yourself every day, start with 5 minutes if that's all You can do, then work it up to 10-15-20 minutes. **Save Space for Source**. With Your BFE and You together, the best days will happen. Save Space for Your 2nd Bestie which is Your physical body, 5-10-15-20 minutes every day to acknowledge, love and play moving Your body. You will start to trust Yourself a little bit more and then Your fears will decrease. You already know that You always have Your BFE to trust and that's the *Main Energy of the Universe*. To help You grow and move forward, You will always have Your Source and Energiez at the beginning, the middle and at the start of the next great thing in Your life. They have always been with You and They'll be here forever for You. There is no person in between *You, Yourself & Source, Your Spirituality,* **ever**.

I am, I feel.

I feel, I have.

You cannot be something that You are not & You cannot have what You wish for, if You are not.

Chapter 31

Good Vibes &

The Best Company

You have to live with a good vibe to have a happy life, right? On the Happiness Scale, Your vibration needs to be one of something higher than satisfaction and this is how We/I vibe now. If You live with these higher vibrations or emotions or even close to them, just think about the possibilities for Your life.

It does affect You, Your life, and the environments around You from the choices that You make about any situation. There are always at least 2 sides to choose from, so which one are You going to focus on? First of all, know that You asked for those choices in the first place, somehow. If it is something You didn't see coming, ask Yourself, *'is it something that I want? This is unexpected, which one will make Me happier this one or that one?* Try both of them if You want, sure, give things a chance. Let it go at Your pace on Your little timeline and just remember, even if You've been down the road before it's still a new choice now. You are an innocent.

It is a new potential with every choice that You make throughout Your day, so give Your life ease of flow.

One way to start making *You* feel at ease and raise Your vibe is to make sure that Your paradise, no matter where it is, is a happy place. Get rid of or change around the things that You don't appreciate when You look at them. Keep it clean and fresh, and who cares if You have a lot of things or if You live as a minimalist, as long as You keep it balanced and so full of love. Just say, *'no negative energy is here anymore because I am happy and aligned, and We're going to make My little paradise so great'.* Love where You are right now, give it a 'good vibe' and then this will start to help You feel better.

Wake up, and if You have children wake them up in a happy, giggling manner instead of the same normal way and raise that vibration early in Y'allz day. Get up just a little bit early so You have that little 5-10-15 minutes for *You, Yourself & Source.* Having Space for Source and for Yourself is non-negotiable if You want to live on this Earth with good vibes, the best company, and the life You wish for. It has to consciously be started and practiced and played with every single day. They say go within when talking about hanging out with Your Best Friend, because when You go within to Your Spirit, to Your Soul, You are just right there with Your BFE. Make it happen even more. Meditations are Your prayers, Your laughter, Your giggles, Your quiet time, Your work out sessions, Your loves and all of the positivity You can find.

Take a moment to watch and listen to the children or animals play or just walk in nature or through a place that brings You peace and calm. Observe them and they will change and uplift Your emotions and mood to a higher vibe.

Doing things that You love to do or learning something new will definitely raise Your vibrations.

Make sure for *You, Yourself & Source,* that You keep the Best Friends who uplift You, who You have fun with and those that make You laugh. You need independence sometime and You also need dependence on friends, but only the ones that You are happy to see. Your friends change along Your pathway, along Your journey and that is okay, and it never indicates that You don't love them. It just means that they're not keeping up with You being You and that is absolutely perfect. Be in that great vibe and bring Your friends with You if they are ready to play Your game.

Don't wait though, hang out with people who make You feel good. The more You take care of Yourself and the happier that You are in the way that You want to be, Your special friends will find You. If You want to meet somebody like 'this and this and this', then You better be that way first. Gather Your Pride, bring them to Your table and have a great time. I am a Leo, so I call mine, *'My Soul Pride'*! For My pride, it is the people who seldom complain and who don't talk about or judge other people. The friends who don't always talk about their problems and who try to stay positive for the most part. It is not disregarding the realities of life; it is making Our realities positive.

If You want better health, better well-being and positive vibes, then involve Your energies, they will help You get rid of the stuff that doesn't need to be there. Don't leave *anything* bottled up inside, because that is just like holding things in Your digestive system that You're not digesting. Extra things, especially negative ones become toxic whether they are thoughts in Your mind, undigested food or bacteria, viruses, parasites, or whatever else lives in You. I counted 15 elimination systems that work every nanosecond to help clear things out. There is not one second of the day that

Your elimination systems aren't working for You, so You have to help them out too by eating well, drinking good fluids so You can absorb the right nutrients and so Your microbiome and Your cells can actually do their jobs. You need to keep everything clean from the outside in also. Your skin expels and absorbs a lot of things, and sometimes it goes straight into Your blood stream and not into the liver to be detoxified. Be careful, keep what goes on Your skin and what You sleep on, Organic. Keep those elimination systems cleaned out so Your 7 circulatory systems can do their jobs too. Please do watch My podcast on **'The Stickiness in Our 7 Circulatory Systems'** on You Tube under My name. Thank You so much. With better nutrition, getting up off Your butt and a positive attitude with Your Source involved, You will sleep a better, which in turn decreases Your stress hormones, which starts a beautiful positive cycle. Physically You know what doesn't feel good. Mentally, You know what is true for You because You know if it makes You feel good or not. Mentally, because Your mind affects Your body, You know what doesn't feel good physically because of all those symptoms We experience. Your physical side will follow along with what You feel, believe and act upon. Listen to Your body and change the way You feel about it. Change the way You see You, know that You are going to be positive about it and help Yourself with a happier attitude.

If Your vibe is lower, whether it's from day in and day out negativity, criticism, etc., or from one single overwhelmingly traumatic event that would change Your life, in both instances You can lose confidence, self-worth and even Your health. Rooted thoughts are entangled within Your reality. With people having low self-esteem, it is hard to be grateful, happy or even satisfied with other people, situations or even to Ourselves. Just thinking this, doesn't it make Your vibe feel all sorts of negative?

When trying to change something most people's attention first goes to the problem or what is wrong, I too would start there. Yes they are true, but it doesn't have to stay that way because You're here now and You are not that same person. And why is *it* wrong or bad? Because somebody told You that it is, because You know that it is wrong in Your heart, because somebody gave You that label or that diagnosis and now it has become a reality? You can see it, You can feel it, but what else can You also do? You could focus on the bad things, the terrible things, the long-lived things that have happened and could still be occurring or You could focus on something better, a little bit more positive. I am not saying ignore things at all, take care of Yourself please, but if You could just change Your thought processes about that subject or not think too much about it. The main way to change anything is how You perceive and react to it, because it is *All about the True You.* It is not about what they tell You about You. You are not a symptom, You are not Your diagnosis, You are not Your addiction, it is just a part of You, a very small part of You, because Your physical body is a very, very small part of You compared to Your bigger aspect, Your Living Spirit.

So, with Source and all that backup with You, all that power, all those good vibes, do You still think You can't? Yes, You can! Just the fact that You made the decision to want to do it, is a huge stepping stone. Concentrate on releasing those negative energies, those negative thoughts or emotions that You have about any aspect of Your life. Rearrange Your mind about 'it' when You can and focus on the good things that are happening. Change all of Your thoughts to good vibe ones. To come out of a physical lower frequency into a higher healthier vibe, You need to use Your Spirit. To come out of a negative mental or mind frequency, You've got to use Your Spirit. You will come out of both of those situations really quickly if Source is involved. No problem! Use Your mind last. Connect with Your Spiritual side first, second and third and You'll get out of anything. If You do this then every aspect of Your life is going to progress with a positive start for a more positive result from any new segment. 🧡 Be happy about All of the things that are right with You, and with the Law of Attraction, no exceptions, with the Law of Attraction, that is what You will bring towards You. *You* are part of an excellent Team with a great vibe. The more You love, the higher and faster You will soar.

Your connection to Your Source is so important, it has to be at the top of Your list in every situation of Your life. Yes, every single time.

Chapter 32

Create Something New

Writing Your Own Book

To live and create Your life, You need to write Your Own book, molding it from what is happening around You, for You and because of You. Our stories tell Our lives, and Our tales try to make sense to another of what We have been through. Who should it be to tell Your story if You are writing it? As You are living Your book, are You a character or the main lead? Is Your persona true to You or is it someone that society will say is good or Your family would say, "Yep I agree'? This is about You and only You, it is Your story. When You are drafting Your book make sure that You are living those scenarios, make sure that it is 'You' that You are talking about, and when You are ready then bring it out and share it with the world. We are all actors and actresses in Our lives and the more You stay true to You, Your life story is going to have more fun, more love, more adventures, better opportunities, more laughter, abundance will come to You and anything else that You need too. You Must Act the part, Feel the part and Play the Role as Happy and as Positive as You can, then Your life will be even more blessed. Your story can work 100% of the time for happy endings and new beginnings.

To create something, to start a new segment with any aspect of Your life, You have to get to the cocreative part, an idea between You and Your Source, #2. This is a mental thought charged by Your relationship with Source. Every time You imagine something, Y'all are digging up an idea together, a desire, a thought and then You have something to work with. These ideas start a plan or a habit for You to practice and play for the reality that You want to live in. Some of the tales should include all of Your dreams and desires coming true and how much more happiness You are going to feel doing the things that You love. Think of where You truly want to be, how You wish to live and who You want to be with. Imagine it and know that it is paid for in full, with the best people, having fun and sharing love. It is ok if You don't have all the answers, because there will always be new questions along Your path and the solutions will come when You need them. The answers to any questions that You have, any dilemmas that You have, You are going to realize them with Your Source. You are going to find it with

Your Energy and using everybody else's Energy too, which has nothing to do with their opinions. Using the opinions of others, because You asked or You looked like You needed help, is a great sharing experience, *Bilateral Learning*. They have to compare You to them on what You're doing to what they're doing, to what they have heard and how they feel. Take their ideas to heart but don't give away Your power too much by letting them be too concerned about You. Don't let others control Your life from how much they love and care for You, they can take some of Your power away. Yes, You can ask people their thoughts about it, but the ultimate action and answer is going to be found between You and Your Best Friend. When You write Your story don't let Your ego mind limit You and don't let anyone else manipulate what You *write* either. It has to be Your story, not Your family's. Use other's opinions and make them Your Own, only if it makes You feel good to create something new with it.

All segments, stories and tales start with a not knowing and being a little lost, an innocent. Life is going to continue to expand and something that You believe one day or within a couple of days, could be something totally different. *No stories or their endings are carved in stone.* Within a second or a couple of hours, You can change Your mind 180'. If it is a 360' turn around, You can always start from another view point and begin again. You can't really make a 'whole' new version of Yourself anyhow; change will be only in some aspects of Your life. You can however make a whole new edition of Your situations or Your environment. Your desire, which is unknown to You, just because it hasn't happened yet, *is already a reality* in nature and in Spirit.

This is a life path and if there are things that You need to leave to yesterday, then that's what You need to do. Reality is infinite and guess what? *What You know for sure is the reality of Your life right now.* The past, a second ago or in the older past, is not reality anymore but You can recall the situations to here and now as a memory if You choose to. If You do reflect, then look for the things that You had an advantage in or only the good stuff. Memories should comfort You, strengthen You and bring You peace where You are right now and if not, it is Your choice not to think or talk about it. Pick out the best variation from Your story that You have learned, moved forward from and made more positive for You right now, and write that down.

Creating something new, while doing things that You don't like to do, You are going to have to change Your ordinary mundane habitual things into something that is fun to complete: like cleaning the house, doing the laundry, doing the dishes, the yard, whatever it is for You and We can name so many. You can do them with a smile, You could add in music, or You can take that road instead of the other way, it is all going to lead to the same place, Your goal. Again, what I do is habit stack. Since I know to have a happy life, I have to find the ways to make it better for Me. I realize that by making My environment wonderful and clean and fresh, that makes it positive for Me, and since I don't really have time somedays to work out because I have to do other things in My daily routine, I do both, something for My physical body and My surroundings. So, I just start the laundry first and while the laundry is washing or drying, I can get a lot of things done. While dusting or doing the floors, I can work out absolutely! While washing dishes or vacuuming be in the moment right here and now, not thinking about what You would rather be doing, because the dishes need done, vacuuming needs done, so make it fun. Feel the water, feel the soap and the bubbles and how soft it is on Your hands. Look how clean and shiny Your dishes are waiting for the next time that You're going to eat a good nutritious meal or pizza, doesn't matter, right? What about the laundry, washing, folding and smelling the clothes. Love and accept what You are doing right now and then see what happens because of the fun in doing those things that You have to do. Now, the chores that I have to do are done for a whole week and I have gotten a couple hours of workout or play time in with My physical body and it is so happy. There is such a variety of ways to get all Your tasks done, and if there is other family around and they live there too, they can and should help. I mean even Your kids will see how much You enjoy doing house hold chores and they won't mind doing their part as much. They are watching You; they are feeling Your good emotions no matter what needs to be done around Your paradise. For Me at the end of the day, My environment feels wonderful and I have loved on Me. Show in that chapter how much fun You have in any endeavors and the results that stand out in Your everyday life.

You can't always be serious either, You have to have play time and I am telling You that the more play time You have, the more You make it appealing to You and the more You appreciate it, the more fun that You are going to have. When You start having more enjoyment with more happiness and more positivity in Your life, then more of all of that will come on in. Once You get started, momentum kicks in and hello! The other things in life that You are doing, without even trying, will have more happiness because of the Laws of the Universe. So don't be serious all the time, One must play. Didn't somebody say that at some point?

If You dream it and live on the path with Source to Your desires, You might not want to switch things up as much as You think You do now. You're going to be so happy on the journey and as You get closer, You will realize that You are having the most fun and then all of a sudden, **boom**, You will be fulfilled for this time frame. If You think that You are missing signs from the Universe, You might be. Turn those filters off or at least clear Your filters and look at life through a different lens. The segments of Your life, especially those things that do not make You feel good can be changed anytime to make You happy. If You start changing Your attitude, Your environment is going to change, the people around You are going to change, the way You look at the drive to work, the buildings, anything that made You feel icky before, will change. All because You altered Your attitude and perceptions. If You play with *You, Yourself & Source* at the beginning of the day, then the whole day is just better, it's funner, it's more productive, and it's more creative. That continuation of Your life story, all those new chapters and titles can be rearranged and start and end anytime that You'd like. Let that communication flow and open up to You being Your normal, beautiful True Self. If You need something, it's already given to You, and if You say that it is just a coincidence when something happens, it is because You don't believe it is really supposed to be happening for You or You don't believe that You actually have that much control over Your desires. When You ask Your Source for help, it is done & You receive the answers by the paths they show You. If You are positive, more positive will come in towards Your wish. Finding joy in Your life, more joy can come to You along Your path. With happiness & love in Your life, the more happiness & love can come to You Blissfully! Self-respect, self-worth and loving You first are all just bonuses. You can only achieve true balance for Yourself when You start reflecting on You and when You change Your attitude. You just have to kind of let go of the outside noise, the outside distractions and concentrate on You. You have to try to figure out how You can find Your outside in the environments of everyday and be the best that You can for You. When You value Yourself, Your reaction times will become more balanced. You will be more kind and friendly and You will be quicker to forgive others or situations. If You want a better life for Your future to add into Your book, then You just have to accept all of those infinite potentials and realities that You can't even measure at this time. You can have all Your chances and if they make You happy, that is all that matters. There is an unlimited number of options that You can have. Why? Because You can change Your mind and You can adapt to who You are for Yourself and for Your Source. Don't say, *'I'm too old, I've done this My whole life; I can't do this; what about My friends, family, My spouse, My boss, coworkers, My community, they won't understand'.* It matters less what the reality is that You are living right now at this moment in time, physically or mentally with any aspect of Your life, if You want it changed. At the end of the day or the end of Our lives, everything is it going to be okay and wonderful anyway.

When You are You and not trying to be somebody else by playing a role in any aspect of Your life, You will get to know Yourself a little bit more with every segment. It's so much better for You to be You always, because then life becomes easier and funner. It's *always* better to be You, just like it's always better to tell the truth because the next time it comes around, You don't have to really try to remember what the h*** You said the first time. The truths will always come out. You decide how You want to take every segment, every situation, every time. Because of You living Your life, it all starts with You and Your opinion, and it is never totally changing everything, it is just switching up the things that don't make You feel good anymore. The funniest way to do this is to definitely learn new things, use Your options and yes, You can start again, You always have a second, a third or a fourth chance.

Stillness is the key to the friendship with YOUR BFE, the mainline of communication with the other part of You and meditation leads You to the cocreation of the life You want. If You work on Your Spiritual part first and daily, that special relationship between You and Your BFE, any new challenges or dilemmas will be followed with new pathways that will come to You easily and with more fun along the way. Trust who You are being led by and whether You realize this or not, it is Your Spirit. They're always going to show You the right path, always! Even if You don't believe in God, or in a higher Source being with a powerful energy, controlling things by using the Laws of the Universe and helping You out, They still believe in You. You don't have a choice in that matter. They are here for the purpose of Your life. To Me this is the best thing in the whole wide world, it is the most important aspect in all of this, *'I became more aware of My Source, of My Energiez, of Our Energiez and My life changed for the better, the much better'.* Become more aware and awakened and Your life will flourish on this Mother Father Earth and between You and Your BFE. Everything that You have asked for, everything that You have prayed for is reserved there for You. You just need to pick the right pathway for You, and again, the easiest way to know if You're following the right one is if You feel good or not. What a great energy to follow, what a perfect lead in Your book with You and as a Best Friend for life. Oh! Yes, Please. When You realize that the unconscious is more powerful than the conscious when You desire something, because Your mind holds You back, You can play with another 80/20 game. 80% of the time be unconscious of how it's happening and 20% of time just know that it's going to happen, because You ask for it. All of this can happen for You and for anyone because We are part of the Universe, You are part of that energy. Anything that You want exists in the Universe and there is enough for all of Us. Everyone deserves it and is worthy, especially the ones like You, who work on themselves with Source first.

Start Your Negativity Detox now at this time and create a new chapter, don't procrastinate. What are You waiting for? Release the Energies that do not let You be You and it doesn't matter *who or what it is*. Don't hold on to lower frequency emotions, move up the scale, Your scale, one or multiple feelings at a time. If You are new to this, start simple and do-little bits at a time or jump right on in, either way it will be fun, it will be successful and there will be a happy segment to the start of Your next book. If a negative emotion comes, take a deep breath first and help Your physical body calm itself, it lets You live the life You want. Be aware and love on Mother Father Earth always. Look for all the beauty, kindness and love around in Your environments. Have unconditional love for All the Organics. Save Space for Source and for You daily and take as many times as You need to in the course of the day to connect. Find the positives in all people and situations. Tutor Your kids and they will also show You the way. Smile and Laugh several times a day. Have the courage because You have the power. Get out of the maze or the labyrinth of society most of the time, find Your space and stay in the higher frequencies A Majority of the Time. Never be totally satisfied, life will flow. You needn't make any decision that You choose, final. It is never a whole paradigm shift; it is a succession of Your happiness to further and further fun and joy in this life. This is what We are trying to do, have a great time in most of or all of Our segments. Persist with playing out Your novel. Please know, even if these ideas are new for You, that all of the happiness is already inside You. Live peacefully in Your Fairytale true to Yourself and document it as You go. You can revise Your plans anytime to make Your autobiography wonderful for You. You need to be the hero or heroine in Your Own book of Your life story. In the next few chapters, here are some practices that I play to help You move on up to knowing You. Yes, You will also have help from Your environment and from many Energies, and Your Source is always working behind the scenes getting things ready for You, but You are the only One that can do something about it. Work together with Your Mind, Body and Spirit and keep the Spiritual part, Your Best Friend at the at the lead in Your exciting, one-of-a-kind, never-ending story…….

Write Your Own story. Slant Your T's and heart Your I's...

The more that You are with Your Source, You will know what You want & will not accept anything less, but You will accept better...

Chapter 33
Meditation, Y'allz Time

Find Yourself and then relax into it... Meditation is a practice of focus, using that piece of Your mind that a lot of people have not been in contact with for a long time. To meditate is to withdraw Our conscious awareness from what is happening in Our lives. If You take Your attention from everything else in Your life, it brings You to the right here and now, right where You are. When You Meditate, You surrender Your thoughts, Your worries and doubts, and what is left is a happy silence, full of peace and calm for Your mind and Your body at the same time. When You calm Your mind and Your body, You're inviting Your Spirit, Your Source to come even closer to You through Your heart. When You meditate, You are setting up space for Spiritual enlightening, an awakening and the joining of You, Your Source and Your Universe. This is when You and Your BFEs are gonna click in the strongest ways. With meditation You are just talking to Your Best Friend, Your other half, Your higher part. We say higher because it's energy. You have Your physical body and

Your mind on earth, then You have Your Source and Universe. This is the energy where You started from, and when You meditate, You're just kind of going back home for a little while and saying 'Hey' to the family and asking, 'what are We gonna do today?' During meditation, You are choosing which consciousness that You want to live in for the rest of the day, so which part of Your being, the happy or troubled one, are You going to play with in the Universe today?

This is My version of connecting to the *resources* available to all of Us. Within any lecture, class, podcast, webinar or other things that You go to broaden Your horizons, some people will get it and some people don't. With this, everybody can achieve it, *if You practice a little bit every day, if You play a little bit every day.* The more that You do Your meditations or pauses with Your Source, the more Your Source is going to make sure that the time is available for You, because They want to spend that time just to relax and move Your Energiez together. I promise You; I guarantee You, that Your life is going to be better for every single one of You who plays.

Meditation is for many different things and in meditation many different things can happen. It has been proven by science, healthcare and religion, that meditation does reduce stress and generates an inner peace within Us while linking Our Soul with its higher self. While You are operating without using Your mind, Your Source is working with Your physical body, relaxing it, calming Your blood pressure and decreasing Your heart rate and Your respirations. There have been studies that show longevity with people who meditate. Meditation will keep You living in the here and now longer, if Your body is healthy and can handle the environment.

Meditation enhances Your quality of sleep, so give Your physical body a pause at any time, a good night's sleep and little naps too. Feel great about having those occasional naps to link You in with Source.

With meditation You actually realize more and it expands Your consciousness. Meditation is a power charger and it gives You creative feelings and that better communication with Your Source, Your intuition. When Your intuition kicks in, You are going to know things even quicker. Yep, just like that and then Your life, Your whole life, every single aspect of Your life is going to change for the positive. Work with Your intuition, work with Your heart and they'll show You which way to go.

Meditation expands Your sensual activity. Afterwards, all of Your physical senses will be elevated. For Me My mood is lighter, I have a smile on My face. I see brighter colors and I hear more harmonic sounds. I have an awareness of tantalizing aromatic flavors that seem better when I eat, and a sensation of touch that makes Me have a tingly sensitivity. So awesome.

I'm always saying You need to release Your ego, but it doesn't mean the ego that is calm, that does protect You and make You think a little bit. In society and living on this Earth, You need Your ego. The only time You really need to calm Your ego, which means quiet Your mind, is when You are with Your Source during meditation or any other time Y'all are together. No matter how many times that You meditate during the day, or take Your pauses, or say Your prayers, then and only then can You give up Your ego, because You don't need it at all. You are safe with Your Best Friend Energy. When You do need to use Your ego or Your thinking mind, they will be calmer because You have been quieting Your mind.

I believe concentrating on Your breathing should be at forefront of everyone's meditation. Breath work initially, because it brings You closer to Your Source. It makes You sit up in a good posture, so Your spine is straight, so Your energy centers are free-flowing. Breathing in starts the energy flow to You and exhaling releases energies and toxins out of Your body that no longer serve You, and it leaves space for more goodness. I am bringing in love and wonderful Pure Positive energy from Mother Father Earth and from the ethers and I think about how great the oxygen is going through My 7 circulatory systems, to all of My trillions of cells and trillions and millions of microbiomes in My body. Just like when You start something and You shake things up. When You do Your breath work, You're shaking up Your cells. You are shaking up Your microbiome, because You have raised Your energy. You know, breathing kind of gets You excited, it makes Your heart rate a little fast at first and then it really calms it down and You slowdown in the end. Good oxygen and nutrients along with a quiet calmness and relaxation, then all the sudden My mind is clear. Breath play is so important to start before any meditation, during a meditation, after meditation, before any workout, cool down or warm up. You also should practice before prayers, before You walk out on stage to do a presentation or before You help somebody, and many more to think of. Before You walk into a temple or place that is sacred to You, breathe, release what You need to release, know that You are sacred and then ask permission, 'May I enter?' When do You need to meditate? Whenever You need to calm Your mind and to set up Your day or a situation. Especially in the morning, that's the best time to just say Hi to Your Best Friend and then again anytime that You feel overwhelmed or You feel worried or doubtful, which could mean that You are impatient, so take those little pauses too. I do several *'pauses'* I call them, throughout the day, just for a few seconds or more. Close Your eyes, put Your palms towards the ground and take a deep breath and say Your word or take a breath and hum. You decide what You are going to say or do, any ideas You have are just perfect. Your little pauses throughout the day are just to remind You that You're not alone. *'Yep, We got You'* is what Your Source and Mother Father Earth say. Acknowledge Them, have fun, giggle and let it be an inside joke between You and Your Best Friend Energiez.

You have conscious ways to meditate to help You through the day and You also have unconscious ways to meditate when You sleep. During Your slumber You are always with Source and They're healing Your physical body. Your body is also working, subconsciously and You are manifesting, just multi-dimensional. Since You are energy and Your mind is not there to argue with You, You are going to do what the heck You want, where You want to and since You are with Your Source, that's where You'll find some answers. Don't look for them however, just ask the question before You retire to bed.

When You daydream, that is also an unconscious snooze for the most part. You are with Your Source right there, telling them what You want out of life and how You want to feel. You're writing that story or that movie with Your Source.

Your mind along with Your imagination has an incredible capability to form a picture or colors to go with Your thoughts. You can form all these images positively or negatively, because You still do have that control in Your mind of what to focus on while You are meditating. If You do start seeing faces, colors or pictures forming in front of You, enjoy them for a moment, but then come back to Your center, concentrate on Your breathing or on the sounds that You chose for this session and blank out Your mind. You also have total control of Your physical body at any time before, during, or after Your meditation.

While You are doing Your meditation, You can also dream and be on Your vacation. Why not take 1 or 2 minutes during Your meditation to be on that little vacation that You would love to go on. Your mind is very powerful, so go on Your little mini-vacation and live it within Your emotions for right now. Do Your little spa retreat, feel the massage on Your back and on Your feet. Oh, My Goodness! Something different and exciting every day, all because You sat quietly with Your BFE just for a little while.

There are many avenues of meditation and I lumped them into three different types. Guided, Through Your Heart and Quieting Your mind. Most people start out with a guided process. Listening to someone, to a sound or to music. In the beginning, since I talk so much, I used guided ones and concentrated on the dialect of the person or one specific sound that didn't let My mind drift. I could not use a running stream or water sounds, because I would always think about what was in the water or I would suddenly have to go to the bathroom. Soooo, choose wisely. :)

You can also meditate with Your mind, or Your body and mind together. Why not work out that way sometime, get two things done at once. Focus on each part of Your body, tensing, relaxing and healing. Meditation could also be a time when You make use all of Your senses. One feeling from each sense, for each body part, with You being calm and at peace.

The second kind of meditation is by living Your purpose. Using Our Happiness Scale, there is a conscious way to reflect too. Every time that You are joyful, finding the positives, the beauty, You are meditating. Focusing on things that make You smile is a type of Mediation. Reading is a type of meditation. The time being with Your Source also includes when You play all of Your hobbies and the things that You do to have fun. Every time that You are happier and higher on that Happiness Scale of more than satisfied, You are meditating and making the world a better place too. Being appreciative of the World and the Universe and letting others know how grateful You are for them, are all kinds of meditations.

The most important one, the 3rd one, I think is the best kind, and yes anyone can do it. This is *'Our Quiet time together"*. Put Your phone down and on silent. In these moments, imagine and feel Your body in the comfortable position it is in now. Don't think about what You have to do next and do not think about what happened the days before. Thinking about here and now will naturally get all the other stuff out of Your mind. Every time, I start with a Thank You to Mother Father Earth for the grounding, healing energiez and love. I give a huge Thank You to My Source, My Winged men and any other ancestors or Energy that wants to come party. Then I focus on My breathing and core, bringing in the Pure Positive Energy and releasing what does not serve My highest interest. My surroundings always become still, silent and peaceful, and when I start running My mouth, (or My mind), I come back to the attention of My breathing. Even if I only shut up for 3 of the 15 minutes, I did great. Every day and every meditation is different. I am so happy for the variety of contemplations to try. You can choose for Your meditation that day, something new or whatever You naturally are drawn to. There are so many types and they are all wonderful, look them up, pick Your favorites and play.

Jose Silva suggests to train Your brain into Your subconscious mind and meditation. Start by counting down from 100 for 10 days, then from 50 for 10 days, then from 25 for 10 days, and then from 10 down for 10 days. This daily practice will help You get into Your quiet space for Your special time with Source.

One of the 1st things that people say, and it is what I said too, when I talk about meditation and quieting My mind is, *'oh I could never do that, I can't quiet My mind, it is always runnin'. Ummm Hullo, they named Me Chatty Cathy when I worked in the Emergency Department and there is a reason for that, and because I can do it, so can You.* On some occasions, still after several years of practicing and playing, at the end I say, *'boy We talked a lot today, My goodness. It was still beautiful and wonderful. Thank You Source for spending this time with Me'.* This is what They want the most too, acceptance, some of Your time and Your acknowledgment of Them, just as much as any Best Friend would love to receive.

If You are not use to being with Yourself for a little while during the day, if You've been way too busy thinking about other people, taking care of others and not Yourself, just realize that it was the way that it *was* supposed to be and You kind of got side tracked for a little bit or a lotta bit of Your life. Everybody deserves their little time throughout the day so You just need to start right here now. This is between You and the other part of You, and You can always find that little bit of time and You deserve it. And yes, You do have the time. There are a lot of times during the day that You are alone, like when You go to the bathroom. That is why it is called the *'rest room'*. Right? Feel the way that Your Best Friend is feeling now that You are coming home finally. It's about time and You are going to giggle and laugh and have the best times more often. Your Best Friend is going to be so excited that You wake up and You go to sleep with them every single day, every single night. If You want to take care of somebody else, take care of You and Your BFE and see what happens for You along the way. All Good, all Great. So, give Yourself some time for You, even if it's just for a couple of minutes, those do add up during the day.

If You need to work on Your reactions, then take more pauses throughout the day also, along with Your daily calm time. This will help You to be able to compose Yourself very fast. When You're trying to figure out an answer to a question, or You get into a little tizzy, or something bad happens, You'll be able to react in the right way and at the right time. When You have practiced and played for a little while, eventually You'll be able to relax in times when You use to flip the f*** out. Now You will be like, *'yeah, it's all good, it is going to be okay, We got this'*.

Give Your mind a break, quit giving it things to think about and conjure up. When You start to practice and play with Your meditations, You will be able to recognize what Your mind goes back-and-forth towards each time, and that will let You know what You need to work on later.

Oh yes! You have to do Your meditations every day, if only just to release things that are going on in Your life for a small amount of time. Make sure that it's the right time for You, but do it as early as You possibly can after You wake up. Invite Your Source to join You, Your BFE, even though they are already right here waiting for You to cocreate Your day. When you meditate, You're basically being trained in everything that You should have known since You were born, and You can catch up really easily. Just remember the other part of You that You are, whether You believe it or not, and start living as a whole, *as 1*. Energy and Source, Spiritual and Physical, with Your body and mind. When You do Your meditations, pauses, grounding and Your positivity games or even Your affirmations, whatever You do to make Yourself happier and better, just know that You are celebrating Yourself. Start with 10-15 minutes a day, it is just for a little while out of Your 12–16-hour day and even if You only have quieted Your mind for 2-3 minutes, that is excellent. If You continue to play and practice for a little while, You will want that 15 minutes to count and You will crave more time, because that's when You will be falling in love with Yourself again. Realize that You are absolutely beyond anything, cherished and adored by Your Source. Live the rest of the day as You are a treasured, precious breath of energy person on this Earth, loved beyond measure by Your Source. Walk around strong and confident and self-assured about this, it is a fact.

If You work with Yourself and Source for 15 minutes every day for the minimum of 3 months and enjoy it the whole time, You will start learning so much about Yourself. It may take You 2-3 months to notice a difference and some people sooner, so keep on playing. You will feel that knowing, You will have that clarity and believe that You will succeed, because You have Source on Your side with none of the side effects that slow You down from living on this earth with people, their opinions and programs. Decorate Your special little area where You do Your meditations the way You want it. Anything to celebrate You every single day. Make it in the perfect place, with the right colors, the right comfort, the right pillows, the right pictures, calm lighting and even the right music. You also can light Your candle, because sometimes You go to Your shadow side while calming Your mind, to the place that You don't want to be or one that You're trying to get out of. If You open Your eyes, the light is always right there, if You close Your eyes, Your Source is always right there, because in that unknown is always Your Source. For You to build Your meditation space and for it to be sacred, You also have to know and believe that You are sacred too. Every part of Your human body is one with Your Spirit, who is already sacred, just as You are. Be true to You, and the Universe will do the rest.

After Your meditations, the way that You feel is beautiful, happy, lighter and full of confidence and power. You will remember what those feelings are, even if You haven't had them for a while. Please do this every single day and feel Your Own Love for Yourself. Shift Your Energiez on purpose. Have Your special ceremony for Yourself every single day because when You do, You are also celebrating Your Source. The most important idea in this little space of time, is that You are here and You are able to be here with You and Your Source quietly, not thinking about anything unless it is something that doesn't mean anything. Nothing about Your human life just for these mere few minutes a day and with just those few conscious moments, You will win.

Do You trust Your Best Friend?

Do You trust Your God, Your Source?

Then let it be.

Make Sure You Save Some Space for Your Source.

Meditation Rights

You have the right to remain silent. Anything You say can and will be used for You in Your life. You have the right to talk to Your Source for advice before You answer any questions. You have the right to have Your BFE with You during questioning. If You think You cannot afford Your Source, They will still be here for You before any questioning if You wish. If You decide to answer questions now without Your Source present, You have the right to stop answering at any time.

Sincerely with Power, Your Universe

Yale Kamisar, Supreme Court, 1966

Chapter 34

Grounding or Earthing

One of the biggest resources that We have, with the most powerful Energy around, besides Our Spirit, is Mother Father Earth. Our planet is so much closer to You than You realize. Mother Father Earth is Our core, it connects *Us* All and it also connects *Us* to the Universe with Our Interstitial Matrix.

Grounding or Earthing has been present throughout history in most cultures and in societies for generations. With any place or structure, if it is built from or on Mother Father Earth, it can be sacred, if You know Yourself to be sacred also. Some people believe that a separation from the Earth is unnatural, and so do I. I believe it could be harmful to Your physical body if You don't live with Your natural Source and be linked to Mother Father Earth at least for a little while on a daily basis. Since You are a part of Earth; You need that Energy to live, and there are several ways to accomplish this. The basic playtime with Your world, is just to walk or stand barefooted on Mother Father Earth!

I also believe that a separation from Your Source is unnatural too. It feels bad to go in a different direction from Your Source, it is also the same for the Earth. Both detachments make You feel negative emotions and some people even develop diseases and illnesses.

The Earth's energy is enormously strong and as I always tell Myself, My BFE and My Mother Father Earth, *'there are no boundaries separating Us, nothing in between Our Energiez. Not My shoes, My car, or the buildings I am in'.* Even just by Me saying it, 'there are no boundaries between Us, I love Your Energy.' You will feel Yourself sink down. I don't care, if You are on the 32nd or the 100th floor, make Your grounding as strong as You need it to be. There are no limitations between Your Energy and Mother Father's Energy, no matter what people tell You. They say that You can't ground with rubber shoes on. Yes, the electricity is slowed down. Yes, it can be stronger at times, but if You need it, there is always something related to Earth around You that will help You to ground. Energy can be slowed down or sped up, even quantumly, but never stopped. It is actually up to You what You want, You have that power. Just imagine keeping up with the strength that

You are a part of. That's why it feels so heavy and warm to Me to ground, all wrapped up in safety, love and wellness.

We are made of microbiome and cells, but Our greater make up is that of Energy. Breaking down the atoms, results in Pure Energy. Our body is all electrical. We have an electrical rhythm in Our hearts, read from an EKG. We have electrical rhythms in Our brain, spinal cord and nerves, read from an EEG. The electrolytes in Our bodies, that must be replenished and balanced, all have electrical charges too. When You eat, the foods and drinks also have an electrical charge and an effect within Our cells and microbiomes. When You ground, they have found a neutral charge to Our bodies, no charge, a stability, and Your body feels and reacts to the environment better. When You gather up all that good negative energy from the Earth, it restores Your body's natural internal electrical rhythms.

The soles of Your feet have over 1300 nerve endings per square inch, more than any other part of Your body, so Your feet absorb that loving, healing Energy from Earth. As You are grounding, electrons take a little while to rise up. To Us they're moving slow, but to them, they're moving fast, in an instant and continuously. As You step on the ground, You could feel the tingles in Your legs.

Grounding supports specific functions of Our tissues, organs and their systems. While Earthing, the electrons decrease the free radicals in Your cells, and when You are healing, they help to reduce the inflammation throughout Your whole body. You need the electrons when You are working out and when You need energy for Your mitochondria. You will have less discomfort and down times after injuries will decrease. When You are grounding it thins Your blood, because when the electrons get into Your body, they coat the red blood cells so they cannot clump together as readily. If Your blood is circulating freely, the nutrients will flow in and the waste products go out easier. Your blood pressure could go down and Your heart rate is probably going to slow a little too. Aahhh! Calmness. Just to be clear from societies point of view, 'grounding does not cure You of any disease or condition', (yet some believe it can), but it does reunite You with the natural, body needed, electrical signals from Our Mother Father Heavenly Body.

Being grounded also helps You with Your intuition, Your special communication with

Your Source. Your perspectives also change to something more positive for You, and You will be able to see the things that You need to see to move forward in Your life. You can receive all sorts of messages, but if You want to really, really hear them and use Your intuition, use Mother Father Earth's energy too. *'Hey, I'm here. Use me. I know You are cleaning Me up and You're doing a great job. Thank You so much for taking care of all My Organics, so make Yourself at home. Use My energy please and make Yourself stronger. Oh yes, I am here for You to live the best life that You can, just love me back. That's all I ask...'*

If You feel unsteady, if You are tripping, falling or feeling off balance, then maybe You are not grounded to Mother Father Earth. Please let Your doctor know of course, do not wait and in the meantime, try grounding several times throughout the day. You cannot overdose and there are only positive side effects.

If You think You can't handle an Energy or a person, ground with Mother Father Earth and use her to maintain Your support. Your Source will be there with You already.

You can ground at any time, even if You have a flight or fight, save Your life kind of situation. You still have those seconds, a half of a second, a millisecond to ground Your mind. Your physical body is already attached to Earth and now with an even stronger bond.

If You need lovin from Earth in a time where You're feeling a little anxious or a little overwhelmed, *'stop for a moment, take a deep breath, release it slowly and just say, 'Mother Father Earth, there are no barriers between Your Energiez and Mine, I need Your support right now', a*nd the Energy will just come right on up, envelope You and make You feel so calm, safe and satisfied. Whenever You link with anything that is Organic, it immediately connects You to the Universe's Energy. When You ground or hug a plant, You immediately get Yourself embraced by the Universe. It all works together in Your favor, all in My favor. Just think, when Your dog rolls around on the ground or lays on the ground all spread out, guess what they're doing? Getting all that love and support and healing from Mother Father Earth and the Universe.

If You feel bottled up Energiez, ground to Mother Father Earth by doing Your *little pauses* and I say, *'Hey, how You doing? You look beautiful today.' 'I release the Energies that are pent-up inside Me, that Me, Myself can't handle very well. My mind doesn't appreciate it. My body tells me, 'I don't appreciate it', so Thank You for Your help', and then whatever You want to do with that Energy go for it.* Mine grows foliage and greenery in places that need it most, so We can bring rain to that part of the Earth. It is just so automatic for Me now, but I still say, *'releasing all the energies that no longer serve Me and give the bestest to Momma and Poppa Earth'.* The stronger all Your Pent-up energy is, the more Mother Father Earth appreciates it and uses it gently and calmly for its benefit. Thank You so much for Your Energy releases to help Yourself and the World. Do this as many times as You need to and then You will find Your emotions calmer and on the top area of Your Happiness Scale more often.

Grounding can be drinking good water and eating root vegetables. Grounding itself is like eating a handful of fresh fruits and veggies with their antioxidant's health benefits. Our Earth also says to eat more fruits and vegetables, not just Your mother or Your practitioners, because if You eat more whole foods, then it will be able to make more, according to The Law of Attraction. *If You eat, it will make.* Mother Father Earth will provide more nutritious, adaptive Organic foods. Love on Your Mother Father Home, imagine the greater things, talk to *it* nicely, appreciate and notice all the varieties to choose from. You'll be more powerful because Mother Father Earth is freely giving You healing and strengthening Energiez.

If You do Your physical activities outside, You will feel different then when You work inside. Open up those other Energy centers in You to allow all the Pure Positive Energy into every part of Your body that You are trying to make healthy. Use Your Universe. They are here for You in every single episode of Your life. You just have to ask for it and believe in it with so much love and acceptance.

A strong protection shows up for You when You meditate or ground. Everything that You receive, all the knowledge and the love from Your meditation, You need to set that into Your physical body and into Your mind, and the best way to do that is to ground it in. Meditation while grounding is very powerful and beneficial to Your physical body. With the negative charges from the Earth's surface and the positive charges from the Ethers, You are receiving both updates. Do what comes natural for Your physical body, for Your mind and for Your Soul. You don't have to study years for this or even 6 months. But You do need to practice and play. After 6 months or so, You have built the playtime in. It is done.

If You can't touch Mother Father Earth, there are other ways to accomplish this. You can ground to Mother Father Earth with a grounding Mat. There are also grounding sheets, that way You're doing it all the time. You can ground to Mother Father Earth by imagining a symbol, or holding Your token close to Your heart and feeling it within You and in Your energetic field. You also can practice this at the same time that You are walking barefooted on Earth. Carry Your precious stones, crystals or trophy, and say Your special mantra. Add in all those powers to be utilized together, You don't have to only use one at a time.

Change is the only constant; **I don't think so.** Source present every moment of Our lives, that is a constant. Our body starting to heal right after an incident, constant until the end. Mother Father Earth is Organic or alive and has 2 sides, a physical side that is adapting to the Universe and an Energy side. Just like We are physical and Source Energy, Mother Father Earth is also Spirit and shifts energetically, because any-*one* who tries to change anything physically, also has to play with the Energy side too. The Earth repairing itself and transforming to the situations that We are causing; this is another constant that will continue, because Mother Father Earth wants to adapt so that We can live and have the things that We need on Earth. All the plants and animals are adapting too, which means spiritually and physically, and they are also adjusting to the customization of the new Earth. I believe that the Earth is doing a great job. Some people would not agree because things are getting lost, Organic lives and homesteads, but adaption is what is happening. The Earth is doing what it needs to do, so it can further nurture Us with an abundance of fruits, vegetables and objects that We can use for safety, housing and living. We just need to listen more openly.

Happy to Me is being a human for this beautiful Mother Father Earth. This is My home base for right now, so I'm gonna make the most of it. I think one of the most important things that *We should ALL take responsibility for, is Our Earth*. You have to be conscientious of Your planet and help, it cannot. Use gentle nudges to help people clean up and if not, then Thank God that You're there to be able to pick it up, right? Nourish it, just like You do Your physical body. Everybody can do just a little part. *Mother Father Earth says, 'love Me every day, appreciate Me every day, replenish what You use and keep Me clean'.* So, what are You intending to do to help Our Mother Father Earth? Even if all You think You can do is to recycle. Yeaaee, absolutely. The garbage that I throw away is hardly anything anymore, because I recycle everything I possibly can. I'm doing something great for the Earth. For all of Us, even if We say, *'Thank You so much' to all of the Captains of the boats that are out there removing trash out of the oceans and waterways so the animals there can thrive again'. I am so happy seeing people plant more trees and all sorts of gardens while cleaning up all sorts of messes. Add to Your prayers to say Thank You for everybody that loved on Mother Father Earth today in the Whole Wide World.* That love from You grows exponentially in the Universe. You are doing a great job assisting Our planet, be proud of Yourself. It is now, and it is going to be okay, because We got a lot of people and Energiez working on it.

Beautiful Energiez are all around Our environments. You should crave to go outside and ground in nature daily. Mother Father Earth and Nature can get You to a different positive place so fast. Take time to appreciate Our Earth. Every person out there, every time You look out the window, every time You think about a beautiful place that You've been to or that You wish to go, smile big and appreciate it more. Walk barefooted, love on those plants, roll in the sand or mud, lay in the dewy grass, swim in the waters and let Mother Father Earth show You the way. Be grateful as You ground to Mother Father Earth and absorb all that good energy. Ground before meditations or ground pretty much before You do anything, and Your life will flow with Healthy Energiez. Throughout the day, I do My little pauses and say, 'Thank You to Mother Father Earth'. Just like Your Source is waiting for You, Mother Father Earth is waiting for You also.

It's Good to be Grounded, 24/7.

Chapter 35

Eat Healthy & Move

To get started in a life that You choose at this time, You consciously have to do it. To make Your life better for You, You have to willfully make that choice and then in time, it will become more and more automatic. Imagine if You opened up to this combination of Your Spirit, Your physical body and Your mind all working together for Your health and wellness.

When You're trying to change part of Your life, let's say losing weight and becoming healthier for Your physical body, You have to remember it's not just *'food and move'*, it is also making Your environment better for the new You. Changing Your scene also might mean the people that You hang out with. If You're the only one ordering something that is healthy, don't feel bad about them and don't feel threatened if they don't get it. You will hear the criticism, teasing and certain joking remarks and underneath, some are not nice. They just want You to stay with them, healthy or not, and they will say anything to keep You in their space. If all Your friends and family eat the things that

You don't want to eat because You know better for Yourself now, this is what I say about it. *'I don't really want to eat that anymore; it doesn't do anything for Me at all except to make Me and My digestive system more sluggish and then I can't get the c*** out and I will absorb those toxins'.*
Sometimes this means that You might have to be with *You, Yourself & Source* during those meals. You never, ever eat alone anyway, You always have somebody there to talk to, Your Source and they will appreciate what You're doing for Your physical body.

If You have to feed Your family at home, make sure that there are plenty of healthy choices. There can always be something that's good to munch on and then every once in a while, sure a treat, but don't keep it in the house. This should be an outside family trip. *That's what I do, this is My secret. If I knew that I would eat it, it didn't stay in My house, nope. I would go out and get it if I really wanted to, but then after a little while, when My microbiome became more balanced, I didn't want it anymore.* If it is a family affair all of the time, and if there is no junk food, then You won't eat it and they won't get it either, and everyone will be healthier and eventually won't want the fillers anymore. I've had people say to Me, '*I have to buy that because I have kids and they won't eat'*. No, You don't, no You do not! If it is not healthy for You it is definitely not healthy for a new growing body either. Nobody is gonna starve to death, they might whine a little bit and not eat as much at first, but soon they will, because they will see how much You are enjoying it and how much happier You are. Even if they are not overweight and can seem to eat anything, You know what is not healthy to eat and You know that eventually it *Will Catch Up With Them*. No matter how much they grumble at first, they are not gonna wither away. Live with Your moral authority, working on Yourself right now, loving the new tastes and feeling better. They will see Your light. Your family will see the difference in You and they will also learn that some things You can chew on and eat and no matter who says what about it, is not going to keep You healthy. Watch My podcasts on You Tube under *Cathy Copperthwaite*, there are many that speak of how Our food and drink sources really are and the impact they have on Our bodies and on Our pet's health too. Try to substitute more and more good foods into Your diet daily. Get a couple recipe books and have them pick out one at a time to make with You. Make all parts of meal time a family affair. The preparation, the meal, and the clean-up.

One thing that You're going to have to add-on to this diet, is to make Your wishes and desires known to Your Source. Don't write down the goal of *'losing weight',* because just that sentence of *'going on a diet to lose weight'*, Oh, My goodness, what a powerful, negative saying, and how many times have I said it? Geezzz. It makes You think things like, *'I can't ever eat that, and oh, My gosh, is this time going to work?'* You can't worry about losing weight and getting into that body shape that You want, You just have to go on the pathways that make You feel good about it. A friend said to me, *'I just eat it if it is going to be healthy for My body and then sometimes I eat things that I know do not supply enough good nutrition'.* You know, those occasional cheat dayz! If You deprive Yourself of things that You desire to eat and You focus on not having them, guess what? You are going to desire them even more, then You will feel guilty when You eat it. When You do occasionally eat Your favorite foods, You do have to give up any negative feelings that You have about it during and after You eat them. If the emotions are of guilt, regret or failure, yea, You had a bite, You ate the whole thing, Oh Well, it is in the past. *'My body absorbed whatever nutrients were available, the rest will be released with nothing stored and the next time, I just won't.'* Make sure that You are not upset and that You are relaxed when You eat. Feel good about whatever You are piggin out on. Concentrate on the positive parts of well-being and that changes Your thought process about losing that extra sub q tissue. Talk about Your extra sub-Q tissue for Your benefit. *'Oh, My all that extra energy just for Me, Thank You and whatever is left over, Thank You for Your reserve and protection'.* Even if You cannot see them yet, the positives are here and becoming more abundant. For everyone You see suffering, angry, unhappy or unhealthy, there are just as many doing just the opposite, making themselves and the world better. *Make sure You are happy; enjoy it and let it satisfy You no matter what it is.* **It then will have the highest chance of being digested and not stored.**

And of course, there are a few things of food and drink that You do need to change or omit with *My Negativity Detox diet*, because You do have to decrease the inflammation in Your body for systems to work correctly. If You can't decrease the swelling in Your body, nothing can flow through right? Certain foods, drinks and emotions bind up Your systems and then when You do eat 'healthier', You don't absorb the nutrients that they're saying are in the food. Some foods are so sticky, they are making Your digestive system less absorbent, not functioning correctly and then Your digestive system stores toxins and leaks into any other body system. You kinda know what foods they are too. Either You don't or maybe take a bite and then say, *'that is good, I have had My fill'.* You have to clean out all of Your elimination systems daily, sometimes hourly. You can change Your body so easily, if You are not sticky physically or mentally.

To help You out a substantial amount, cut out the s***, it really is, cut the man-made junk. You need to stop eating those things that are filling You up, that give You an immediate gratification, with less benefits, less nutrients, and also that really don't satisfy. These are the choices people are eating at every meal and for snacks. After a healthy, nutritious meal usually You wouldn't eat again for several hours, but with the junk food, that message doesn't get received in the brain to stop because of the artificialness and preservatives, and then You eat again before Your first meal has been digested. If

You eat again to soon, You are not giving Your body a chance to digest and rest. It takes a little while to break down Your food and it is different for every individual. There are other foods that fill You up better for the long run. If You eat the things that fill You up and that are more nutritious, then You are not going to need to eat every 3 or 4 hours. Also, some of the time, You might not really be hungry, just thirsty, so listen to Your body and quench with good water or juicy fruits and veggies. Your body is going to work more efficiently, Your elimination systems are going to start working better and then Your circulatory systems will flow easier and You will feel the difference.

You don't have to give up Your favorite drinks all together, but You do have to add up those calories at the end of the night. You know, 3 or 4 glasses of wine is 300-500 calories or more and it gets broken down differently. Your liver and Your body don't want those 'wasteful calories' to break down and detoxify. As long as You are drinking something, like good ole fashion distilled water, that is what I drink, You will be satisfied. Put it in a wine glass, martini glass or beer mug if it makes You feel better.

You should knowingly feed Your 2nd Bestie, Your human body, good tasting nutritious meals and consciously get up and move. And if You can, walk for 15 minutes after a meal to help Your digestive system work better. Show that You do have vitality and that You want the best life in this human body, through the actions of giving Your 2nd Best Friend minutes a day to get up and move. Use Your Spiritual connection with Your BFE, talk to Your Source and an ultimate reason will show itself and You will have the best work outs. It will be more calming for You, more peaceful and You'll feel relaxed, at ease and stronger for the rest of the day. One thing I tell Myself about working out or giving Myself and My 2nd-Best Friend that 7 to 30 minutes every single day, is that if I do not use My muscles they're going to feel neglected and they are not going to be strong for Me when I need them. Use Mother Father Earth, the Universe and all Their support when You wish to. Get the motivation from Your body and Source. Feel that soreness, not pain and then the next day do something different.

I believe that everyone should do some strength training. There are muscles in every aspect of Your body, even if You haven't seen them for a long time. Wouldn't You want to tighten them up and admire them again? They want to be flexed and extended to promote blood and lymph flow and to grow a bit. Isn't it nice to see that little bicep on Your arm after You have given it some attention? It kinda wants to make You work out some more. I try to work My muscles about 15 minutes before I eat, because it helps to burn Your sugar and some fats. If I use weights to build a little muscle, I add more protein in that day. Just think about that muscle You want to motivate, talk to it sweetly like, *'My …muscle is engaged and I feel stronger now. Look how cute My lil muscle is. I love to get up and move every single day and I love to choose which play session that I want to do'.*

You can do Spiritual workouts too. Regular workouts involve Your physical body for the most part, because that's what You're trying to fix up and a little bit of Your mind and ego. Meditative workouts involve Your mind, body and Spirit. You will get more out of a Spiritual Balancing workout with Your BFE, to help Your heart, lungs and musculoskeletal systems to be able to endure more. That special time with Your Source while You are working out, means a lot more stretching and flexibility. Yes, You can have bursts of things like running or weight training, but the rest of the time You are stretching and breathing, and flowing and balancing. These are the best workouts because You're involving Your Source, through Your kind of Meditation. Change up Your workout a little bit and add in Spirituality or Meditation.

I do not perform very much intense cardio exercises anymore, only because I am implementing breathing exercises with the other movements and My heartrate does get elevated. Walking, dancing, or jogging in place at intervals is the best for Me. Slow, fast, then medium intensity and repeat. It is just for a few sessions and usually in between, is weight training.

What I started doing about 15 years ago, was just working out and doing stuff at home. I have My Own body weight to use, some dumbbells, a yoga mat and Mother Father Earth. I talk to My body and to Mother Father Earth while I am showing love to My 2nd Bestie. I say, *'Thanx Mother Father Earth for Your grounding while I am moving around and playing with My muscles. I know I don't have heavier weights, so when You add in The Law of Gravity, My body becomes heavier and My muscle has more resistance.'* Think about the muscle, add in gravity and bammo. Oh Yes, this works great and the closer You are to the ground, the denser Your body part will be. I also have Momentum too, another Law of the Universe, because if I am moving forward in a way and I'm thinking about it, I can go farther. If I really think about the muscle that I want to work out, or the muscles that I want to move and show, it seems to give Me some extra force there. There are so many different things You can do in Your paradise, just put some great music on and move that bootie.

If You choose to work out at home, make Yourself a little special workout area, just like Your meditation space. Make it Yours, bring that Energy in with You and do it. Put on Your tennis shoes, You will work out in some way.

You don't need to go to the gym to get in shape. Some people say, *'well I go there because I need the motivation, or I need to get out of the house, or to socialize, or they have more equipment'. Are You happy going there? Is it really beneficial for You? Are there positive variations showin up with Your body and mind?* If the answer is yes, yes, and yes, then by all means go to the gym, but don't overdo it just because You are there and the equipment is available, or Your friends are there and watching. Over exertion or over exercising is Not Good for Your Body. If You believe that You have to go to a gym for motivation, then You are not ready to change Your life for You. If You need the motivation from society, or from societies ideas for Your ideas to get up and move, come on, who are You letting control You? We should work out because it feels good and it is valuable for Our mind and body. You want to go to the gym only with positive reasons to work out. The reason I went to the gym was to be healthy, to feel good and to be in shape using their equipment. Not to socialize, but that is what a lot of people wanted to do with Me, so 'nope'. I have My Best partners to work out with, My Source, My body and Mother Father Earth, because Their energiez are with Me all the time.

There are so many You Tube videos from a variety of people with all different play times. One essential idea for Your safety is, *Please watch videos with credible people, at Your level, that will give You the right poses and stances for Your protection. Another point that **must be** followed is You must let Your practitioners know what You are starting. They will be so pleased.*

Breathing is number one every day. You have to concentrate and breathe. I always make sure that I exhale longer than I inhale and hold it a few seconds at the peak. And no matter what the instructor is saying when I am practicing a guided meditation, or if I am performing a mentored breathing exercise, or a coached work out session, it doesn't matter, I always breathe at My pace, because with some of those You can feel really, really dizzy. Do a lot of natural breathing too, only in Your style.

When I do My breathing exercises I tell Myself that I'm also working the muscles in My core. Core is not just Your abds, it includes Your whole trunk. Your core is the most important area of Your body, it supports the whole of You so Your pelvis is straight, so You are not losing Your organs to gravity or peeing or dribbling at certain times, and so You are not straining Your back with daily movements. If You bend over and pick something up that is 20 pounds, like Your little doggie or a bag of veggies, if You don't bend Your knees and use Your legs and bootie, You are picking up around 200 pounds with Your back. The times will add up. Tell Yourself and practice, *'I am going to remember to use My core muscles, especially if I lift something or bend. I will do this automatically as I'm tightening up any of My muscles during exercise'.* While living daily, I encourage My whole trunk to be involved and I think about My breathing. Again, core movements and breathing practices I do every day, and then I alternate working with My other body parts. Make sure You change it up, do not do the same extremity or core groups each day. With My core playtime, I do stimulations of each muscle with My Source. Which is just tightening My abs, My back and chest, all while supporting and tightening with Kegels. I want to stand up straight and I don't want My bladder or My insides to sag and fall through certain holes as I get older. One of the Laws of the Universe, Gravity, is going to do what it is supposed to do, to pull everything down. So, if You pee on Yourself, when You laugh, or You sneeze, or when You cough, that's Your body's way of saying, *'Hey, do Your Kegel exercises'.* Kegels are for women and men. Who dribbles, who can't start the stream sometimes, who is constipated? *Yes, this is for all people, because everybody has a muscle down there to keep things up.* So don't forget about Our Kegel exercises. Anybody can do them and it doesn't matter what age You are either. It is easy, it is in Your control and Your responsibility, or You can go get surgery, or take a pill, it's up to You.

Saying it more positively is even better. We should always find a happier sentence for anything that doesn't make Us feel good. So, the sentence, *'I was laughing so hard urine came out, I need to do My Kegels', change to 'I almost dribbled, Thank God I've been doing My Kegel exercises'.*

There are only certain times that I don't do Kegel exercises. When I am in any body of water, You do not want to accidently suck that stuff up in there, or when You are urinating, You don't want to stop that flow. I know some people say to do that because it does tighten up the muscles so You don't tinkle on Yourself when You cough, sneeze, or laugh out loud, but it also reflexes the urine, the bacteria, and the dead cells that You're trying to get out of Your body, back up in Your tubes and bladder again.

Any activity that You do, never put Your body under too much stress for long, because that is detrimental to Your physical body. Doing too much of anything is not good for You, even the stuff that is good for You, even the positive stresses, You know. Don't do the same activities every day, switch it up. Your body and Spirit love adventure and variety.

Your mind is the only thing that likes routines and habits.

You have to relax before & after any movements and there should always be a grateful warm up and cool down. Do a little something every day, then imagine how strong, flexible and thriving You could be.

If You don't have the 7-15-30 minutes to work out, during the day while You're doing other things, You can be thinking about that muscle. Even while sitting at Your desk. You can do a conscious, mindful exercise. Tapping Your foot gets You moving and also stretches Your foot and calf. You can always be tightening up some muscle and breathing with it. If You have Your thought process of how great this is and utilize all Your resources along with Your movements, guess what, You've done Your workout, You didn't have to drive anywhere and You have pretty much moved Your whole body with the best exercises. Remember also to habit stack, engage in some practices while doing other things that need done like the household chores or some work aspects.

Now You know some ideas to do to make Yourself Your physical body healthier and if You're not doing it, for whatever reason, then You must like to be playing the victim.

You could say that *'I just don't want to do it. I'm too lazy. It hurts to much, I can't do it, it takes up too much time'*. Deep down under, You want to be the victim for some kind of attention. By now You know, that if You don't take care of You and think differently about it, Your life and body are going to progress to something else for You to really be a victim in. The lower You feel, the higher that You are supposed to soar. You have a huge power, Your Source behind You that will help You. If You are being too hard on Yourself, that's another reason to step back and quiet Your mind. Appreciate and love Your physical body no matter what shape You're in right now, because You know it can always change, even if You've been trying for many, many, years, it doesn't matter. You must purposefully start saying positive things to Yourself and positive things about the world, the environments around You and what You wish to change. Just a little bit nicer and then full-blown love. You have to find the positive parts about Your outside, love You and then that's when things start changing a little bit for You to see. Start with being happy right now with Yourself and Your situation and then They will show You more of the happy person that You are and that You want to be. *Save Space for Source.*

Consciously sit down to meditate and add in some walking and stretching for flexibility, some resistance training and nutritious input. These will help You to be balanced physically and mentally. Workout Your mind to appreciate and love it when You practice and play. If You can decrease the inflammation in Your mind about what You think about things, Your circulation of energy is going to be able to flow true and easily. If You want to really live, You must play the lead part and then a healthy, great life You will have, and because of the Laws of the Universe You will be drawing in only those blissful moments to You. Getting up and moving is Your body's and Your mind's meditation time. Do Your 7-30 minutes for Your physical body and find Your strength, because as of right now in this moment, Your already strong, so now the only thing that You can do is expand forward and become stronger. Dream about a healthy mind, body and Soul, smile about them and don't tell people yet. These desires are Yours.

Be careful what You consume physically and mentally. Changing the ways that You think and altering Your mindset have even more of an impact on the outcome than what You change about Your habits. Work on Your mindset, work on Your Spirituality, play with

Your Best Friend and They will help You exponentially to change and evolve in the way that You want to grow to accomplish Your goals. To get this done once and for all, You must start at the top with Your Spirit and then Your mind. It is always Your mind that needs to change to become healthier in the ways that You wish to become healthier. Don't overthink it and make Your wish. In any case, You don't need to make a wish and check it twice, They got it, They feel it with Your emotions and it is being worked on from Your Source and Energiez and from Your body in positive ways. Your physical body will follow Your emotions and thoughts about Yourself, and when You change the foods and drinks that You consume that cause swelling, the inflammation will decrease in Your body. When that starts happening, Your metabolism will increase. Decreasing inflammation increases Your digestion, absorption and elimination of the crap that does not need to be stored, ever! Listen to Your body, which is already directly linked to the Universe and Your Source, and supply it with good water, air, nutrients, movement, positive energy and thoughts, cleanliness, sunlight every day, and the moonlight at night.

Our body is self-regulating & self-healing, it does not wait for Us to decide, because it has always been attached to Source & to Mother Father Earth..

Chapter 36

Intention and Freedom

Your life ~ continuous, progressive and cumulative. Your expansion can be big or small, that is All up to You. The journey can be fun and exciting or the opposite. What are Your intentions? This is about *You* evolving and being healthier in all 3 aspects of Your life, *Body, Mind and Spirit,* and if You use Your Spirit side to help You, it's going to work, 100% of the time.

In Your physical body and in Your mind, You have to be flexible. Sometimes You need to update Your beliefs, which means You have to go back and change Your thoughts about things that You've learned and lived. If that belief or that thought does not make You feel good anymore, that's another indication that You need to change Your thought pattern. You have to give up some of Your habits of criticizing, judging, jealousy, guilt, regret or blame if You carry them. For Your peace of mind, You might need to give up things that make You frustrated or sad or anything on the negative side of the Happiness Scale. That might even include stepping away from some people, because right now it's about

You. It's kind of hard to step away Your family though, You know the people that really get on Your nerves, but You might have to, at least for a little while. Change Your vocabulary, which will change Your emotions, which will make You happier, which will increase Your belief, which will raise Your vibrations, which will make everything else positive in Your life and also the World.

We live in the here and We are in the now. If You do talk about the past, You want to talk good about it, because Your reality right now is a manifestation from Your past. All those memories from Your past that You need to bring with You to the right here and now, for whatever reason that is, You need to make joyful and be grateful where You are right now because of those things. It is so important to change those things that still bother You about then, and what You want to remember a little bit different, You just kind of change the memories around a tad bit. Ask Yourself why they need to be live with You now? Are You trying to chase Your past and be the same person to live like the old You, or even to look like the same person that You did then? You don't want to be the same as You were in Your 20s, 30s, 40s, etc., if You are not there now. Yes bring smidgens with You, but otherwise grow and expand. If You find Yourself slipping back into the old habits, spend time with Your Source, play more games and get back on track having fun. *'Oh, My goodness, I can't believe I did that again'.* Make it fun, don't get mad at Yourself and don't condemn Yourself; no, no, no, no. Just start playing with the situation and You will get through it. Don't talk bad about Yourself and do not cut Yourself down. Even if You say, *'I'm just joking'. No, You are not!* Joke around with only funny things that We all can giggle about that are true. Have joy in doing something that You love and get Your mind off of the negatives. Start out small and then You'll be up to 24 hours of keeping Your mind off *old stuff,* and You will feel Your life changing.

One of the first things that You can do is shut off Your TV more often than not. If You need to know something, You'll find it out. If You must watch the news then also add in the other perspective, the other 180° turn. Whatever chaos and mayhem and negative things that are going on in this world, there is positive going on in that situation that they're not telling You, that they probably are not even aware of themselves. When You get caught up in all those stories, all the 'what if's' like, 'what if that was happening to Me?', it will make You unsure, doubtful and afraid of the world and of Your life. If You do watch, make sure You turn that TV off afterwards saying to Yourself, yes it's what We saw, but I noticed this and these little positives about it, and on this side of the country or of the world these wonderful moments are happening. Try not to listen before You go to bed, because it will affect Your dreams and Your sleep cycle, and don't watch it when You first wake up in the morning either to find out what terrible things happened while You were sleeping. The first thing You should think about in the morning is *You, Yourself & Source* and what kind of great day that You are going to have, not something that is going on with the world that is probably not good and that You cannot do anything about. Don't start Your day out with fear of some kind, because that's what will go out into the world from You and it will also recycle more things to be afraid of back at Ya! If You are hearing negativity on the news, send Your Love and send Your peace to everyone, including the speakers, and live that for Yourself throughout the day. That action in itself will bring more peace and positivity to the World.

You might have to get off Facebook or cut down on Your social media too if there is too much negative in Your life or if You notice hours going by while You scroll. Social media and the participants impose their standards on You over and over again with ads and their thoughts about situations, or what they were told to say. While watching social media, You compare Yourself and it makes You constantly evaluate Yourself. Your ego will never be happy. Stop trying to impress other people and who cares about the trends. Some of the stuff You want to know and the other stuff, well, is other people's businesses. Get to know You and You'll start believing what We already know, 'You are all gonna be ok, if You change where You receive Your perspectives'.

If You find Yourself unhappy, if You are stumped, if You feel like there's a barrier or a blockage or You don't feel good doing something anymore, then don't. If You just don't have that appreciation and anticipation of an idea, that just means You really need to step down, and the worse those feelings are, the more You need to step back, but not into the past.   ; } You get that little, You know, ickiness in Your gut, that's one of Your first brains saying, *'step back a second, and then Your ego mind might jump in and say, 'but this needs to be done and we have bills to pay and we have a timeline'.* You also have the outside side effects making it have to be done even more hurriedly. That is Your ego plus double, triple from Your environment, from Your bosses and whoever controls that part of You. Don't rush Yourself, You will be miserable. You need to consciously calm down Your ego and say, *'I'm going to be fine, I'm going to be great, it all will get done and work out great, because I have this huge Source, My big Energiez, My BFE around Me all the time'.* If it's making You upset or if it stresses You out, that just means to slow down and don't make that decision right now. Slow it down, way down if You need to sometimes, and step aside for minute, an hour or a day. From the outside *side effects*, to the responsibility *side effects*, which are closer to You, You are still the one who has to change that little mindset and break it down into even smaller pieces to complete, but not for You to analyze and not for You to try to figure out right now either. There's You and You have to do You first, and if You have those outside effects that do not get it, then You might need to move on.

One idea, is that You shouldn't be trying to make Yourself feel good, if You just can't, and usually You don't need to, but circumstances and Your ego say 'stay'. If Your intention is to feel and be joyful, and the environment is not giving You that, if it is something that doesn't make You feel good, just stop it for a little while and see how You feel about You. Have no guilt. because You are self-soothing Your mind.

If You're drained of Your power or actually, if You feel drained of Your power, You're not going to feel like or be Your True Self. By the way that You talk to Yourself, if it is not positive, eventually You are going to drain the power of Your physical body too, and then You are going to have to work harder on being healthier. Take Your power back, and it is not actually getting it back again either, because You never lose it, it's just letting it out. It's in there, whether You want it to be there or not. Your Source, Your Energiez are with You all the time too. Believe it or not. If You feel like You are having problems getting something done, then be compassionate to Yourself. Your Source already knows You can do it; You are the doubter. You can feel it very easily too if You wish, and don't be afraid of it either, because it is only positive. It only can be good with fun and happiness involved. Let it out a little bit, or if You can, Oh My

Goodness, let it all out and in at one time. That could be overwhelming for a lot of people, so use some of Your God given patience. The best times to use patience is when You are on the lower end of the Happiness Scale. Patience will calm You down, and keep You from regretting or being guilty for something that You have said or did for the rest of Your life. A moment of calm, a little deep breath, a little pause in a minute of anger, or when You are frustrated, or when You start to feel overwhelmed, You know. Catch it ahead of time, before You plummet further and further, and You'll be able to get out of things easier. Make it individual and live Your True Self, by having a little bit more fun during Your days with Source and the Laws of the Universe helping. Just stop for a minute and remember who You are and who You are attached to, instant Power.

What about those things You do that are unnecessary, like over analyzing? If You think of it, over analyzing is a form of procrastination, so why are You waiting? Overanalyzing anything is Your ego not letting Your Source do the walking for You. Most of the time it should be intuition over logic. If You are working too hard as to figure something out, *You are going to be workin hard to get the answers.* Let Your intuition step up. Let Them show You the insights and little snippets using Your intuition. Now math, the sciences, those are fun games to learn (?) and You should use both logic and Your intuition for the best outcome. Anyone can do it if they practice with Source. People who get it, they think it is exciting, where others are like, *'Oh My God, Maaath, I don't get it, where do they get this….?'* Try to make anything You do fun, it will be different, and give Your Source a chance to let Them do the analyzing for You. They know the best way to get there and They will help You get the job done better than You can ever imagine, and You'll have so much fun while You're doing it too.

When You ask for something, You get excited and Your feelings soar. If You're too expectant and can't wait, You could become impatient. If You don't practice patience, You might not find the joys, or see the beauty, or have as much fun on Your journey. What does this mean? *'Stop, listen to Your environment and to Your body and see what Your Source is trying to show You'.* If You are ready and listening to Your guidance system, You will have strong thoughts or an *intuition* to, *'Come here and go this way, how about this, what about this? You will know it is right because You can say, 'I feel good this way, I feel good doing this, let's go this way or, I'm not so sure, it doesn't make Me feel good, so I won't go that way right now or ever.'* The more excited You are, the more You have to relax and slow Yourself down so You don't miss the good stuff that *Will Show Up for You*.

Sometimes You ask and then You totally miss it also because You were worried about it. If You worry and stress about something that You've asked for, or You complain to other people about it, or You criticize and judge other people and get angry because they have it, that just means You're afraid that You are not going to get it or that You will be left out. Along with Your fearful emotions, Your mind starts thinking about it more and that is where You start messing things up trying to figure out the when's and the how's to take action. Don't add in that negativity. You know it doesn't make You feel good to even read that paragraph, so why think it or say it? *Gary Keller said, 'the majority of what You want, will come from the minority of what You do'.* So that means let the Universe do most of it. Use an 80/20 rule I read, 80% of the time or most of the time, let Your Energy or Your Source do the work and 20% of time, You do what You need to do to stay in contact with Your Source using Your' conscious mind and continue with Your purpose of happiness, joy, peace, and love every day. If You just do 1% improvement a-day for whatever Your wishes are, it all adds up. This is what they say now, *'most habits don't form in 14 days or 30 days, it's 60 to 90 days for full on change'.* If You can handle that one little aspect of 1% a day, and then in 100 days, You will have 100% improvement in whatever Your dilemma was.

As far as the resources and references that come to You, ask Yourself, *'are they headed in a direction that I want to go in, or am I just here to learn from them for a moment'?* Don't block the ideas when someone is trying to show You something, even if You know Your idea is better. Don't argue because You already know that You are right, because in their opinion, they are correct too. If You really know that You are accurate, then You are correct, and at times, it should stay between You and Your Best Friend Energy. You do not have to convince anybody of anything either, unless it is a life-or-death event. Convincing is an argument. You can always state Your opinion and keep doing what You say, and then they'll see it true for themselves, eventually. In this journey to love Yourself, make sure You ask for help, not from people but from Your Source, from Your Angels, and from Mother Father Earth first. You will not second guess Yourself anymore. Instead of second or third presumption, You will know right away. *'Yep, this is good'*, and Your BFE will be beside You the whole way with the best ideas and outcomes.

Everything that is alive or everything that is Organic is an Energy and You come in contact with many Energiez throughout the day. The common denominator in all of those scenarios is You! It's Your attitude and Energy in each segment, whether You're walking by a plant, an animal or insect, or a person in Your different environments, how the aspects of Your life are going to play out. Start with loving Yourself first and start loving other Organics too. If You can't do it that way then concentrate on the other Organics that You do already love. Start to be nicer and kinder to every little thing in Your path. People giggle when I hug My plants, so what, the love I actually feel back, Oh My goodness. I also say Hi to flowers, I smell them and say, *'oh My gosh, how beautiful You are'.* Why not let them brighten up too. The people that were laughing at Me because I was talking to the plant, some would take that as a negative. Nah, not Me, that's not how I take it. It is all about how You absorb others Energiez. I only take the positive parts of their Energy. *A laugh is a positive thing every time, if You Let It Be* and if they really were laughing at Me to be mean, then that's on them. I don't give a crap about stupidity, jealously or fitting into the crowd. I am not going to stop being kind to all the Organics and doing the things that make Me feel great, and don't ever stop being Yourself either. Just smile and know that You are not hugging and giggling all by Yourself, Your Source is here too, making Your heart feel so full and happy, which brings in more love and increased happiness into Your life.

'You become what You think about most of the time.'

Earl Nightingale

What You think about Yourself, is also what You see in the world. That's the Law of Attraction playing around. Words and emotions that don't have a positive link will give You limited beliefs about Yourself. Since We are what We think, don't think about it if it is not a happy thought. The things that You say about Yourself condition You to be that way and that Energy will come forth. The things that You say to other people about You, is what they're going to start thinking about You too, authentic or not, and if it is a negative connotation, then it is certainly not a true reality. When You repeat, *'oh I only have this, or that didn't happen, it will never happen, I can't do this, I am fat, this… part of My life sux, I might have this forever, or it is going to be hard'*, You are putting boundaries around Yourself. You cannot say that just because it happened before and then it happened again, that the same will occur now. It just wasn't the right time and now You have learned more. If it is something that You really believe in and have that undeniable passion for it, the next time will be better. Focus on the great things that happen for You every single day, even if it's *almost* the same things over and over again to get You started, and then add in the other positives that You notice. Now, imagine how the Law of Attraction and the Law of Momentum are going to kick in and help You out. Your whole life can change in a second, for the better.

For Your best life, live every day in Your True reality. You have to look both in the mirror and through a glass window at how You see the world, because what You think of other people is what You think of Yourself also. Try to see Yourself from an outside view, looking through the window and loving Your life, and also while You are looking through the looking glass, smile at Yourself. Usually, what You are thinking about in reference to others, is not Your biz anyway, sooo... Sometimes the people You attract are not of Your highest, loving level, but they need and are drawn to You. Love Yourself every day, Love them and be safe. Give Your physical body time every day and make sure that the nutrients that You're putting into all of Your energy fields and Your physical field are positive for Your vitality. While You are living here on this Earth, say 'Hello' to the things that support You every single day, which is every single Organic on this planet, including Mother Father Earth. Living on this Earth, Your life should be good for Mother Father Earth too. We are all connected that way. You're connected to Source more, if You are connected to Your energy more. If You live through Your Source, there will be less individualization, because You will be as one with the collective, which means You will judge, criticize or compare Yourself to others less. What a happier life You will have, releasing that part of Your psyche. Have fun, find the joy, find the positives in everything that You possibly can. Be humble and empty Your basket to release things when You are trying to learn something new, so You can fill it back up again using Your resources. When You're releasing and clearing out things that no longer serve You right now, replace it with something positive, something to play with, so Your mind is like, *'okay, now do I feel great'?* Replace it with something that is going to make You smile in a second, that is gonna make You say, *'oh that's good, let's go there'*. So, assess and acknowledge, and release and replace.

If something is out of Your hands, it should also be out of Your mind too. Sometimes, actually most of the time, that is all We should do. In the meantime, making the life that You do live in, Your reality, a good and positive one and step over to the Source's side. The answer to any question, is that it has to be good for You, Your mind and good for Your physical body. I always say when I tutor on My ideas of, **Preprevention and AlignAge** *that My Spirit is very old and My body is getting Younger and healthier every day, it is just My mind that needs to keep up with US.* Change is going to happen and it should, and You can pick which directions

Your expansion will be towards. If You want true freedom from anything, You have to start with Your mind. You have to *intentionally start changing Your attitude towards Yourself for a happy piece of mind*. Be open and truthful, especially to Yourself about how You feel on certain situations and if You do that, then Your life is going to be so much better. If You've been living *those* segments over and over again, change it up, find the good stuff in there and look elsewhere for new. You'd be surprised what You can discover on the outside. One day just sit around and be an observer. Don't talk as much to people and just listen and observe. Use all Your senses and see what amazing things that You can find in Your environments. Even ones that You've been in many times before and You just never noticed the good stuff. Speak Your positive truth and live that way and then Your life will become exactly the way that You are and wish it to be. Oh, My goodness, You'll be able to handle any little thing that comes along with ease, grace and enlightenment. You know whether it makes You feel good or not. It's Your choice to be happier, it's always Your choice. You just have to get started and it has to begin with You, and in some cases it just means that You just don't do *it* anymore. If there are things that You need to do, make it simple and let Your Source show You, which means You do less. Make Your wishes be clear and know it is here for You. Give Your Source times every day. You do Your part and They will do Theirs, and You will have already won before You even faced it.

Sooowwhhaa, how are You going to talk to Yourself so that You can see things differently, so that You are happier when You look at the world? How are You going to view Your environments so that You Yourself can benefit the most? This is what You have to think about to get this playtime started, because it has to start with You first and then You can actually see the world through those rose-colored glasses or whatever color is Your favorite.

Start Your negativity detox right now. Easy, fun, fast or slow, it is up to You. How much fun do You want to have? How much fun can You handle in one day? How much fun can You handle in 1 hour? How much laughing can You do in 15 minutes? Are You ready to laugh Your ass off and have Your face hurt from smiling most of the time? Just how much bliss can You handle?

Chapter 37

Practice and Play

Negativity Detox

Ahhhh, the last chapter in a book *all about You!* I hope You have grown and learned to love Yourself and Your BFE even more, just like I did and will continue to do. I was so excited that I stumbled across this information and said, 'that sounds weird, let Me look some more', and then it was and is, 'that sounds true, let Me learn more', and now it is, 'Holy crap, I must tell everyone.' During this time, a little over a year, I also recreated Me, to the real Me and I am experiencing how We are all supposed to be living. Yes that life of joy, happiness and peace, and since it has to do with Source, it is only associated with and out of love.

So Yep, You are going to have to change to keep up with Yourself and the world. As We designed this book, imagine how much I practiced and played and altered My life. Yes some new differences, all wonderful and great, and some parts of My life stayed the same. The main idea is, *'it was and is all My choice'.* We grow and add new ideas into Our life all the time, and the most important ones to Us, We hold on to. The programs, traditions and rituals that We grew up with from the past, are the ones that can be brought forward to now, and some of them might need to be updated a little bit. Some old ways and old beliefs are actually going away with an even older knowledge coming back in, Thanks to Me and to others. These ideas that We are supposed to know, but have not been taught or even been aware of during Our lives. It should be natural and effortless to live, play and expand, and it's very freeing when You can let something go with love in Your heart.

To live the life that You want, sometimes You might have to reset some rules. Those conditions that really just do not make You feel good in Your heart and gut anymore, but You follow them because Your third brain says, '*this is the way that it's supposed to be, this is the way it has always been'.* Even Your beliefs can be limited, if You let them be. In this life system, some Organics practice judging and separating, a survival of the fittest. We humans sometimes tend to take it to extremes, and then Our minds need to put those in its memory for a reference so We can move forward. Your ego mind does the thinking and the replaying of Your thoughts, all secondary to what You've experienced, or what You have heard of, and it pushes You to take action. To deal with the past, learn as You go because You just can't stay there and be fulfilled here. So, does Your mind need to release anything that is going to hold You back from seeing new perspectives? You might have to interrupt some of Your Own rules, especially those controls that are based on fears or doubts associated with the unknowing of what is coming in the future. Fear and doubt will ruin Your dreams and desires more than a failure, and the future, well it is coming. Live Your life, in all of Your segments right now, because this is the only time that You can do anything about anything anyway, and when they say to, *'follow Your heart',* that is really what You need to do.

Most people have 4 to 7 different environments that they have to live in every single day, and yes those numbers could be higher or lower dependent on You. Well, how many of those settings are exactly the way that You want them to be? You can make any place that just is not right for You, a perfect atmosphere. After You do You, then start with Your home, and then move on to Your job space, or You can do them simultaneously, it is all up to You. Make Your house a *happy and clean house*, and one of the happiest places in Your house should be Your bedroom. What's the first thing You look at when You wake up in the morning? Is it dull and drab, or beautiful pictures and bright colors? And what alarm do You wake up to? Is it something that makes You happy to be awake, all ready to get up and move around and start Your new day? My alarm is always music, it makes Me ready to play any games that day with My BFE. Switch it up and make All of Your dwellings a paradise from Your heart, one place at a time, always starting with You.

Since You are in control, that means You are the joy bringer, the happy donor, the person that lights up the room to Your life. **Yes that is You!** You don't have to try and access Your power, it is there. It was inborn before birth; You just have to let it out. Which means You can't be afraid, You cannot be doubtful, and You should not listen to Your environment some of the time. It is essential, yes, occasionally to hear it, but to listen and absorb daily the same negative things is unnecessary and so unhealthy. I would say that in 80% or more of Your external environments, are things that You do not need to put Yourself in a place of.

That means social medias, TV, groups, and some people. Most of the stuff that You listen to is not going to directly affect You right here & now, or ever. If there is something that You need to really, really know about, that 20% or so, Your BFE will bring You the right resources, the right people and the right inklings to let You know about it. So, since You are already not going to worry about it, because there is nothing that You can do about certain things, why even bother Yourself with it? Why waste Your time with something that is not directly Your business? Turn them off, some people included, and get back with the Organics in this world and spend more time with Your Source and the ones You love. Source will let You know if it is important to You, and the rest of the time should be Your time, not societies. I would rather get that 80% from the cosmos and not from WIFI or the TV shows anyway, it is funner, and that 20%, I will let Source contemplate that too. They'll let Me know what I need to know, when I need to know it, because We have this special communication, Source and I, and We made it up Ourselves, and it was just the way that I wanted it to be. The most important thing for You to clarify is just knowing the way that You want to live on this Earth. The way that You want Your life to be. How You would want that day to go when You get up in the morning and how You would love it when You go to work. How would You love to interact with Your family, Your friends and when You are out in Your community centers like church, the gym, the grocery store or wherever else You go. While living, You will attract Your Own fate and if You want something to come into Your life, You have to clear the space for it. The material things We would love to have in Our lives are all recyclable and there is enough, there is plenty to go around for everyone.

As You continue to move forward in this happy life, playing around with Your new BFEs, all the resources and everything that You need right here at this moment will come to You, and You will see and feel it easily with Your intuition and with Your 5 senses. All for Your benefit, all for the life that You want to live. To help You along the way, don't ever try do it by Yourself or just with people, You always need Your Source. You do that first and then everything else works out better and easier. We can all be the smartest in the class, if You stay in touch with Yourself and Your Source, the smarter part of You. Along Your paths, wouldn't You want to receive advice from someone who knows all the answers? You always want to talk to the wisest person and now You know You have one, a Best Friend that is Your Spirit. An enlightened entity was with You freely at birth. You were kind of born with an instruction manual set-in place, full of everything You need, in every different language and manner. Hopefully this will strengthen Your belief in *'how You do have the power to allow Yourself to have a better life'.* Your Elders know best, so ask the informed ones, the geniuses, and We are all geniuses, You just have to tap into them. So put Your fun, positive, crazy ideas out there in the world, into the Universe and maybe not to Your family or friends just yet, You know. Plant Your inspirations and see how positively that You can change the world. *You, Yourself & Source* have that much power, and the reason You have that much power is because now You are aware of who You are and the way that You want it to be.

I know Who I am in this life and I know how I want to feel in this lifetime.

Everybody's purpose in this life is the same; to live with joy, fun, happiness and love. For Your individual purpose in life, You have to do the things that You love to do and then it will expand even further. Because of the Laws of the Universe, Our opportunities multiply as they are used, and You are going to grow and expand anyway, so which way are You going to go? On a pathway that You don't feel good on, or on one that You do feel good about and can say to Yourself, *'yes I would enjoy that'.* Your Source is always leading You on another path, and then another one, and then…. for the best times of Your life. Use this simple idea of feeling good or not, and You will find Your sole (Soul) purpose and Your individual Dharma. *With this method, You will find Your unique higher purpose.* Don't try to name what it is yet if You don't know, just do the things that You like to do already, and the roles You must do, play in a more positive, fun way. There are only 2 answers to any questions, not problems, that occur. *I feel good about this, or I do not.* Plan and practice with Your mind, think before You act, and consciously ask Yourself with each segment, *'does this make Me feel good or not' and Your Best Friend will help You make that decision.* Learn to use Your emotions, because Your BFE loves those. Don't hide them, because this is what will lead You further and further, and faster and faster along to all of Your wishes and desires. Open up Your heart and eyes and look for the key aspects directed towards You. They are easy to pick out because You chose them ahead of time. Cocreating with Source amplifies the fact that You do love Yourself. You do deserve a happy, fun life, to do what You want, to explore All of Your passions and to *'go for the gold'*.

Learn about Your masculine and Your feminine sides. We All have both, and We should be on the feminine side most of the time, and then when You do take action (masculine), it should be positive for You and fun every single time. In the ebb and flow, or in the changing of the seasons, or in the cycles of life, You are going to go in and out of Your masculine and feminine roles, and because Our masculine takes it to the max sometimes, try to be mostly in the nurturing spiritual part of living. The letting great things happen side of life, the calmer aspect, Our feminine zone. You have to consciously make that choice to 'let it be' throughout Your ups and downs in Your life here on Mother Father Earth. And consciously means, You have a choice to do it or not. Start believing in Your potential and begin to *Practice and Play.* You will know when to take actions and You will also know when not to, if You listen to Your Spirit and not involve people or Your protective ego too much.

If You think it's a darker season in Your life, that just means *it's a more Soulful season for You.* Life is hard for everyone at times, but it is always supposed to get better and that choice is Yours alone. *'It is all in Your mind',* and it is the one part of Us that tries to be in control most of the time. Have more adventures between You and Your Best Friend Energy. Spend more conscious times between You and Your Source. This is *Your Spirituality; You, Yourself & Source,* and it's only positive, it is only good, and it is for the benefit of You and of humanity. If You want to feel Your Source more often, especially in Your 15 minutes and in those pauses throughout the day, then clear Your mind of any negative thoughts and that leaves *'Space for Your Source'* to come and enjoy You in peace. They want You to talk to them and to hear how Your day went, even though They have been with You the whole time. They live life on this Earth through You, so make it fun and do what They love, which is anything that makes You happy. This will make such a better friendship, and there will be less frequent and shorter durations of Our shadow times. In the face of adversities about any situation, if Source is more in Your life during those criticisms, hate, or the grief around You, You will be able to stand more confidently in positivity and light, and then more delightful, easy times will happen for You in pretty much every single segment. Do not ever be ashamed for being You, or for having fun, or for doing the things that You like to do. *It is nobody else's business.* You are You, and You are so unique and so wonderful, and Source, Your Best Friend loves You more than You can possibly imagine. Indivisible infinity is a great way to describe Your Energy and You. Know this to be real and to be true. This is the most important part, *'the Spiritual association between You and Your Source and for You to always remain consciously aware of Your Energiez every second of the day'.* Your Source is with You 24/7, always looking for the positives, always cheering You on, always trying to show You beautiful signs that You, Yourself have caused.

I know now that I do not have to go through another person to talk to God, My Creator, My Energy, My Heart, I can go straight to the Source, because I am part of Them. You are part of that Energy too. You are more a part of that Energy than You are a human body, so just go directly to Your Source, to Your Angels, or to Your Energies. They are all around You and Us. I talk to Source all the time and say things like, *'that was fun, did You see that? Oh My gosh, We just laughed My a** off, My face is sore from smiling, Geeezzz, what another great time today'.*

What else is with You 24/7? Well, Your physical body is with You every second, *and* it's already directly linked to Source. Your physical body is pretty much ready for You to join in and have fun with Source being healthy, as soon as You wake up. Your mind is really the only thing that needs to be upgraded and to be aligned with Your Best Friend, with Your God, with Your Source. Your physical mind is with You for those 12-18 hours a day while You are awake, and then when You're asleep is when Your mind is with Source, and You guys have so much fun. Fall asleep with nothing on Your mind except for, *'Thank You for the great day, and oh My gosh, tomorrow is gonna be even better. Thank You for healing My body this night'.* If You wake up in the early am, is it restroom time, a hot flash minute or is it time to connect consciously with Your Source or maybe all 3? In My case, why not habit stack? At this moment in time, Your ego is already calmed, so open up and relax for Your few minutes. This will not happen every night, and You will not be as tired as You think You will be.

You always have the choice to be happy, to be positive, and to stay in those higher frequencies. Don't be Happy because of the conditions, be Joyful most of the time, and then momentum grows those positive feelings. When You are happy and having fun, You are more confident, motivated, calm, and flexible. You will be masterful enough to pause, observe, relax, and not to react unless absolutely necessary. When You stay in higher frequencies, You are happy most of the time and You can easily find the positives in any situation. I would not wait around to let others or a condition make Me happy anymore, I know that I am that powerful to change My here and now.

*An expansion and growth from where You are right now, always **never** reaching Your goals all the way, because there are continually other 'somethings' to think about and to wish for every day.* Believe that Your desires can happen and that You are the reason for it.

As the world is changing, guess *who* is changing the world? You ARE, that's how strong and powerful You are, whether You believe it or not, whether You knew it or not.

Well, now You know. I am telling You, and You cannot ever say truthfully that You do not know now, even if You don't believe it yet. *So how are You going to change the world for future generations, and so You live the rest of Your life with ease, fun, happiness, joy and bliss? You know, just the way that You wish. What would that price be for You to change Your Universe to the way You want to live?* If You want to keep up with the adapting world so You expand and grow in a good way, then change Your thoughts, revise Your words, Your emotions, and exchange Your beliefs for the *New You*. You can reinvent Yourself at any age, it doesn't matter. It is just Your thought processes and Your emotions about it, how You move forward. For You to keep up with the world, You cannot be the same person that You were 10 years ago, You have to expand with Yourself. You can't even be the same person that You were 5 or even 1 year ago. Going through life, there is so much to explore and so much more to discover between *You, Yourself & Your Source* that is constantly changing, and that is the best part. Life changes again and again, and We have to start playing different games each time. Your whole life is a continuation with new beginnings, and every time You learn something new, Yes You can absolutely add in Your positive, generational-honored customs also, but at that moment in time, that initial second, release everything else and start as an innocent, start from scratch. You will see it in a different light. To plan Your future, You have to learn as You go. It's so much more exciting to start something new to keep that brain working on trying out unfamiliar ideas. Something new every day, every week, or something new every month. That was My deal with God when I would go to work in the Emergency Room. If I learned a new idea, I would have to come back tomorrow, and I would always learn so many new things, from so many different people. It was awesome, this little game I use to play with My BFE. For Your games, they have to start with Your world, and then You will have an effect on the whole world. You impact Me. We are all connected, We are all one, all that is Organic, which includes Mother Father Earth, all the Energiez, and Source. No One is excluded in this family, unless they choose to be. Nobody will be left out. Other Organics in the world, except for humans, because We have that big old, massive thinking about all the crap brain, already lives using the Laws of the Universe. The plants don't ostracize other plants, they all work together. Animals work together, and the same goes with insects, even if they eat each other, it's still a part of the 'life of belonging'. You know that Your Source gives Happiness, Joy and Love to every Organic You come across, so what about You?

To summarize it all up again for You and add just a smidge more for thought, here Ya go! My Negativity detox is for any human that needs it, and it works 100% of the time if You decide to Play. It can be fun, easy and entertaining, all for You, if You Choose It To Be!!! You are going to need to be open and receptive with no doubts, no worries and You are going to need to give in and play more in Your reality now. You have to surrender knowing that it is all going to be great, with happy, wonderful outcomes. You need to be satisfied where You are right now, and when You believe that, *'Yes You Can',* then better things just happen while You grow into Your awesome life. In the middle of all this, You're going to say to Yourself, *'wow, I didn't really think My life was like this. I was not as happy and joyful as I thought I was, because now that I've changed a few little things in My life, I see the differences and I am aware of the Universe in an uncommon way now. The world can be different than what I believed about My life. So much better, so much funner. So much more abundant, prosperous, enjoyable and any other positive words on 'My Happiness Scale'.* **Don't You want to really be a part of Yourself more now?** There are so many people doing these activities, playing and practicing, waking up happy, knowing themselves and getting to a place where they want to live. So many people that You and I aren't even aware of yet. All I know for sure is that it is gonna be so awesome. Are You going to be one of them, one of Us? If You open up Your Spiritual mind and Your heart, who says You can't have it all? NO ONE except You! Who are You going to choose to hang out with the most, Source, Your Energy? Or, are You going choose to serve Your ego and society?

So now with all the stuff that You have learned about You and what You should do about You, what are You consciously going to make Your priority every single day? Are You going to make sure that You have Your special time, every single day for You & Source, Your Heart? Will You also give Yourself Your little pauses to ground and say, 'Thank You and Hello' to Mother Father Earth and all the Energiez around You? Could You sit back and respond in calmer ways? Are You going to find Your positivity in situations and stay high up on the Happiness Scale?

Are You going to do the things that make You feel good every day? Can You dream, imagine and support Your Subconscious, Your Soul, or Your Spirit? Can You be like Your inner child and be a healthy innocent and know that You never have to heal Your Inner Child, You just have to change Your mind about it? Is Your priority gonna be to laugh and giggle, and to find beauty in most things? Are You going to choose to have fun and play more? Will You get up and move Your physical body, Your 2nd bestie, and fuel it nutritiously? Will You look to see the divinity in people, by acknowledging Our similarities, and give Your Unconditional Love? Can You focus on Yourself most of the time? Can You Love Your Whole Self? Will it be Your intention to see the beauty, strength, diversity, gorgeousness and the adaptation of Our Mother Father Earth and the nature around You and assist where You choose? How will You use Your power? Can You let things go from history and live *Right Now*? And yes, We need our past because We kind of go back-and-forth remembering what We like and what We don't like, just don't hang out there. You shouldn't be worried about the future either. You just can't be, because You are focusing on something that could....... See, You can't even finish the sentence yet. You are troubling Yourself about a potential, that will probably not happen, when You could be making it great right now and changing that trajectory. Isn't that easier? Just live in the now, have a great time living Your purpose and then the future takes care of itself. As Reverend Ken would say, 'leave all Your woulda 's, shoulda 's, and coulda 's back there, can You do that? Are You capable to stop thinking about what You don't have, and just desire and manifest? Will You choose to hang with those that You like to be with, or that like to be with You? Could You give Your mind a rest, consciously and purposefully so it too can adapt? Will You be Your True Self in any situations? Are You prepared to make You a priority in Your life for *You, Yourself & Source* so that You can lead others home? All this seems like A Lot to think about and revise hu? Well, it is a wonderful thing that the greater part of You is already *Livin that Way*. Talk to Your Source just like You would Your Best Friend, and now You can no longer say, *'it is easier said than done, because if You play with Your BFE, what is said, is done easily.'* Love Your life right now and then imagine even more. How much Freedom do You want? Relax and let Them do it, let Them play, They're on it.

You are Your best right now, so make it amazing. Leave the majority of the action up to Them and You will get everything that You want, every single time, and if You don't get exactly what You wanted, it is going to be something even better.

Imagine if You did all 7 things in My Negativity Detox: use Your 15 minutes every single day, do Your little pauses several times a day, and make sure that You are grounded as much as You can. Get up and move Your physical body most of the time, and feed it only the best. Decrease any kind of stress. Your body and mind to not differentiate excited stress, worry stress, or routine stresses. It will have similar reactions for Your protection, and will eventually be a hurdle for You to be healthy. If You are struggling or if You think that something is an obstacle, then make it an opportunity, an unexpected benefit. Y'all are playing this game of life with Your Source, using the Laws of the Universe, so make sure that You are smiling most of the time, even if at first, it is just in Your mind. Make things fun, enjoy Your life, feel good about this or that, find Your positives and do things that You love to do. Build up all that ++ momentum while You are living Your life, and it will come back to You. Keep on imagining what is next and get excited, but live most of the time right here and now. *We can practice all of this in the Play Shoppe Journey and Journal coming next... this is where We can play together for the betterment of You.*

So, who are You today? What kind of life are You going to cocreate with Source right now? Be with both of Your Best Friends: Source and Your Physical body and don't worry, Your mind won't feel left out, it will always come along for the party.

Love, Learn & Take Control

Sincerely with a Giggle,

Love, Chatty Cathy

&

Me, Myself & Us